Money and
Capital Markets

Money and Capital Markets in Postbellum America

JOHN A. JAMES

Princeton University Press

PRINCETON, NEW JERSEY

Library of Congress Cataloging in Publication Data will be
found on the last printed page of this book

Publication of this book has been aided by the Paul Mellon
Fund of Princeton University Press

This book has been composed in Linotype Times Roman

Printed in the United States of America by Princeton
University Press, Princeton, New Jersey

To M.

Contents

CONTENTS

List of Tables

List of Figures

Preface

THE period after the Civil War in the United States witnessed dramatic changes in the financial system. One of the most notable was the pronounced convergence of regional interest rates during the period, which has usually been taken as evidence of the development of a truly national financial market in short-term capital, especially in view of the fact that the antebellum period appears to have been characterized by large and quite stable differentials in local interest rates across the country. This book is a study of the structure and operation of the postbellum banking system and the forces responsible for the narrowing of interregional interest rate differentials.

In spite of the extensive and fundamental structural changes that took place in the American economy after the Civil War, the postbellum period has received relatively little attention from economic historians until quite recently, in contrast to the more glamorous antebellum era. Similarly, even though monetary questions were heatedly contested both before the Civil War, such as in the Jacksonian period, and after it, as in the greenback and silver controversies, for example, economic historians have devoted relatively little study to financial development in the nineteenth century and its role in promoting economic growth. This study therefore attempts to analyze an important, but neglected, area of nineteenth-century American history, the postbellum banking system and the short-term capital market. A discussion and explanation of some nineteenth-century banking terms and financial instruments, which might prove useful in understanding the operation of the nineteenth-century financial system, is included in the text.

The forces behind the convergence of regional interest rates are studied using the approaches and techniques of the so-called New Economic History. Explicit hypotheses are framed and then tested against historical data. In this case, in order to evaluate the competing hypotheses, a new, more accurate data series for local interest rates for the period is presented; its derivation is discussed in Appendix A. Even the most dedicated new economic historians, however, have increasingly come to realize that institutions are also important. One cannot study the functioning of, say, the nine-teenth-century economy without considering the institutional framework within which the economic agents operated and which influenced their decisions. Consequently, in examining the operation of the short-term capital market, the structure or framework of the banking system is also explicitly considered. Moreover, because institutional arrangements are not immutable, the evolution of financial institutions over time or the process of institutional change in response to both legal and real constraints also merits examination. The book is, then, in part a study of financial institutions and institutional change or adaptation, as well as an exercise in the New Economic History.

In order to make the work more accessible, the more esoteric aspects of the New Economic History, the econometric work underlying the hypotheses tests described in Chapter 6, are not reported here. The regression results and tests are discussed in detail in "Banking Market Structure, Risk, and the Pattern of Local Interest Rates in the United States, 1893–1911," *Review of Economics and Statistics*, LVIII (November 1976), and "The Development of the National Money Market, 1893–1911," *Journal of Economic History*, XXXVI (December 1976). Permission to draw upon their results in Chapter 6 is gratefully acknowledged to the *Review of Economics and Statistics* and the *Journal of Economic History*. Material in Appendix B originally appeared as "A Note on Interest Paid on New York Bankers' Balances in the Postbellum Period," *Business History Review*, L (Summer 1976); permission to reprint it is acknowledged to the *Business History Review*.

The present work is based on part of my MIT doctoral dissertation. My greatest debt is certainly to my principal thesis advisor, Peter Temin, who in earlier stages offered many useful suggestions and criticisms and in later stages proved to be a discerning editor and organizer. The opus was substantially improved through his efforts. This should not, however, overshadow my debt to the other members of my committee, Duncan Foley and Richard S. Eckaus, for their assistance and suggestions. The manuscript benefited from the comments of many others, among whom I would especially like to thank Lance Davis, Paul David, Jeffrey Williamson, Bruce Greenwald, and Richard West. William Breit and R. M. Hartwell also deserve special recognition for services rendered. Responsibility for all remaining errors, of course, must rest with the author. Steve DeCanio obligingly supplied part of the data, and Emily Albanese skillfully keypunched legions of numbers for the regressions. A special debt is due Mary C. Gubbins and Cynthia Annunziata for competently and cheerfully typing the manuscript in its various stages of development, and also I would like to thank the Thomas Jefferson Center for supporting the typing of the manuscript. Finally, I would like to thank my wife Marylin for encouragement and forbearance, but most of all for her editing and indexing skills.

December 1976   J.A.J.

Money and
Capital Markets

CHAPTER I

Introduction

THE development of an efficient financial structure plays an important role in the process of economic development. The accumulation of capital in itself does nothing to promote growth in income or output if that capital cannot be successfully transferred into a productive use. A financial structure that leads to an efficient allocation of funds is one of the necessary conditions for growth in per capita income. The importance of finance for development in the United States has perhaps never been articulated as well as by J. S. Gibbons in 1858:

> Anyone who has travelled among our country villages, out of the immediate influence of cities, has occasionally been struck by the neglect of natural advantages, the lack of energy, the rudeness of life and character, and the almost savage features of the common people. But on visiting the same place after an interval of a few years, he has seen a total change; a larger population, a better class of buildings, an air of thrifty growth, and a manifest increase of comfort. The old lethargy has disappeared; a new life has been infused into everything; even the countenances of the people are softened; a less brutal and more intelligent spirit beams from their eyes. A *bank* has been the starting point of this new career; the mill-dam has been built across the little streams of capital and the social machinery is brought into play.[1]

The United States in the postbellum period, the period between the end of the Civil War and the establishment of

[1] J. S. Gibbons, *The Banks of New York, Their Dealers, The Clearing House, and the Panic of 1857* (New York: D. Appleton and Co., 1858), pp. 12–13.

3

the Federal Reserve system, experienced significant and far-reaching structural changes in both the composition and location of economic activity. The process of industrialization that had begun in the antebellum period continued after the Civil War. From 1869 to 1899 the share of agriculture in total commodity output fell from 53 to 33 percent, whereas the manufacturing share rose from 33 to 53 percent.[2] In addition to this substantial shift in the composition of output from agriculture to industry, there was a regional shift within manufacturing from the East to the Midwest going on as well. Value added in manufacturing in the Northeast amounted to 66 percent of total manufacturing value added in 1870, but fell to 51 percent in 1910; meanwhile, the Midwest share increased from 18 to 25 percent during the period from 1870 to 1910, while the Western share rose from 10 to 13 percent.[3]

These changes in the composition and regional distribution of output were paralleled by shifts in the distribution of the labor force. From 1870 to 1910 agricultural workers as a percentage of the labor force fell from 52.9 to 31.4 percent, that is, from over one-half of the labor force to under one-third, while at the same time workers in manufacturing increased from 19.1 to 22.2 percent.[4] At the same time this sectoral shift was taking place, a westward shift in the distribution of the population was occurring as well.[5] Concomi-

[2] Robert E. Gallman, "Commodity Output, 1839–1899," in Conference on Research in Income and Wealth, *Trends in the American Economy in the Nineteenth Century* (Princeton, N.J.: Princeton University Press, 1960), p. 26.

[3] Harvey Perloff et al., *Regions, Resources, and Economic Growth* (Lincoln: University of Nebraska Press, 1960), p. 153.

[4] Stanley Lebergott, "Labor Force and Employment, 1800–1960," in Conference on Research in Income and Wealth, *Output, Employment and Productivity in the United States after 1800* (New York: Columbia University Press, 1966), p. 119.

[5] Richard Easterlin, "Interregional Differences in Per Capita Income, Population, and Total Income, 1840–1950," in *Trends in the American Economy in the Nineteenth Century*, p. 136.

tant with the growth in the relative importance of manufacturing and the relative decline in agriculture was a marked migration into the cities. Between 1870 and 1910 urban population as a percentage of total population almost doubled, rising from 25.2 to 45.7 percent.[6]

The general shift in the composition of output from agriculture to industry, the migration and change in composition of the labor force, and shifts in regional demand for funds, due in part to the shift of industry from East to West and also in part to the increasing capital intensiveness of agricultural production, all marked significant changes in the structure of the American economy. Efficient mobilization of financial resources required a transfer of funds from relatively stagnant to rapidly expanding industries, as well as from relatively capital-abundant areas to relatively capital-scarce areas.[7] Consequently, efficient allocation of financial resources called for both intersectoral and interregional trans-

---

[6] Perloff et al., *Regions, Resources, and Economic Growth*, p. 126.

[7] Gallman and Davis argue that financial intermediation affected not only the spatial and industrial mobility of funds, but also the size of total savings, which was a function of the relative elasticities of the demand for and supply of capital in each region. The deficit sector, in this case the West, probably had a fairly wide range of investment opportunities and thus a fairly elastic investment demand function; on the other hand, much of the Western saving was probably done by persons directly involved in the firms, so Gallman and Davis argue that the supply of Western savings was relatively inelastic. In the capital-surplus area, the East, there was probably a narrower range of profitable investments, while savings were less attached to particular firms and hence more elastic. If the demand for capital in the deficit sector, the West, is relatively elastic and the supply relatively more inelastic than demand and supply in the surplus region, the East, total savings will increase. Thus, they argue that the transfer of funds from East to West in the postbellum period was an important factor in explaining the upward shift in the savings rate in the postbellum period. Robert E. Gallman and Lance E. Davis, "The Share of Savings and Investment in Gross National Product during the 19th Century in the U.S.A.," in *Fourth International Conference of Economic History, Bloomington, Indiana, 1968* (Paris: Mouton, 1973), pp. 437–466.

5

fers of funds. At the same time the economy as a whole expanded very rapidly during this period, with net national product rising fivefold between 1870 and the beginning of the Federal Reserve period, while real per capita income almost tripled.[8]

These substantial changes in both the quantity and composition of output placed great demands on the financial system. The development of large-scale industry with its increased demands for external financing required the raising of unprecedented amounts of capital. One result was the rapid growth of the open market for funds in the late nineteenth century, especially the New York stock and bond markets, which were no longer limited to railroad issues. Another institutional development that resulted from this need to mobilize large sums was the rise of the investment banker. Private bankers, such as J. P. Morgan, were able to assemble much greater amounts of capital than ever before, as evidenced, for example, in the creation of U.S. Steel. Financial intermediaries, such as mutual savings banks, building and loan associations, and life insurance companies, grew rapidly and played significant roles in the mobilization and transfer of long-term capital from surplus to deficit areas, as also did mortgage companies.

A variety of institutions therefore were instrumental in mobilizing and transferring long-term capital. On the other hand, the market in short-term capital was primarily the province of the banking system, to which it was restricted by both sound banking theory and legal regulations. An open market in short-term funds, the commercial paper market, did spread rapidly during the period, but its principal customers were the banks. Commercial banks were by far the most numerous and important financial intermediaries in the postbellum period. The banking system had two important functions: the creation of the means of payment, and the mobilization and transfer of short-term capital, as op-

[8] Lance E. Davis et al., *American Economic Growth*. (New York: Harper & Row, 1972), p. 34.

posed to financial intermediaries in the long-term market, which were not allowed to create money, either in the form of bank notes or deposits. The adequacy of the banking system in fulfilling these functions had direct effects on the growth and stability of the American economy, and the post-bellum banking system has been severely criticized for its performance in both areas. That record of performance will be examined here.

In the late nineteenth century questions of banking and monetary policy, such as the appropriate type and volume of bank notes to be issued, the proper basis for the currency, the level of rural interest rates and the existence of banking monopolies there, were subject to more public discussion, debate, and outrage than in any other time in U.S. history, with the possible exception of the Jacksonian period. The national banking system was widely criticized as being unsuited to the needs of the country. Detractors pointed to its tendency to concentrate balances in New York and its resulting susceptibility to panics, and also to the unresponsiveness, or "inelasticity" in the word of the time, of the currency to seasonal or cyclical shifts in demand. Indeed, the banking system throughout the nineteenth century has been almost always pictured as a promoter of instability rather than of economic development.

This book will examine the structure and operation of the banking system in the postbellum period. Structure here will encompass not only such quantifiable features as the number of banks and bank density but also the legal framework and constraints under which the banks operated. In addition, the way in which practice frequently differed from legal requirements will be studied. In the process of portfolio selection, for example, banks were often able to evade or sidestep legal restrictions. Consequently, studies of the development of banking legislation, such as Knox's well-known *History of Banking*, can be misleading as to the actual workings of the financial system.

The National Monetary Commission in 1911 complained

that "no satisfactory account of the operations of European banks, no penetrating examination of the great credit institutions or of the organization of credit" was available, so its studies were designed to provide "more accurate and concrete information in regard to the actual practice of banking in these countries than has ever been published before."[9] These same criticisms apply equally well to studies of U.S. banking in the late nineteenth century, which have considered only the legal and theoretical constraints under which banks operated.

The demands of the postbellum economy, which was growing rapidly and also changing in composition, spawned a variety of financial institutions to meet its needs, in both the long- and short-term capital markets. The development of the open market in commercial paper represented one response to the need for interindustry and interregional transfers of funds. Several provisions of the National Banking Act established legal barriers to some profitable opportunities of banks. In addition to being a study of institutions, this is also a study of institutional change, in which the process of adaptation of the banking system will be examined. It will be shown that the banking system, through the development of the commercial paper market and the correspondent banking system, adjusted to mitigate the effects of the barriers to the mobility of funds, as the growth of state banks avoided the legal barriers to profitable operations imposed by the National Banking Act.

Just as the postbellum banking system was widely believed to be an accomplice, if not a promoter, of instability, it was also pictured as having been an imperfect and underdeveloped structure for the mobilization and transfer of short-term capital in the face of widespread barriers to interregional capital mobility. Lance Davis, for one, has argued that these pervasive barriers to capital flows were significant in American development, asserting, "In the United States

[9] U.S. National Monetary Commission, *Report* (Washington, D.C., 1911), pp. 4–5.

such immobilities distorted the pattern of growth throughout the entire nineteenth century; but they became much more important in the postbellum decades."[10]

Evidence of these barriers to capital mobility was well known in the postbellum period. In an efficient national short-term capital market, interest rates would be equalized across regions and sectors after allowing for differences in risk. Areas with high interest rates, indicating a high marginal product of capital, attract funds from relatively low interest rate regions; capital is thereby transferred into the region in which it may be employed most productively. At the same time, the inflow of funds reduces interest rates and consequently the differential between regions until in a perfect market interest rates are equalized.

Short-term interest rates, however, were not uniform across the United States in the postbellum era. Substantial differences among regional interest rates existed and were taken as evidence of the misallocation of financial resources. Logan Roots, president of the Arkansas Bankers' Association, noted in 1892 that in Little Rock it was often difficult to borrow on good security at 8–10 percent, whereas in Boston it was often difficult to loan at 3–5 percent, and noted, "The condition is well known. . . ."[11] More systematically, in an 1898 *Political Science Quarterly* article, R. M. Breckenridge compiled average weekly rates of discount from reports from selected cities as reported in *Bradstreet's*, which are reported in Table 1. These figures were supposed to represent the local discount rate on loans of the same quality—prime, double-name paper.[12] So, to the extent that

[10] Lance E. Davis, "Capital Immobilities and Finance Capitalism: A Study of Economic Evolution in the United States, 1820–1920," *Explorations in Entrepreneurial History*, Second Series, I (Fall 1963), p. 89.

[11] Logan H. Roots, untitled address, in "The Convention of the Arkansas Bankers' Association," *Bankers' Magazine*, XLIV (June 1892), p. 944.

[12] R. M. Breckenridge, "Discount Rates in the United States," *Political Science Quarterly*, XIII (March 1898), p. 122.

Table 1

Average Weekly Rate of Discount in Selected Cities, 1893–1897
(in percentages)

East		Midwest	
Boston	3.832	Cincinnati	5.012
Hartford	4.602	Pittsburgh	5.838
Providence	4.982	Cleveland	6.376
Portland, Me.	6.000	Indianapolis	6.369
New York	4.412	Chicago	5.740
Buffalo	6.007	Detroit	6.415
Philadelphia	4.642	Minneapolis	6.903
Baltimore	4.567	St. Paul	6.607
South		Duluth	7.253
New Orleans	5.853	St. Joseph	6.969
Richmond	6.000	Kansas City	6.911
Memphis	6.103	Omaha	7.980
Nashville	6.673		
Louisville	6.826	*West*	
Charleston	7.026	Denver	10.000
Galveston	7.311	Salt Lake City	8.000
Mobile	7.957	San Francisco	6.216
Savannah	7.992	Los Angeles	7.057
Atlanta	8.000	Portland	8.000
Birmingham	8.000	Seattle	9.969
Houston	8.000	Tacoma	9.273
Little Rock	8.015		
Dallas	8.342		

Source: R. M. Breckenridge, "Discount Rates in the United States,"
Political Science Quarterly, XIII (March 1898), p. 126.

the quality of loans and discounts was poorer in the interior and thus commanded higher rates there, this table understates the differences in average loan rates between regions. Breckenridge commented that these local differences in discount rates were so wide that "they must seem to many astonishing and inexplicable."[13]

[13] Ibid., p. 123.

What were the contemporary explanations for these differentials? One popular theory was that the regional differentials were due to the "disinclination of capital to migrate," which an interest rate difference of about 2 percent was necessary to overcome.[14] Breckenridge rejected this argument because the lack of an efficient mechanism to transfer funds between regions seemed to be much more important. The persistence of the differentials must be ascribed to "the failure of the American organization of credit adequately to mediate, with equitable charges, between those who need to borrow and those who are able and willing to lend."[15] In other words, the financial system provided no efficient mechanism of domestic arbitrage to equalize discount rates across regions.

This lack of formal mechanisms to promote interregional transfers of funds was a widely criticized aspect of the national banking system. The National Monetary Commission, charged by Congress to inquire as to what changes were necessary or desirable in the U.S. monetary system, noted that "there is a marked lack of equality in credit facilities between different sections of the country reflected in less favored communities, in retarded development, and great disparity in rates of discount. . . . Our system lacks an agency whose influence can be made effective in securing greater uniformity, steadiness, and reasonableness of rates of discount in all parts of the country."[16]

The prohibition of interstate branch banking was often identified as the institutional barrier to an efficient distribution of capital. The Indianapolis Monetary Commission observed: "Bank capital is in nearly every other country distributed largely by means of branch offices. No where save in the United States is there such a multitude of small and unconnected institutions."[17] Branch banking was argued by many to be the solution to the problem of the interregional

[14] Ibid., p. 129.   [15] Ibid., p. 141.
[16] *Report of the National Monetary Commission*, p. 9.
[17] *Report of the Indianapolis Monetary Commission* (Chicago: University of Chicago Press, 1898), p. 376.

allocation of capital;[18] an extensive system of branches across areas could efficiently allocate funds to the best advantage in contrast with the actual system of unit banking in which banks were small, isolated entities not participating in national markets.

Extensive studies of the branch banking systems in more than a dozen countries were done by the National Monetary Commission, and the tightly interconnected networks of branches in such countries as Canada, England, and Scotland were often cited with approval. In spite of the low population density, the rate of discount in Canada did not vary more than 1 to 1½ percent across the entire country, in sharp contrast to the United States.[19] These barriers to interregional capital mobility in turn were said to have had serious consequences in the misallocation of resources: "Even the strongest and most flourishing enterprises suffer from the lack of some efficient machinery for simultaneously borrowing in the accumulating, wealthy and investing sections of the country and lending the means thus acquired in the sections where opportunities for investment are more abundant than capital."[20]

However, it will be argued here that just as consideration of legal restrictions alone gives a misleading picture of nineteenth-century bank operations, an erroneous conception of the nature and extent of the short-term capital market will be acquired from examination only of the legal unit banking structure of the national banking system. Notwithstanding the prohibition of interstate branch banking, a com-

[18] See, for example, Breckenridge, "Discount Rates in the United States"; *Report of the Indianapolis Monetary Commission*; Thornton Cooke, "Branch Banking for the West and South," *Quarterly Journal of Economics*, XVIII (November 1903), pp. 97–113.

[19] Breckenridge, "Discount Rates in the United States," p. 130.

[20] Ibid., p. 141. Jeffrey Williamson, however, has recently estimated the effects of these distortions to be small in his model of nineteenth-century American development. Jeffrey G. Williamson, *Late Nineteenth-Century American Development* (Cambridge: Cambridge University Press, 1974), pp. 134–135.

plex and extensive network of interrelationships for the transfer of funds did exist among banks; they were not isolated entities. Jonathan Hughes was closer to the truth in observing, "By the end of the 1870s there existed a giant American financial system; virtually a national market for money."[21] Again, the banking system proved to be quite responsive to profit opportunities in spite of legal constraints.

Nevertheless, it is not enough to know that institutions existed for the transfer of short-term capital. In addition, we would like to know how successful these mechanisms of the interregional capital market in fact were in promoting the development of a national market. A study of the structure of financial markets and data on the size of interregional capital flows alone will not reveal the success of these channels in integrating local markets into a national one. One also needs to know what effects those flows had. In other words, the performance of the market, as indicated by interest rate movements, must be assessed as well as the structure.

The postbellum era experienced a remarkable convergence of regional interest rates, indicating the development of a national capital market over a relatively brief period. Our investigation will be confined to the short-term market, although Lance Davis suggests that the same process of interest rate convergence also proceeded in the long-term market at a slower pace.[22] Davis has derived regional series of gross and net returns on earning assets for both country and reserve city[23] national banks for the postbellum period,[24] which have become the standard measures of market performance in this period, serving as proxies for local interest

---

[21] Jonathan R. T. Hughes, *The Vital Few* (Boston: Houghton Mifflin Company, 1966), p. 360.

[22] Lance E. Davis, "The Investment Market, 1870–1914: The Evolution of a National Market," *Journal of Economic History*, XXV (September 1965), pp. 373–387.

[23] See Chapter IV for a description of country and reserve city banks.

[24] Davis, "The Investment Market," pp. 357–359.

13

rates. Consider Figure 1, which presents the movements of net returns on earning assets of country national banks by region[25] for the 1870–1914 period. Even though the figures

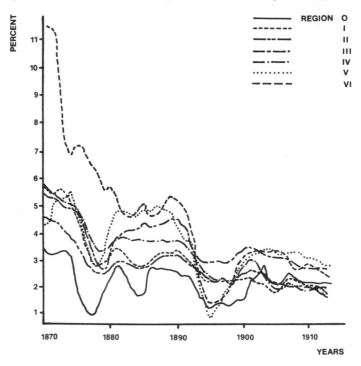

Figure 1. Three-Year Moving Averages of Net Returns on Earning Assets for Country Banks. Source: Lance E. Davis, "The Investment Market, 1870–1914: The Evolution of a National Market," *Journal of Economic History*, XXV (September 1965), p. 368. Reprinted with the permission of Lance Davis and the *Journal of Economic History*.

[25] Region I—Maine, Vermont, New Hampshire, Massachusetts, Rhode Island, Connecticut; Region II—New York, New Jersey, Pennsylvania, Delaware, Maryland, District of Columbia; Region III —Virginia, West Virginia, North Carolina, South Carolina, Georgia, Florida, Alabama, Mississippi, Louisiana, Texas, Arkansas, Kentucky, Tennessee; Region IV—Ohio, Indiana, Illinois, Michigan, Wisconsin, Minnesota, Iowa, Missouri; Region V—North Dakota, South Dakota,

are only proxies for the true interest rates, the trend is evident. Over the postbellum period interregional differentials narrowed substantially and a national market evolved. In Appendix A the construction of a series of local interest rates more precise than both Davis's gross and net return on earning assets and Smiley's recent postbellum regional interest rate series for the shorter 1888–1911 period is described.[26] Figure 2 presents these estimates of regional short-term interest rates[27] for country banks in the period 1888–1911. The regional interest rate series are weighted averages of the average rate on loans and discounts of country national banks by state, the weights being the relative sizes of the loan and discount portfolio.

Figure 3 presents the movements of the differentials between the Southern, Midwestern, and Western series and the

---

Nebraska, Kansas, Montana, Wyoming, Colorado, New Mexico, Oklahoma; Region VI—Washington, Oregon, California, Arizona, Nevada, Utah, Idaho.

[26] The series discussed in Appendix A are more accurate than those constructed by Smiley, even though they are based on the same sources—earnings statements and balance sheets of national banks reported annually by the U.S. Comptroller of the Currency. These series are semiannual rather than annual. In addition, the Smiley series in reality are rates of return on private earning assets, whereas in the present series items such as stocks and bonds are separated out; similarly, losses here are separated from the Losses and Premiums account. Finally, a correction is included to take into account the growth of the size of the loan portfolio in the derivation of the series reported here in order to avoid biasing the computed series downward. Gene Smiley, "Interest Rate Movement in the United States, 1888–1913," *Journal of Economic History*, XXXV (September 1975), p. 595.

[27] East—Maine, New Hampshire, Vermont, Massachusetts, Rhode Island, Connecticut, New York, New Jersey, Pennsylvania, Delaware, Maryland, District of Columbia; South—Virginia, West Virginia, North Carolina, South Carolina, Georgia, Florida, Alabama, Mississippi, Louisiana, Texas, Arkansas, Tennessee, Kentucky; Midwest—Ohio, Indiana, Illinois, Michigan, Wisconsin, Minnesota, Iowa, Missouri, Kansas, Nebraska, North Dakota, South Dakota; West—Colorado, Wyoming, Montana, Idaho, Nevada, Utah, New Mexico, Arizona, California, Oregon, Washington, Oklahoma.

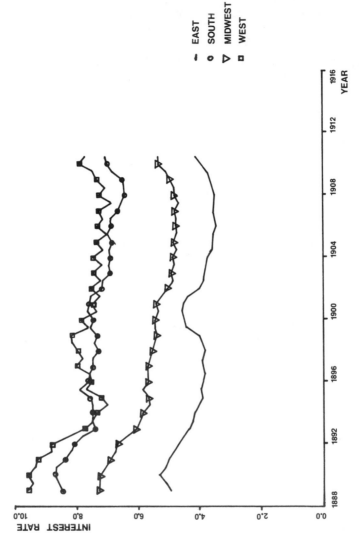

Figure 2. Five-Period Moving Averages of Semiannual Regional Short-Term Interest Rates for Country Banks.

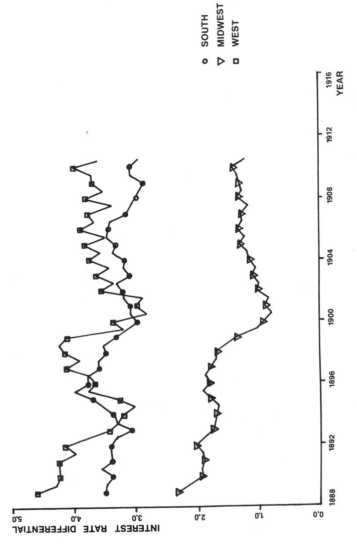

Figure 3. Interregional Short-Term Interest Rate Differentials with the Eastern Region, Country Banks.

Eastern series. In Figure 4 we see the differentials between interest rates in Regions II–VI and Region I rates, that is, New England regional interest rates. There clearly seems to be a decline in interregional interest rate differentials over time, and thus a gradual evolution of a national short-term capital market over the period. Figures 2 through 4 are in terms of nominal rates; the unsmoothed series and real rates are reported in Appendix A.[28]

In our period, average Middle Atlantic country bank rates are very close to those in New England and usually somewhat lower. Rates in Region IV, the North Central states,

---

[28] Figure A1 in Appendix A presents movements in regional real rates of interest. Nominal rates are composed of two components— the real rate and the expected proportional rate of change of prices:

$$r_n(t) = r_r(t) + \frac{\Delta P^e(t)}{P(t)}$$

To compute the real rate we impose a priori a lag structure for the determination of price expectations following the procedure of the Federal Reserve Bank of St. Louis. Their technique is simply to subtract a simple average of monthly rates of change in the implicit GNP price deflator over the previous 24 months from nominal rates. We may note that the movements in our real interest rate series correlate fairly well with the pattern of long swings or Kuznets cycles. In the period 1888–1911 the pattern of long swings shows a peak in 1892, a trough in 1896, and a peak in 1907. In the real and nominal series we see a high point in the early 1890s. However, the trough in the nominal series comes around 1896, but in the real series, not until around 1900. The next peak, in 1907, shows up quite distinctly in every region in the real series, but no upward movement at all is evident in the nominal series around that date. Davis finds a peak around 1901 in his series, which is also present in the movements of our nominal rates. On the other hand, the real series shows no turning point around 1901 and thus is consistent with long swings trends, which show no peak there either. For the calculation of real interest rate, see William P. Yohe and Davis S. Karnosky, "Interest Rates and Price Level Changes," *Federal Reserve Bank of St. Louis Review*, LI (December 1969), pp. 19–36. For long swings, see Richard Easterlin, "Influences in European Overseas Emigration before World War I," in R. Fogel and S. Engerman, eds., *Reinterpretation of American Economic History* (New York: Harper & Row, 1971), p. 393; Davis, "The Investment Market," p. 369.

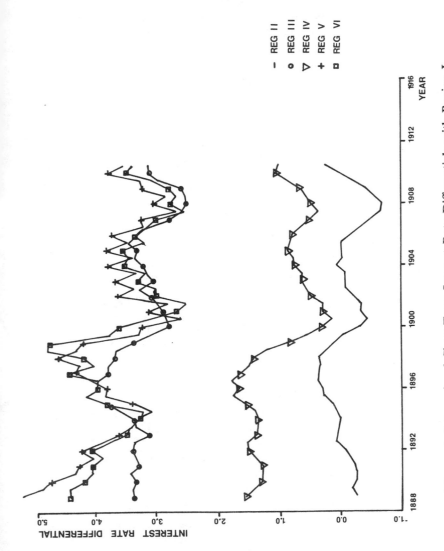

Figure 4. Interregional Short-Term Interest Rate Differentials with Region I, Country Banks.

narrow the gap with New England significantly in the late 1890s. By 1900 North Central and New England rates are virtually equal; after 1900 the difference is always less than 1 percentage point. However, here Midwestern rates do not fall below Eastern rates as Williamson finds.[29] Farther west, the differentials are larger, but the decreases are dramatic. For Region V, the Great Plains and Mountain states, the differential decreases from over 5 percent to less than 4 percent, a fall of almost 2 percentage points, or almost 40 percent. The differential for Region VI, Mountain and Pacific states, falls around 1 percentage point, or around 25 percent. On the other hand, Southern differentials show a somewhat smaller decrease of about 0.5 percentage points, or around 15 percent.

The postbellum period witnessed a movement toward the establishment of a national short-term capital market. In view of the fact that the antebellum capital market exhibited large and persistent interest rate differentials across regions, appearing to be a continuous state of disequilibrium, and that substantial structural changes were occurring in the postbellum economy, the convergence of regional interest rates and the narrowing of interregional interest rate differentials is all the more striking. How can this interest rate convergence in the postbellum period be accounted for? What forces were at work in promoting the development of a national money market? Was the integration of the regional capital markets into a national one the result of institutional changes promoting interregional flows of funds, as Breckenridge had argued was necessary?

This study will also investigate the process of short-term capital market integration in the postbellum United States and the forces underlying it. The analysis of the structure of the interregional capital market indicates that interregional financial flows were taking place, so local capital markets were at least partially integrated. However, the existence of

[29] Williamson, *Late Nineteenth-Century American Development,* pp. 135.

interregional interest rate differentials do not necessarily indicate the existence of an imperfect or segmented market. If there were transactions or information costs to the transfer of funds across regions or differentials in the riskiness of local loans, then interest rate differentials would exist even if there were no barriers to capital mobility, a perfect capital market. Could decreases in the riskiness of Southern and Western loans account for the narrowing differentials in the postbellum period, so that a perfect capital market had existed in fact, promoted by existing institutions, for the interregional transfer of funds? If local or regional capital markets were segmented to some degree, what forces contributed to the narrowing of interregional interest rate differentials and the erosion of monopoly power of local banks? Two major explanations of the process of capital market integration based on the existence of segmented local and regional capital markets will be tested—the institutional change hypothesis of Lance Davis, which emphasized the westward expansion of the commercial paper market in weaving local markets into a national one; and the market power hypothesis of Richard Sylla, which emphasized the role of local monopoly power protected by high legal barriers to entry in the National Banking Act in explaining observed interest rate differentials.

The following pages, then, will be a study of the structure and performance of the postbellum banking system. They will examine the functioning of both the individual bank and the banking system in the mobilization and transfer of capital, as well as the banking system's success in achieving a perfect short-term capital market. Chapter II will describe the banking system as a whole, whereas Chapter III will focus on the individual bank portfolio; Chapters IV and V will investigate the mechanisms for the interregional transfer of funds; Chapter VI will analyze the extent to which this structure for interregional transfers was employed and the forces behind regional interest rate convergence; finally, Chapter VII will summarize the findings.

21

CHAPTER II

The Growth of the Banking System

THE EXPANSION OF DEPOSITS

THE composition of the money stock changed dramatically in the period after the Civil War, with the proportion of deposits held relative to currency in the total money stock rising dramatically. In the mid-1860s deposits constituted somewhat less than 60 percent of the money stock, but by 1914 the share of deposits had risen to over 88 percent;[1] the public, which had held $1.50 of deposits for every dollar of currency after the Civil War, by the beginning of the Federal Reserve period held almost $9 of deposits for every currency dollar. Indeed, this remarkable downward trend in the ratio of currency to the total money stock continued until 1930, in spite of the fact that national bank notes were protected against loss from bank failure by the backing of government bonds, whereas depositors in general had no similar insurance.[2]

[1] The money stock here is M_2, defined as currency held by the public plus demand and time deposits at commercial banks. Milton Friedman and Anna Schwartz, *Monetary Statistics of the United States* (New York: Columbia University Press, 1970), pp. 4–13.

[2] Strangely enough, notwithstanding this rise in importance of deposits, most of the debate about the monetary policies of the time centered on the role of notes and currency, virtually ignoring deposits. One of the recurring criticisms of the national banking system was that the system of note issue for which it provided was inelastic with respect to changes in the demand for credit. Thus, when the demand for credit rose in the crop-moving season, the autumn, the supply of notes did not increase proportionally, as a result leading to stringencies. Little notice was taken of the fact that the volume of deposits was quite responsive to changes in demand.

Similarly, groups wishing to raise the price level focused almost exclusively on expanding the stock of currency by issuing more notes

One possible explanation for this sizable and sustained shift toward deposits in the period after the Civil War is based on the ending of the frontier. As population increased and transportation and communication improved in rural and remote areas, increasing numbers of farmers may have moved from self-sufficient operations to production for the market. Barter transactions and production for own use would have been supplanted by the expansion of the monetary economy, and along with it the growth of the banking system.[3] This extensive spread of the monetary system cannot be identified directly from available data, but it is unlikely that this effect would prove to be a major one here. Although the monetary economy may well have spread across the frontier, population there was so sparse relative to the rest of the country that only a small part of the total decline in the currency-deposit ratio could be accounted for by it.

Most explanations for the substantial increase in the ratio of deposits to currency emphasize the role of demand. Increases in the demand for deposits by the public lead to a rise in the deposit-currency ratio and ultimately to the expansion of the banking system. Friedman and Schwartz accord primary importance to the rise in real income per capita in accounting for the doubling of the deposit-currency ratio during the period 1879–1897. They argue that de-

---

(the Greenbackers) or by increasing the coinage (the Silverites). Very few recognized, as Charles G. Dawes argued, that questions of changing the price level could not be answered with reference to the currency stock alone, because it constituted only a small part of the money stock. The role of deposits also had to be considered. Charles G. Dawes, *The Banking System of the United States* (Chicago: Rand, McNally and Co., 1894), pp. 23–24.

[3] The shift from an agrarian economy to an industrial one with the concomitant transformation from a self-sufficient barter society to one based on a monetary economy has been advanced as the explanation for the rapid development of the Swedish commercial banking system over almost the same period, 1871–1913. Lars Jonung, "The Behavior of Velocity in Sweden, 1871–1913," Nationalekomiska Institution, University of Lund, 1976.

posits are regarded as a more satisfactory vehicle for holding substantial sums than currency, so that as incomes rise the public will substitute deposits for currency;[4] in other words, the income elasticity of the demand for bank deposits is greater than 1. However, the rate of growth of total deposits, demand and time, before the turn of the century was so great that the income elasticity in question would have had to have been substantially greater than 2 for growth in real income to account for all of the observed shift toward deposits.[5] In light of recent evidence on the demand for money, such a figure appears to be extremely high,[6] so most likely other factors influenced the relative growth of deposits in addition to the expansion of real per capita income.

Another frequently mentioned cause of the shift in the demand for deposits relative to currency is based on a change in taste by the public. It is argued that the public, who, in general, in antebellum times preferred to hold their money balances in the form of currency, gradually became willing to hold them as deposits, as evidenced by the spread of the use of checks. During the last part of the nineteenth century

[4] Milton Friedman and Anna Schwartz, *A Monetary History of the United States, 1867–1960* (Princeton, N.J.: Princeton University Press, 1963), p. 122.

[5] This calculation uses Gallman's estimates of GNP. Robert E. Gallman, "Gross National Product in the United States, 1834–1909," in Conference on Research in Income and Wealth, ed., *Output, Employment, and Productivity in the United States after 1800* (New York: Columbia University Press, 1966), p. 26.

[6] Goldfeld estimates the long-run income elasticity of demand for demand deposits to be about 0.6. Figures for separating total deposits into demand and time deposits are not available before 1914; however, in that year time deposits made up only a little more than 30 percent of total deposit holdings. It is generally acknowledged that the elasticity for time deposits is greater than that for demand deposits, but in this case it would have been very high indeed to have produced an income elasticity of demand for deposits greater than 2. Friedman and Schwartz, *Monetary Statistics*, p. 14; Stephen Goldfeld, "The Demand for Money Revisited," *Brookings Papers on Economic Activity*, 3 (1973), p. 606.

the increasing acceptance of the use of checks thus led to the expansion of deposit banking. This explanation will be discussed in some detail later in this chapter with regard to the growth of state banks, where it will be argued that checks were already widely in use by the end of the Civil War and spread very rapidly thereafter, so that this could not have been a significant influence on demand over a long period. Finally, one other effect influencing the growth in deposits over the period, suggested by Cagan, was the increasing urbanization in the United States.[7]

This dramatic increase in the use of deposits after the Civil War is reflected in the growth in the numbers of banks. Table 2 shows the expansion from 1850 to 1910 of the

Table 2

Number of Commercial Banks
in the United States, 1850–1910

Year	National	State	Private	Total
1850	—	830	398[a]	1,228
1860	—	1,579	1,108	2,687
1870	1,612	261	1,903	3,776
1880	2,076	1,051	2,318	5,445
1890	3,484	2,830	4,365	10,679
1900	3,731	8,696		12,427
1910	7,138	17,376		24,514

[a] Estimate for 1853.

Source: Richard Sylla, "The United States, 1863–1913," in Rondo Cameron, ed., *Banking and Economic Development* (New York: Oxford University Press, 1972), p. 238. Reprinted with the permission of the Oxford University Press.

three major components of the postbellum banking system—national banks, state banks, and private banks. National

[7] Phillip Cagan, *Determinants and Effects of Changes in the Stock of Money, 1875–1960* (New York: National Bureau of Economic Research, 1965), pp. 126–128.

banks were chartered by the federal government, more specifically by the Comptroller of the Currency in the Treasury Department; state banks were chartered by state authorities; private banks were unincorporated, with generally no responsibilities to any government.

The growth in the use of deposits necessitated the spread of local banks. In the antebellum period a state bank could issue enough notes to satisfy the currency-holding preferences of individuals over a wide area. On the other hand, it would have been very inconvenient for all of those widespread individuals to maintain deposit accounts with one bank in one location. Deposit banking meant local banking. Because branch banking was prohibited to national and most state banks, however, the spread of deposit banking together with the spread of population led to a rapid increase in the number of unit banks.

The growth of the banking system, as evidenced in Table 2, however, was not simply a response to increases in the demand for deposits relative to currency by the public. Changes on the supply side, as well as on the demand side, were important. Banks generally became easier to establish during the postbellum period. The National Banking Act was based on a policy of free banking, whereby any group fulfilling the specified conditions could obtain a bank charter rather than having to apply to the legislature for a special charter. Such a policy, introduced by New York and Michigan in the late 1830s, greatly facilitated entry into the banking system. Moreover, many states liberalized regulations, such as capital and reserve requirements, also making entry easier.

Thus, Friedman and Schwartz attribute the increase in the deposit-currency ratio after the Civil War to "the rapid spread of commercial banking and hence to the greater usefulness of bank deposits." Similarly, the more widespread availability of checking facilities in the period 1879–1897 is identified as a contributing factor to the observed rise.[8]

[8] Friedman and Schwartz, *A Monetary History*, pp. 56, 122.

Needless to say, it is extremely difficult to disentangle the relative importance of the demand and supply effects, but undoubtedly more liberalized chartering provisions had a significant role in promoting the growth of the banking system. Now we shall examine the growth of the major components of the banking system in more detail.

NATIONAL BANKS

The National Banking Acts of 1863 and 1864 established the framework of the national banking system. Their principal purposes were to provide a market for government bonds issued during the Civil War and to establish a uniform national currency based on national bank notes, replacing the heterogeneous mixture of state bank notes that had characterized antebellum note circulation. National banks could issue notes only if government bonds had been purchased as security for them. However, in the nine months after the passage of the 1863 Act, just 134 banks availed themselves of the opportunity of obtaining a national charter, with the number rising to only 450 after sixteen months.[9] Additional incentives for state banks to convert were provided by Congress in the passage of an act levying a 10 percent tax on all state bank notes issued after July 1, 1866. As a result, by that date most state banks had converted into national ones, so that the national banking system encompassed 1,634 banks.[10] The number of state banks fell from 1,562 in 1860 to 247 in 1868, and finally began to rise again only after 1870.[11] For a detailed description of the origins and antecedents of the national banking system, one should consult the National Monetary Commission publica-

---

[9] Charles F. Dunbar, *Chapters on the Theory and History of Banking* (New York: G. P. Putnam's Sons, 1901), p. 161.

[10] Ibid., p. 162.

[11] George E. Barnett, *State Banks and Trust Companies since the Passage of the National-Bank Act* (Washington, D.C.: U.S. Government Printing Office, 1911), p. 11.

27

tion appropriately titled *The Origins of the National Banking System*.[12]

The rapid demise of the state bank in the mid-1860s is generally taken as evidence of the importance of the power of note issue. Around the Civil War, it is argued, notes were still widely preferred to demand deposits as a form of holding money and consequently one of the bank's most profitable operations, functioning as a bank of issue, had in effect been restricted to national banks. Thus, national and state banks were not perfect substitutes. Richard Sylla has argued that the effective prohibition on state bank note issue functioned as a very important barrier to entry in the banking system and attributed the slow growth of state banks after the Civil War to this loss of the power of note issue. "The habit of writing checks, which seems so simple today, was slow in coming to the rural districts of America in this period and so, therefore, was pure deposit banking."[13]

Just as the restriction on state bank note issue insulated national banks from state bank competition immediately after the Civil War, other restrictive provisions of the National Banking Act of 1864 made the entry of new banks much more difficult, and thus restricted competition among national banks themselves, especially in small towns. Relatively high minimum capital requirements were established for national banks. A national bank's minimum capital stock had to be at least $50,000 in towns with a population under 6,000, $100,000 in cities with a population greater than 50,000.[14] In many towns the amount of business was not sufficient to enable a bank to earn a reasonable return on a capital of $50,000. Consequently, the high minimum capi-

[12] A. M. Davis, *The Origins of the National Banking System* (Washington, D.C.: U.S. Government Printing Office, 1910).

[13] Richard Sylla, "The United States, 1863–1913," in Rondo Cameron, ed., *Banking and Economic Development* (New York: Oxford University Press, 1972), pp. 244–246.

[14] A. T. Huntington and Robert J. Mawhinney, *Laws of the United States Concerning Money, Banking, and Loans, 1778–1909* (Washington, D.C.: U.S. Government Printing Office, 1910), p. 333.

tal requirements served as a severe restriction on entry in small towns.

The other significant entry barrier established in the 1864 Act was the prohibition of mortgage lending by national banks. The unfavorable experience of antebellum New York state banks in using real estate mortgages as the basis for note issue had made many suspicious of real estate collateral. The principal problem was insufficient liquidity, because mortgages were subject to a longer foreclosure process and also because land values often fell precipitously in periods of financial stress.[15] This suspicion of real estate collateral was written into the National Banking Act. National banks were prohibited from mortgage lending, with the ban remaining in effect until 1913. Thus, in agricultural areas, such as the South and West, where land was the principal asset, national banks were not allowed to loan on real estate. Competition from state banks, savings banks, and trust companies, however, forced many national banks to loan on real estate, contrary to the prohibition. Before the passage of the Federal Reserve Act, records indicated that more than 17 percent of national banks illegally made loans on real estate security.[16]

STATE BANKS

The expansion of state banks was severely retarded in the decade or so following the Civil War by the loss of the power of note issue. However, even if notes had been the preferred form of holding money balances by the public, so that state banks, acting only as banks of deposit, were at a substantial disadvantage, this hindrance was relatively short-lived and by no means persisted through the rest of the nineteenth century, as Sylla implies. The use of checks and deposit

[15] Leonard C. Helderman, *National and State Banks* (Boston: Houghton Mifflin Company, 1931), p. 150.

[16] Thomas P. Kane, *The Romance and Tragedy of Banking* (New York: The Bankers' Publishing Co., 1923), p. 321.

29

banking were already widespread during the Civil War and then also expanded rapidly in the period following it, so that soon afterwards state banks were viable competitors to national ones, even though they were only banks of deposit rather than banks of issue.

The timing of the spread of deposit banking is very difficult to measure. One study examined changes in the ratio of total deposits to total liabilities over time of state banks in Wisconsin,[17] but this is clearly an inappropriate measure in the postbellum period. State banks were unable to issue notes, so there is no possibility of observing changes in the relative proportions of notes and deposits in state bank liability portfolios. Thus, there is no reason to believe that changes in the deposits-liabilities ratio reflect changes in the demand for deposits versus notes.

Such a measure of the growth of deposit banking is also inapplicable to national banks even though both notes and deposits were components of their liabilities. It was in relatively underdeveloped areas where this shift toward deposit banking took place after the Civil War, but it was precisely in those areas that few national bank notes were issued, an imbalance often remarked on at the time.[18] Rural areas, such as the South and West, where according to Sylla state banks were at the greatest disadvantage for lacking the power of note issue, were also the regions where national banks made the least use of that power. Moreover, it was in those regions where the growth of state banks was the fastest.

Another, more recent, study of Wisconsin banking used changes in the amount of deposits per capita by county as the index of the spread of deposit banking in the countryside. The rapid increase in deposit holdings across the state

[17] Leonard B. Krueger, *History of Commercial Banking in Wisconsin* (Madison: University of Wisconsin Press, 1933), p. 139.

[18] See John A. James, "The Conundrum of the Low Issue of National Bank Notes," *Journal of Political Economy*, LXXXIV (April 1976), pp. 359–367.

led to rejection of Sylla's assertion that deposit banking spread only slowly in rural areas and to the conclusion that by 1900 deposit banking was firmly established in all parts of Wisconsin.[19] The measure used there, changes in deposits per capita, offers evidence that is certainly consistent with the spread of deposit banking, but it is not necessarily conclusive proof. For one thing, it is only a relative measure, comparing levels over time. Since one cannot identify a particular level of deposits per capita with widespread deposit banking, it might have been the case that it had already been well established at the beginning of the period. In addition, to the extent that the spread of deposit banking is identified with a shift in preferences on the part of the public in rural areas, the measure is ambiguous, because an increase in deposits per capita might also be the result of a rise in a real income, with preferences constant.

Nevertheless, even though adequate measures of the spread of deposit banking are difficult to construct, it is clear that the use of checks and deposit banking were spreading rapidly. Even in the early part of the nineteenth century, the amount of deposits of banks in commercial centers almost consistently was greater than the volume of their notes in circulation,[20] and the practice spread from urban areas into the countryside during the antebellum period. By the 1850s deposit banking was becoming more important than note issue even in such western outposts as Chicago, which had a population of 29,983 in 1850.[21] This increasing use of de-

[19] Richard Keehn, "Federal Bank Policy, Bank Market Structure, and Bank Performance: Wisconsin, 1863–1914," *Business History Review*, XLVIII (Spring 1974), pp. 7–8.

[20] J. Van Fenstermaker, "The Development of American Commercial Banking: 1782–1837," Bureau of Economic and Business Research Series No. 5, Kent State University, 1965, p. 39.

[21] Rollin G. Thomas, "The Development of State Banks in Chicago" (unpublished Ph.D. dissertation, University of Chicago, 1930), p. 45; Fritz Redlich, *The Molding of American Banking: Men and Ideas* (New York: Johnson Reprint Co., 1968), p. vii.

posits continued after the Civil War, so that by the 1880s there is little evidence of barriers to the growth of deposit banking.

The Comptroller of the Currency occasionally collected data from national banks on the proportion of total bank receipts in the form of checks and drafts; these data provide some suggestion of the extent of the differences in preferences for notes against deposits across regions. The higher the proportion of checks in total receipts, the smaller the preference for holding notes in that area. Even if many people did not use banks directly, as in the South, in the course of business transactions funds would eventually work their way to be deposited in a bank; therefore the composition of bank receipts should be indicative of the relative amounts of notes and deposits in the area. Table 3 presents

Table 3

Proportion of Checks and Drafts in Total Receipts of Country. and Reserve City National Banks, 1881–1890
(in percent)

	Country Banks		Reserve City Banks	
Region	1881	1890	1881	1890
I	82.6	87.9	96.5	94.1
II	82.5	85.3	94.4	92.2
III	70.0	79.0	91.3	91.8
IV	74.5	79.2	88.7	90.7
V	72.6	79.6	—	95.9
VI	52.0	69.9	91.8	85.6

Source: U.S. Comptroller of the Currency, *Annual Report*, 1881 (Washington, D.C.: U.S. Government Printing Office, 1881), pp. 17–19; *Annual Report*, 1890, pp. 27–28.

the shifts in the proportion of checks in total receipts for both country and reserve city national banks during the period June 30, 1881, to July 1, 1890, in Regions I–VI.

Not too much faith should be placed in the reserve city

figures, however, because there were so few reserve city banks in some regions. For example, Omaha was the only reserve city in Region V; San Francisco, the only one in Region VI; Boston, the only reserve city in Region I. Also, the addition of new, smaller reserve cities could make it appear as if there had been a decrease in the use of checks, such as in Region II. Nevertheless, the general patterns are quite clear. Checks were received relatively more frequently by banks in cities than by those in rural areas. Eastern rural districts, Regions I and II, showed greater use of checks than Southern and Western regions. The trend toward the greater use of checks is evident in every rural region. However, even in 1881 the great extent to which checks were used in rural areas is striking. Only the Pacific and far Mountain states in Region VI showed the use of checks less than 70 percent in 1881, although the amount of variation within some regions was substantial; in 1881 in Region V, for example, the percentages ranged from 81.1 percent in Colorado to 33.6 percent in Wyoming. The use of September dates rather than midsummer ones does not change the general pattern. In addition, as early as 1871 a study of fifty-two Ohio banks, including city, small city, and country banks done for the Chairman of the House Banking and Currency Committee (James Garfield), revealed that 88 percent of receipts were in the form of checks and drafts.[22]

In 1894 the Comptroller of the Currency reported on a survey of the usage of credit instruments in which 2,465 out of 3,774 national banks reported on the form of deposits of retail firms—in particular, dealers in food, clothing, furniture, and fuel, the combined outlay on which amounted to 72.6 percent of total average household expenditure. Such deposits were taken to reflect the use of credit instruments in normal retail transactions by households. Checks and drafts were used in 58.9 percent of the surveyed retail transactions. There was relatively little geographical variation in the frequency of the use of checks. In fact, the Southern

[22] *Proceedings of the American Bankers' Association*, 1881, p. 45.

regions showed the most frequent receipt of checks,[23] whereas the North Central region showed the smallest proportion, with 54.3 percent of recorded retail transactions made by checks. Similarly there was little variation in the use of checks with changes in city size; 55.9 percent of retail transactions were done by checks in cities of 500,000 and over, whereas the proportion was 55.6 percent in cities below 10,000.[24] The percentages cited here are smaller than those in Table 3 because those figures represented the proportion of checks used in all transactions and hence included wholesale operations, which raised the average considerably. However, both studies probably overstated the total use of cash in retail transactions, because those areas excluded from the study, small country towns with no national banks, were areas where, according to the Comptroller of the Currency, trade was done mostly on the basis of book credit at a general store and little money was used.[25] In addition, in such small towns the use of checks could not have been too difficult, because it was there, as will be shown in Chapter VI, that the growth of state banks was the greatest.

Thus, the use of checks spread rapidly even into rural areas in the antebellum period and immediately after the Civil War, so that by the late nineteenth century it was an established practice virtually everywhere. Evidence on the nature of deposits at national banks shows that checks constituted a majority of total receipts even of country banks in every region by at least 1881. Even though the loss of the power of note issue may have been a serious one during the Civil War, its importance waned rapidly in the postbellum period. At least by the early 1880s, state banks, which were only banks of deposit, were again in a position to be serious competitors to national banks.

Another serious obstacle to the growth of state banking

[23] South Atlantic Region—62.3 percent checks; South Central Region—65.6 percent checks.

[24] U.S. Comptroller of the Currency, *Annual Report*, 1894 (Washington, D.C.: U.S. Government Printing Office, 1894), pp. 18–23.

[25] Ibid., p. 18.

immediately after the Civil War was the difficulty of incorporation, due to the fact that in many states special legislative approval was needed; in contrast, the national banking system was based on free banking. Any group fulfilling the statute requirements could obtain a national charter. State bank incorporation laws will be discussed in more detail in Chapter VI.

The growth of state banks in the period immediately after the Civil War was considerably impeded by the difficulty of incorporation by special charter as well as by the loss of the power of note issue. As shown in Figure 5, the number of

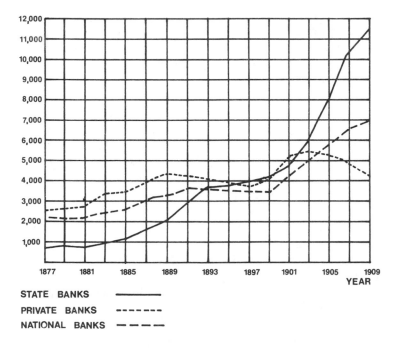

STATE BANKS ——————

PRIVATE BANKS ― ― ― ― ―

NATIONAL BANKS ― ― ― ―

Figure 5. National Monetary Commission Series of Private, State, and National Banks, 1877–1909. Source: George E. Barnett, *State Banks and Trust Companies since the Passage of the National Bank Act* (Washington, D.C.: U.S. Government Printing Office, 1911), p. 202.

state banks rose only very slowly between 1877 and 1883. After the mid-1880s, however, the growth of state banks was extremely rapid, due in part to shifts in the demand for holding deposits, so that as the public began to hold more deposits relative to currency the disadvantage of the lack of the power of note issue became less important, and also to shifts in supply because of liberalized incorporation laws. The rapid expansion of state banks, private banks, and other financial intermediaries, such as trust companies, in the postbellum period represents the response of the banking system in developing substitutes for national banks in order to escape many of the restrictions imposed by the National Banking Act. Just as the National Banking Act was the immediate cause of the decline of the state banking system during and immediately following the Civil War, it was also the spur to its development later in the period because of its restrictions.

Many of the national bank regulations were particularly unsuited for small rural banks. As noted earlier, the relatively high minimum capital requirements for national banks certainly limited entry in small towns and discouraged it altogether in very small ones, because the level of business there was insufficient to yield a reasonable return on that large an investment. On the other hand, capital requirements for state banks were usually much lower, encouraging the formation of state rather than national banks in small towns; the effects of these lower capital requirements will be discussed in more detail in Chapter VI.

According to George Barnett, "There is no more characteristic difference between the state banking laws and the national-bank act than the fact that, in almost all the States, state bank and trust companies may make loans on the security of real estate, whereas national banks are prohibited from doing so."[26] Following the example of the National Banking Act, many state banking laws originally prohibited loans on real estate, but over time more and more states dropped the provision, so that by 1910 real estate loans

[26] Barnett, *State Banks and Trust Companies*, p. 99.

were permitted for all state banks except those in New Mexico and Rhode Island. Indeed, the proportion of the portfolio that might be invested in such loans was limited in only ten states—Michigan, New York, North Dakota, Ohio, Oklahoma, Pennsylvania, South Carolina, Texas, Vermont, and Wisconsin.[27]

National banks were also limited to extending loans of an amount not more than one-tenth of bank capital to any one lender, which in 1906 was increased to one-tenth of capital and surplus. Such a provision encouraged the spreading of risk in the loan portfolio, but at the same time made it difficult for many large firms to be accommodated by their banks. One effect of this regulation was the growth of open-market borrowing and private, or investment, banking.

The excessive loan limitation was also a significant impediment to banks in smaller towns, which may have had only a very limited range of qualified borrowers from which to choose. Once again, however, state banking regulations in almost all cases were made more liberal than the national one. Only two states, New Hampshire and North Carolina, had a restriction as severe as the national act. Other states had limitations of larger percentages of capital or capital and surplus, ranging up to 30 percent of capital and surplus in Wisconsin. No restrictions at all on amounts that one borrower could be extended existed in ten states—Arizona, Arkansas, Delaware, Florida, Indiana, Mississippi, New Mexico, Pennsylvania, Tennessee, and Washington.[28]

Country national banks were required to maintain specified reserves described in Chapter IV, in lawful money or in part in deposits with reserve city and central reserve city banks, as percentages of deposits, which were strictly enforced. State banks, on the other hand, in many cases were under no restrictions at all with respect to the maintenance of a required reserve. In Wisconsin, for example, no cash reserve was required until the passage of the new banking law in 1903, which called for a reserve equal to 15 percent

[27] Ibid., p. 100.   [28] Ibid., pp. 87–88.

of total deposits.[29] Many other states were likewise quite slow in adopting reserve requirements, and the rules that were ultimately adopted were in almost all cases less stringent than those in the National Banking Act. A number of states graduated reserve requirements by city population, with higher requirements in larger cities; different reserve requirements were enforced for different types of deposits, demand and time, in several states. Consequently, compact summary of state reserve requirements is not possible here.[30] In no state did reserves have to consist entirely of cash in the vault. Balances held in other banks could be counted as one-half to three-quarters of required reserves, again there being more liberal requirements in most states than those on national banks.

State and private banks, therefore, in large part developed in response to restrictions imposed on national banks. By 1900 the number of state banks exceeded the number of national banks, although the number of state and private banks combined exceeded national banks even in 1870. The rise of state banks was especially dramatic in rural, agricultural areas, where national bank restrictions had their heaviest impact. In 1910 only 2 percent of New England bank capital was held by state banks; in the South it was 80 percent.[31] It was not until 1906 that non-national commercial bank assets exceeded total national bank assets, so Sylla described the response of the banking system to the restrictions imposed by the National Banking Acts as delayed and drawn out.[32] However, in view of the very substantial initial disadvantages of the lack of the power of note issue and the difficulty of incorporation in many states, the growth of state banks after the mid-1880s appears quite impressive.

[29] Krueger, *History of Commercial Banking*, p. 155.

[30] For more detail see Barnett, *State Banks and Trust Companies*, pp. 110–134.

[31] Helderman, *National and State Banks*, p. 161.

[32] Richard Sylla, "Federal Policy, Banking Market Structure, and Capital Mobilization in the United States, 1863–1913," *Journal of Economic History*, XXIX (December 1969), p. 662.

Even though they had been deprived of the power of note issue, which was quite valuable at least in antebellum times, state banks were by no means inferior investments relative to national banks, because at the same time they were able to operate under fewer constraints. In most cases, state banks were able to operate with less capital and lower reserves, and to engage in a wider variety of lending activities, such as on real estate security, than national banks. For example, during the 1905–1914 decade Chicago state banks earned over 20 percent more on invested capital than national banks, a 10.9 as opposed to a 9.0 percent rate of return.[33]

TRUST COMPANIES

Another institution that developed in response to the restrictions of the National Banking Act in the late nineteenth century was the trust company. Originally established to act as trustees of estates and bond issues, executors, and guardians, in the 1880s trusts began to assume all the functions of commercial banks, except of course for note issue, in spite of the intentions of the state governments that chartered them. The early trust companies, which had the power to receive trust deposits and to loan money, were able to expand into commercial banking because of the difficulty in distinguishing between the exercise of such powers in pursuit of the trust business as opposed to the banking business.[34]

Trust companies, like state banks, were freed from many of the restrictions on the operations of national banks. For example, in New York no cash reserves were required against deposits for trust companies and they were allowed to invest their funds in real estate, to buy and sell stocks, and to lend money on realty, all powers that had been denied or severely restricted to national banks.[35] As a result, trust

---

[33] Thomas, "The Development of State Banks," p. 358.

[34] Barnett, *State Banks and Trust Companies*, p. 16.

[35] Alexander D. Noyes, *Forty Years of American Finance* (New York: G. P. Putnam's Sons, 1898), p. 367.

companies were able to offer interest rates on demand deposits that most banks subject to reserve requirements could not meet. One response to the threat posed by the trust companies was combination, so that it was not uncommon to see a national bank and a trust company operated and controlled by the same stockholders, frequently in the same building.[36]

Less than one hundred trust companies were in existence in 1888, but the number began to grow rapidly after 1900. By 1909 almost 1,100 trust companies were in operation, concentrated primarily in the East. Nearly one-half of all trust companies in 1909 were located in New England, New York, or Pennsylvania.[37] Relatively few trust companies were located in Western and Southern states, where the greatest expansion of the banking system and fall in interest rates occurred. Consequently, because the emphasis here is on the role of the banking system in the development of a national capital market and the promotion of interregional short-term capital flows, trust companies will not be considered further.

PRIVATE BANKS

The growth of the private, or unincorporated, bank was another development in the attempt to reconcile the increasing demands for banking services with the restrictions of the National Banking Act. Indeed, until the mid-1890s the private banks, which operated under no charter at all, were the most common type. Figure 5 shows that between 1877 and 1888 the number of private banks almost doubled, increasing from 2,432 to 4,064.[38] Expansion immediately after

---

[36] Kane, *The Romance and Tragedy of Banking*, p. 169.

[37] Barnett, *State Banks and Trust Companies*, p. 204.

[38] The National Monetary Commission series shown in the figure understates the actual number of private banks as compared with the definitive series in *All-Bank Statistics*. Unfortunately, however, the *All-Bank Statistics* series goes back only to 1896, and the N.M.C. series is deemed to be the next most accurate estimate. See Board of Governors of the Federal Reserve System, *All-Bank Statistics, 1896–1955* (Washington, D.C.: 1959), pp. 22–33.

the Civil War was especially rapid because most state banking laws were repealed or made obsolete by the fact that most of them were intended to regulate banks of issue.[39] Into this void stepped the private banks as competitors to national ones, but unencumbered by such restrictions. In Iowa, for example, the general or free banking law, never used but already obsolete, was repealed in March 1870, and private banks flourished as a result.[40]

Private banks, like state banks, were only banks of deposit rather than banks of issue, although their principal function differed in various areas. In the East many private bankers, including Jay Cooke, J. P. Morgan, and Kuhn and Loeb, were engaged in investment or mortgage banking. Some private banks, such as T. Mellon and Sons in Pittsburgh,[41] operated essentially as commercial banks and were serious competitors to chartered ones, although few were of the size of the Mellon bank. Private bankers in the mid-nineteenth century also functioned as bill or note brokers, serving as intermediaries between buyers and sellers of notes. Although bill brokerage had earlier been only an appendage to the general private banking business or combined with security brokerage, by the 1880s specialized private banks, or commercial paper houses, began to appear.

In interior regions one of the important functions of private banks was dealing in real estate transactions, often serving as local agents for mortgage companies. On the frontier, in small communities the general store normally was the center of business life and often evolved into a private bank, most of the time with little capital backing. Private bankers were usually engaged in another business at the same time, so that there was a real danger if the banker failed as a merchant or whatever that his creditors would take the assets of the bank in compensation. Similarly, although not

[39] Barnett, *State Banks and Trust Companies*, p. 11.

[40] Howard H. Preston, *History of Banking in Iowa* (Iowa City: State Historical Society of Iowa, 1922), p. 135.

[41] Paul Trescott, *Financing American Enterprise* (New York: Harper & Row, 1963), pp. 84–86.

strictly counted as private banks, the general stores in the South functioned as financial intermediaries in the provision of credit and served as another substitute for the chartered banking system.[42] Sylla argues that antebellum private bankers functioned in ways very similar to chartered banks,[43] and there is no reason to believe that the statement does not apply to the postbellum period also. Private banks were substitutes to some extent for incorporated banks.

The distinguishing feature of most private or unincorporated banks in interior regions was the smallness of their capital. Private banks provided banking facilities for small communities that could not have supported a bank with the larger state or national capital requirements. As a result, even very small towns were able to support more than one bank. North Liberty, Iowa, had a population of under 200 in 1915 but had two banks; Battle Creek, Iowa, was a town of 688 in 1915 but supported three banks.[44] In Iowa in 1875 there were about 200 private banks, as compared with 75 national ones.[45] In Wisconsin in 1875 there were 76 private banks, more than double the number of national banks and triple the number of state banks, accounting for almost 20 percent of total banking resources.[46] In Michigan in 1887, of 336 commercial banks 208 were private, only 20 were state banks, and 108 were national banks.[47] In addition to providing credit facilities for very small towns, private banks

[42] For an examination of the role of the general store in the Southern financial system, see Roger Ransom and Richard Sutch, "Documenting Monopoly Power in the Rural South: The Case of the General Store," Southern Economic History Project, Working Paper No. 15 (Riverside, Calif., April 1976).

[43] Richard Sylla, "Forgotten Men of Money: Private Bankers in Early U.S. History," *Journal of Economic History*, XXXVI (March 1976), pp. 173–188.

[44] Preston, *History of Banking*, p. 354.

[45] Ibid., p. 92.

[46] Krueger, *History of Commercial Banking*, p. 126.

[47] T. H. Hinchman, *Banks and Banking in Michigan* (Detroit: M. Graham, 1887), p. 159.

also offered competition for chartered banks in larger ones. For example, Rome, Georgia, with a population of 4,500 in 1883, supported three banks—one national and two private ones.[48]

The existence of high minimum national bank capital requirements, then, did not mean that small towns were necessarily without banking services or even that they had no choice of banks. The rapid growth of private banks until 1888 indicates that even in the early part of the period banks of discount were not at an insurmountable disadvantage because of the lack of the power of note issue. Moreover, most of these unincorporated banks were established in very small towns, exactly the areas where preference for notes as opposed to deposits was supposed to have been the strongest.

In addition, private banks were particularly important in areas such as Texas, where they represented the only institutions providing banking services. Texans had long shown animosity toward chartered banks by prohibiting them in the constitutions of 1845, 1861, and 1866, even though under the 1868 constitution incorporation was possible and between 1870 and 1875 more than forty state banks were established. Under the 1876 constitution, however, the chartering of banks was once again prohibited, with the ban remaining in effect until the passage of a general banking law in 1905. As a result, the number of private banks grew from 86 at the end of 1873 to 421 in 1904.[49]

In most other areas the rate of growth of private banks diminished substantially after the mid-1880s. Between 1888 and 1909 the number of private banks rose only from 4,064 to 4,407. Barnett argues, however, that most of the growth in this latter period in reality was due to brokers' banks, which concealed an actual decline in the number of private banks in small towns. After deducting private banks in New

---

[48] Address of John C. Printup, *Proceedings of the American Bankers' Association*, 1883, p. 66.

[49] Redlich, *The Molding of American Banking*, p. xxvi; Barnett, *State Banks and Trust Companies*, pp. 23–34.

York, Massachusetts, Pennsylvania, and Illinois, where the majority were brokers' banks, the totals decline significantly from 3,050 in 1888 to 2,143 in 1909.[50] This decrease may have been due in part to increasing regulation of private bankers by states as to minimum capital requirements and required reserves, thus reducing the attractiveness of the unincorporated form of organization. In addition, following the action of North Dakota in 1890, by 1910 eight states had banned unincorporated banking entirely.[51] State banking had become much more attractive also, especially with the lowered capital requirements.

The importance of private banks in the commercial banking system should not be underestimated. Unincorporated banks represented an important element in the nineteenth-century financial structure, especially in frontier and rural areas, which has often been neglected. This inattention may be due in large part to the difficulty of gathering data. Unincorporated banks, with no responsibilities of reporting to any government agency, often were not included in banking statistics, or else were underrepresented. What efforts were made to canvas private banks were usually seriously incomplete and inaccurate. Nevertheless, private banks were another important substitute for national banks. Between 1877 and 1888, when state banks were relatively difficult to incorporate through special charter in many states, private banks increased in number by 67 percent. Even in the late 1860s and 1870s alternatives to and competition for national banks existed. However, from 1888 to 1909, during which time state bank charters were relatively easy to obtain, private banks as a whole grew by less than 9 percent, and state banks assumed the role of the principal rivals to national banks.

[50] Barnett, *State Banks and Trust Companies*, pp. 207–208.
[51] Ibid., pp. 209–219.

CHAPTER III

The Individual Bank

NINETEENTH-CENTURY banks have traditionally been pictured as extremely restricted institutions, operating under many legal and geographic constraints. Provisions of the National Banking Act influenced the choice of assets in the bank portfolio by enforcing reserve requirements, prohibiting loans on real estate, and limiting the amount that could be extended to one borrower. Usury laws limited the maximum interest rate allowable on loans and discounts for all national banks and for state banks in virtually every state. Banks were thus constrained on what they could charge on loans, and in addition sound banking practice restricted the types of loans that they could make. The real-bills doctrine, which was the dominant influence in late nineteenth-century banking, emphasized that commercial loans should be short-term and self-liquidating.

Country banks especially were regarded as isolated, cut off from participation in national financial markets, and confined to local markets because of barriers to the flow of funds between cities and the countryside and between regions. Segmented capital markets restricted the range of operation of the bank, reinforced by legal restrictions limiting banks to operation within only one state.

The banking histories of this period have been written almost entirely in terms of these legal and theoretical restrictions. Histories of the national banking system, such as Dunbar's,[1] are based on the development of the legal framework in which the banks operated. Extensive studies of American

[1] Charles F. Dunbar, *Chapters on the Theory and History of Banking* (New York: G. P. Putnam's Sons, 1901), pp. 158–190.

banking, such as those by Knox and by Sumner,[2] are essentially legal histories, chronicling the evolution of banking law. Other studies in the history of banking, such as Lloyd Mints' *A History of Banking Theory*,[3] describe the development of theories of sound banking, rather than actual banking practices.

The implicit assumption made in viewing such studies as histories of actual banking development is that such legal and theoretical constraints were in fact binding, that the operations of the nineteenth-century bank were in reality constrained by these restrictions. However, if there were divergencies between theory and reality, then by examining only the legal and theoretical structure of nineteenth-century banking one cannot derive an accurate picture of the manner in which banks actually functioned. As a result, here we shall examine the way nineteenth-century banks operated in reality. In this chapter we shall see that, contrary to legal and theoretical restrictions, banks had a good deal of leeway in the choice of their asset portfolio; they did not seem to be strict adherents to the real-bills doctrine, notwithstanding its position as the foundation of the sound banking theory of the time. In Chapter IV we shall see that even small country banks were not isolated and cut off from financial markets, but rather were linked with other banks through a quite sophisticated network called the correspondent banking system.

In this chapter the process of bank portfolio selection and the composition of the portfolio will be examined. Table 4 presents a very simplified balance sheet of a national bank.[4]

[2] John Jay Knox, *A History of Banking in the United States* (New York: B. Rhodes and Co., 1903); William G. Sumner, "History of Banking in the United States," in *A History of Banking in All Leading Nations*, Vol. I (New York: Journal of Commerce and Commercial Bulletin, 1896).

[3] Lloyd W. Mints, *A History of Banking Theory* (Chicago: University of Chicago Press, 1945).

[4] For a much more detailed balance sheet with descriptions of entries, see Edgar G. Alcorn, *The Duties and Liabilities of Bank*

Table 4

Sample National Bank Balance Sheet

Assets	Liabilities and Net Worth
Cash	Deposits
Due from banks	Notes outstanding
Bonds for circulation	Due to banks
Bonds for deposit	Capital
Other stocks and bonds	Surplus and undistributed profits
Loans and discounts	
5 percent redemption fund with Treasury	
Banking house and real estate	

The principal difference between this and a state bank balance sheet is the presence of entries pertaining to note issue. Thus the items—"Notes outstanding," "Bonds for circulation," and "Redemption fund with Treasury"—would be absent. These entries will be discussed in the section on national bank notes. "Due from banks" and "due to banks" refer to deposits of bankers' balances, which will be discussed in Chapter IV. Primary attention will be directed to the composition of the loan and discount portfolio. In order to become familiar with the economic environment in which and terminology with which the nineteenth-century bank operated, some of the more important credit instruments of the time will be described. First of all, however, we shall consider the process of asset portfolio selection and the role of secondary reserves.

BANK PORTFOLIO SELECTION

By the end of the nineteenth century, bank asset portfolio selection was becoming a more sophisticated process. It was

Directors (Columbus, Ohio: Financial Publishing Co., 1908), pp. 138–151.

becoming more well known that an asset portfolio composed entirely of commercial loans was not necessarily the most desirable one. Rather, the idea of portfolio diversification, that the asset portfolio should include some fairly liquid assets in addition to relatively illiquid, but higher-paying, ones, such as loans, was gaining in favor.

The traditional concept of liquidity, influenced by the real-bills doctrine, which will be discussed later in the chapter, involved simply the ability of the bank to meet current obligations by virtue of shrewd timing of the maturity dates on its loans. Liquid loans were those that were paid off at maturity. The modern notion of liquidity in bank portfolios, of maintaining some assets that can be readily convertible into cash, although it was spreading in the postbellum period, did not gain wide acceptance until around the beginning of the Federal Reserve period.[5] The idea of liquidity as easy marketability rather than as the state of being self-liquidating in turn led to the concept of maintaining a secondary reserve of readily marketable assets to be converted into cash during periods of unexpected withdrawals.

Charles Dunbar in his textbook argued that the primary reserve of cash "may be greatly strengthened by the judicious selection of securities,"[6] that is, by maintaining a secondary reserve. Such a practice would increase the bank portfolio's liquidity in the modern sense: "It may easily happen however that the bank may find it desirable to invest a part of its resources in some other form [than loans]. . . . In this case it will purchase such other securities as offer not only safety of investment, but the possibility of easy conversion into cash in case of need."[7] In similar fashion, White's *Money and Banking* advised that it was "desirable that a bank should have a portion of its interest-bearing assets so invested that it can be turned quickly into cash to meet a

[5] Br. Suviranta, "The Shiftability Theory of Bank Liquidity," in *Economic Essays in Honor of Gustave Cassel* (London: George Allen and Unwin, 1933), pp. 623–636.

[6] Dunbar, *Chapters*, p. 36.   [7] Ibid., p. 30.

sudden emergency."[8] At local bankers' meetings the advantages of holding several different assets in one's portfolio were extolled. For example, in 1905 the president of the Abilene National Bank urged portfolio diversification, the holding of commercial paper, bonds, and so forth, in addition to loans, at the Kansas Bankers' Association convention.[9] In the same year Minnesota bankers were being warned to keep "unencumbered securities" in their portfolio, which might be easily converted into cash in the face of unanticipated withdrawals.[10] Other local addresses also advocated holding several different assets in the portfolio, such as commercial paper, real estate loans, bonds, stocks, and mortgages.[11]

Just after the turn of the century, a "leading authority" in banking stated that a bank should have a 20 percent of its investments in high-grade bonds, 20 percent in commercial paper, and 60 percent in commercial loans.[12] However, the role of a secondary reserve actually became important only quite late in the nineteenth century. In his study of Chicago banking before 1890, Dailey observed that the most striking aspect of the investment policy of Chicago state banks during the period 1860–1890 was the large place given to loans and the continuous reluctance to build up a secondary reserve of bond holdings.[13] On the other hand, during the 1870s secondary reserves consisting of bonds and call loans were

[8] Horace White, *Money and Banking*, 4th ed. (Boston: Ginn and Co., 1912), p. 210.

[9] G. A. Rogers, "Loaning Money," *Proceedings of the Kansas Bankers' Association*, 1905, p. 138.

[10] Frank L. McVey, "The Relation of the Banking Capital to the Volume of Business," in Walter Hull, ed., *Practical Problems in Banking and Currency* (New York: Macmillan Company, 1907), p. 39.

[11] C. L. Brokaw, "A Study in Bank Investments," *Proceedings of the Kansas Bankers' Association*, 1908, pp. 37–48.

[12] Hull, *Practical Problems*, p. 69.

[13] Don Dailey, "The Development of Banking in Chicago before 1890" (unpublished Ph.D. dissertation, Northwestern University, 1934), p. 446.

maintained at about 20 percent of earning assets in the port-folio of Preston, Kean, and Co., the largest private banker in Chicago, with the role of bonds in the portfolio increasing over time.[14] By 1889 in Chicago securities amounted to 4.6 percent of total earning assets in national banks and 2.1 percent of total earning assets in state banks,[15] so before 1890 secondary reserves did not seem to be a very important factor in Chicago bank portfolios.

The Chicago experience seemed to be representative of that period, although the proportion of securities held as secondary reserves was rising over the postbellum period. In 1863 securities comprised only 0.5 percent of total assets of national banks; by 1890 they made up 3.6 percent. After 1890 the rise is quite dramatic. Between 1890 and 1900 the role of bonds doubled in the portfolio to 7.2 percent of total assets, and reached 8.4 percent by 1910.[16] State banks appeared to maintain about the same level of secondary reserves as national banks. In 1910, 8.22 percent of total assets of state banks were held in the form of bonds. The practice of maintaining secondary reserves was spreading quite rapidly. After the turn of the century, in locations as remote from financial centers as Waukesha, Wisconsin, the president of the national bank held $100,000 of bonds "as a secondary reserve."[17]

Bankers were usually advised against including stocks in the secondary reserve portfolio because of their "more speculative character."[18] Instead, the secondary reserve port-folio consisted primarily of high-quality securities, such as state, municipal, railroad, or corporate bonds, with railroad

[14] Ibid., p. 435.

[15] Ibid., p. 456.

[16] Jacob H. Hollander, "Security Holdings of National Banks," *American Economic Review*, III (December 1913), p. 798.

[17] Testimony of Andrew Jay Frame, U.S. Senate, Banking and Currency Committe, *Hearings on H.R. 7837*, 63rd Congress, 1st Session, p. 703.

[18] Davis Dewey and Martin Shugrue, *Banking and Credit* (New York: Ronald Press Co., 1922), p. 268.

bonds making up the majority. In 1908 railroad bonds constituted 66 percent of bond holdings other than governments of national banks.[19] In addition to bonds, other assets such as call loans and commercial paper were considered quite desirable as reserve assets, although this assessment was based partially on an irrelevant criterion, the self-liquidating nature of these assets.[20]

In 1880 the ratio of bonds held as secondary reserves to loans and discounts of national banks was 1 to 20; by 1910 it had fallen to 1 to 6. This may be taken as an indication that banks were paying much more attention to portfolio diversification considerations.[21] However, supply influences may also have been important in promoting this large increase in bond holdings, because the amount of external financing done by large corporations increased greatly in the late nineteenth century.[22]

BILLS OF EXCHANGE

Bills of exchange were common commercial credit instruments in the nineteenth century, used to transfer funds between locations in commercial transactions. Strictly speaking, a bill of exchange may be defined as an order from one person to another living in a different place directing him or her to pay a given amount of money to a third person. Thus, there are three parties to a bill of exchange: the drawer, the drawee, and the payee. The drawer is the person who makes out the order and directs the drawee to pay a

[19] U.S. Comptroller of the Currency, *Annual Report*, 1909 (Washington, D.C.: U.S. Government Printing Office, 1909), p. 9.

[20] See Rogers, "Loaning Money," p. 139; F. W. Crane, "Commercial Paper Purchased from Brokers," *Proceedings of the Illinois State Bankers' Association*, 1916, p. 132; Ray Westerfield, *Banking Principles and Practice* (New York: Ronald Press Co., 1924), p. 129.

[21] In addition, it was realized that the maintenance of a secondary reserve enabled banks to maintain smaller primary reserves than otherwise. Westerfield, *Banking Principles*, p. 124.

[22] Dewey and Shugrue, *Banking and Credit*, p. 265.

specific sum. The drawee must take formal action before he or she becomes legally bound by the bill by writing the word "Accepted" across it and signing it.[23] Henceforth, the bill becomes known as an "Acceptance" and the drawee becomes known as the "Acceptor."

The drawee who eventually pays out the amount of the bill is most usually a bank, but could just as well be someone in debt or lending to the drawer. The payee is the person to whom the drawer has ordered the payment. Some bills were payable immediately upon presentation or on sight and were known as "sight" or "demand" bills. Time bills, on the other hand, were payable only after some fixed period, such as thirty or sixty days.

Bills of exchange were important in financing commercial transactions. Suppose that a New York merchant sold a quantity of goods to someone in New Orleans. A check on a New Orleans bank is not of much use to a person in New York; he or she desires instead to be paid in New York funds. The person in New Orleans would therefore purchase New York funds, known as New York exchange, from a local bank that has an account with a New York bank. Then he or she would issue a bill of exchange to the New York bank, directing it to pay the New York merchant the amount in question. The banking system therefore played an important role in facilitating trade, and indirectly economic growth.

Similarly, bills of exchange facilitated transfer of funds among banks. Imagine that a check on a bank in New Haven is deposited in a bank in Buffalo. Rather than request the shipment of cash from New Haven to Buffalo, the Buffalo bank might prefer that it be deposited in its own account with a New York bank. The Buffalo bank then would request "New York funds" or "New York exchange." It costs the New Haven bank, say 25 cents, to ship $1,000 to New York, and it deducts this amount as shipping charges. The

[23] Ibid., p. 36.

Buffalo bank in turn passes this charge for collecting the check on to the depositor, which is also known as exchange. If the flow of funds between St. Louis and New York and between New York and St. Louis exactly balances, there is no need for any transfer of cash. As a result, there will be no shipping charges and no exchange charges. The exchange rate between St. Louis and New York is said to be at par. On the other hand, suppose that there is an imbalance in the flow of funds, so that funds have to be shipped from St. Louis to New York. Consequently, a dollar in St. Louis is going to be worth less than a dollar in New York because of the exchange charges. In this case we may say that New York exchange is at a premium, or that the rate of exchange is in favor of New York. The rate of exchange, then, is always against the location that owes the most money and in favor of the location that owes the least.

Exchange charges declined rapidly in the postbellum period. The Comptroller of Currency in 1894 estimated that New York exchange in New Orleans would sell at par or at a slight premium of 1/10–1/8 percent, whereas in 1859 the average rate of exchange on New York from Southern and Western points was 1–1 1/2 percent.[24] It was estimated that total exchange charges in 1890 of $11 million at 1859 rates would have cost the public $195 million,[25] but this, of course, is an upper bound, assuming completely inelastic demand.

Many commercial instruments are forms of bills of exchange. The check, for example, is a bill of exchange directing a bank to pay a specified sum to a designated individual. The trade acceptance, described in the next section, is a time bill of exchange between the buyer and seller in a specified commercial transaction.

The bank acceptance, which rose to prominence in the early twentieth century, is another form of the bill of ex-

[24] U.S. Comptroller of the Currency, *Annual Report*, 1894, pp. 30–31.

[25] Alonzo B. Hepburn, *A History of Currency in the United States* (New York: Macmillan Company, 1903), p. 338.

change. When the drawee of a bill of exchange is a bank or banking house, the bills are called bank acceptances. The bank is the acceptor of the bill. In contrast, when the drawee is not a bank, the bill is called a trade acceptance; of course, the drawee, or seller of the merchandise, can then discount the trade acceptance at a bank. Bank acceptances, like trade acceptances, should be backed by specific commercial transactions according to the real-bills doctrine, and thus should be used only to facilitate the movement of goods from seller to buyer.

LOANS AND DISCOUNTS

The most important entry in the bank's earning asset portfolio is the loan and discount portfolio. A discount differs from a loan in that the interest charge on a discount is collected in advance, whereas on a loan interest charges are collected at specific intervals and at maturity. For example, on a discount of $1,000, the bank actually advances the customer $1,000 less the interest charge, say $50, or $950; the full amount, $1,000, is due at maturity. A discount is necessarily payable at a definite date, whereas a loan may be payable on demand. A discount is usually unsecured, that is, made on the basis of the general credit of the borrower and his or her endorsers. On the other hand, a loan is generally secured by some form of collateral, such as stocks, bonds, warehouse receipts, or bills of lading.

We shall first distinguish between two types of discounts—single-name and double-name paper. In the antebellum period commercial transactions were usually financed by the trade acceptance, which is a bill of exchange drawn to order, with a definite maturity date, where the obligation to pay at maturity has been accepted by the person upon whom it is drawn. The seller may then take the trade acceptance to a bank to be discounted.

The trade acceptance arises from a specific commercial transaction and is a form of two-name paper. Two-name

54

paper is an instrument carrying the obligation of a drawer in addition to that of an acceptor, or of an endorser in addition to the maker. At maturity payment will be sought from the buyer, or maker of the acceptance. If payment is not forthcoming, however, the seller, who obtained the discount, is liable to the bank for the amount involved. Similarly, the endorser is liable for the amount of the discount if the maker defaults. In contrast, only one party, the maker, is liable for payment of single-name paper, which is in effect an unsecured promissory note. When discounts were offered for sale on the open market, usually through a broker, as opposed to being presented at the local bank, they became known as commercial paper.

The trade acceptance was widely used in the antebellum period to finance commercial transactions. Before the Civil War retail dealers customarily made one or two trips per year to commercial centers, such as New York or Boston, to purchase merchandise. Since the size of these orders was fairly large, they usually issued a trade acceptance in payment, with maturities running from about four months to a year. The sellers then endorsed these notes and discounted them at a local bank or else sold them to note brokers.[26] The Civil War put an end to this system of conducting business based on long credit terms. In a period in which the value of the greenback fluctuated widely, it was clearly undesirable to make long-term contracts in fixed dollar amounts. Sellers, therefore, reduced the length of credit terms to thirty or sixty days and offered substantial discounts for cash payments, which, ranging from 13 to 18 percent per year, were above rates charged by banks.[27] Consequently, it was clearly in the interest of the buyers to borrow at a bank and pay cash rather than to issue a trade acceptance.

The cash discount system, given its impetus by the Civil War, spread rapidly in the last part of the nineteenth century.

[26] Albert O. Greef, *The Commercial Paper House in the United States* (Cambridge, Mass.: Harvard University Press, 1938), p. 70.
[27] Ibid.

After the Civil War it became a quite common practice for dealers to sell goods on open account with terms of ten to ninety days.[28] Thus, the credit period was shortened, but at the same time the buyer had the option of paying cash within ten days and receiving a discount for doing so. Sellers who needed funds temporarily until payment was received, and buyers who wished to take advantage of the cash discount, both began taking their unsecured notes to the bank for discount. No longer did the bank rely for its security upon a specified completed business transaction, as in the case of the trade acceptance. There was less insistence on specific collateral and more on the indirect security of a sound business operation, as revealed through its financial statement, for example.

The trade acceptance had been losing favor even before the Civil War, and the change in credit methods brought about by the war hastened its demise. By the middle of the 1860s, single-name promissory notes constituted the majority of Chicago merchants' bankable paper.[29] By the end of the century, only about 3 percent of all domestic credit transactions were financed by the issuance of a trade acceptance.[30] The most convenient method of borrowing to pay cash for merchandise was by issuing a promissory note. Thus, the single-name promissory note began to displace double-name paper, the trade acceptance.

Another force that contributed to the decline of the trade acceptance after the Civil War was the changing system of distribution. The growth of traveling salesmen meant that it was no longer necessary for the merchant to go to New York once or twice a year. Instead, the salesman called on

[28] L. H. Langston, *Practical Bank Operation* (New York: Ronald Press Co., 1921), p. 259.

[29] Dailey, "The Development of Banking," p. 460.

[30] Margaret G. Myers, *The New York Money Market, Volume I: Origins and Development* (New York: Columbia University Press, 1931). p. 316.

him at regular intervals and he began to make smaller purchases at shorter intervals. For the settlement of these smaller orders a trade bill did not seem appropriate.[31]

In the postbellum period, then, American banking began to diverge from British practices. In the United States the short-term, unsecured promissory note became the dominant credit instrument for financing the credit needs of merchants and farmers. In England, on the other hand, the bill of exchange remained the usual form.

Single-name paper came in round sums and thus was somewhat more marketable than double-name paper, which usually came in odd denominations because it was based on specific commercial transactions. The growth of the practice of issuing unendorsed notes was especially rapid in the decade between 1882 and 1892, so that by the latter date a knowledgeable New York banker estimated that two-thirds of all the paper purchased by banks in the city was single-name paper.[32] This expansion of single-name paper, however, did not meet with universal approval. In 1884 the American Bankers' Association was warned that the issue of one-name paper was "illegitimate for the borrower and dangerous for the lender. To the borrower it encourages an extended and inflated style of business. It leads also to business and personal extravagance." When money could be obtained by simply writing a promissory note "without any necessity to pledge security or to ask for a personal guarantee, or even to make personal explanations to the lender, it is scarcely in human nature to use money so obtained economically and carefully."[33] Country banks were somewhat more reluctant in their acceptance of single-name paper than city banks. As late as 1898 a banker from Atlanta, in discussing country bank investments, warned, "Do not permit any loans to be

[31] Greef, *The Commercial Paper House*, p. 72.
[32] Ibid., p. 67.
[33] Address of George Hague, *Proceedings of the American Bankers' Association*, 1884, p. 69.

made to anyone on single-name paper, unless otherwise secured, no matter what the commercial rating may be."[34]

Data collected by the Comptroller of the Currency give some indication of the replacement of double-name paper by single-name paper in national bank portfolios. The total amounts of discounts here include both discounts made directly by the banks and those purchased in the open market, there being no way to separate them. In New York City national banks between 1886 and 1900, the proportion of two-name paper to total loans and discounts fell from almost 50 percent to under 20 percent and remained at the level through the period 1900–1913. At the same time single-name paper increased from less than 10 percent to over 20 percent in the period 1886–1900.[35] Consequently, after 1900 single-name paper constituted a larger part of loans and discounts than did double-name paper. The story is similar, but not quite as pronounced, for country banks. From 1886 to 1900 two-name paper fell from about 50 to 33 percent of the loan and discount portfolio, whereas single-name paper rose from about 10 percent to over 20 percent.[36]

In addition to changes over time, there was also considerable geographic variation in the proportion of single-name to double-name paper held by banks. Consider Table 5. For comparison, the percentage in New York City was slightly higher than 100; in all other reserve cities it was 75.[37] Eastern country banks held only 25 percent as much single-name paper as double-name, but Western states held almost equal amounts. Among national banks the proportion of single-name paper held seems to vary directly with the distance from New York, so that single-name paper was held in much higher proportions in Western states than in Eastern states. The explanation for this regional variation in holdings of single- versus double-name paper is a mystery.

---

[34] Address of W. S. Witham, *Proceedings of the American Bankers' Association Convention*, 1898, p. 130.

[35] Myers, *The New York Money Market*, pp. 322–323.

[36] Ibid., pp. 323–324.   [37] Ibid., p. 324.

The real-bills doctrine was espoused by virtually all nine-teenth-century banking theorists as the basis of sound banking. The theory held that the extension of business credit by the bank should be in the form of short-term loans to finance the production, storage, or shipment of goods. Ultimately, the sale of goods could then be used to pay off the loan. In essence, the commercial loan should be used only to finance commercial transactions. Put more gracefully, the bank is "the bridge that spans the time from one process to

Table 5

Percentage of Single-Name Paper to Double-Name Paper
in Bank Portfolios, June 30, 1910

Region	Country National Banks	State Banks and Trust Companies
New England	46	53
Eastern	26	51
Southern	41	23
Midwestern	52	62
Western	98	73
Pacific	78	80
United States	44	52

Source: Margaret G. Myers, *The New York Money Market, Volume I: Origins and Development* (New York: Columbia University Press, 1931), p. 324. Reprinted with the permission of Columbia University Press.

another."[38] The bank bridges the gap between seedtime and harvest, between the purchase of raw materials and the sale of finished products, the revenues from which pay back the loan. The bill of exchange, consequently, was a credit instrument that was a perfect example of the real-bills doctrine. Because it often took several months for goods to be transferred from seller to buyer, the bill of exchange allowed

[38] William H. Kniffin, *American Banking Practice* (New York: McGraw-Hill Book Company, 1921), p. 167.

a third party, the drawer, usually a bank, to finance the transfer of goods. Bills of exchange were limited to commercial transactions and were self-liquidating because the sale of the goods, after they had arrived, could be used to pay back the loan.

The real-bills doctrine held that the restriction of loans and discounts to real bills of exchange, obligations with their origins in real transactions, would automatically limit the quantity of bank liabilities. Liabilities, then, would vary in quantity according to the "needs of business"; in addition, the bank would be able to meet withdrawal demands because its short-term loans would be repaid continually as goods were delivered.[39] Thus, if commercial loans were restricted to real bills of exchange, the currency would be elastic and the banks would be liquid.[40] Consequently, loans should be short-term and should not be used for the purchase of long-term capital by businesses, clearly not a self-liquidating transaction. In 1876 the Comptroller of the Currency laid down a list of principles of sound banking before the American Bankers' Association. He advised: "As banks are commercial institutions, created for commercial purposes, preferences in discounts should always be given to paper based upon actual commercial transactions. Banks are not loan offices. It is no part of their business to furnish their customers with capital. . . ."[41]

If the bank's loan portfolio consisted entirely of bills of exchange, it would be clear that the real-bills doctrine was being abided by. In the postbellum period, however, as loans began more and more to take the form of single-name promissory notes instead of explicit bills of exchange, it became much more difficult to tell if commercial banks were actually adhering to the principles of the real-bills doctrine. In spite of its position as the basis of sound banking, substantial

[39] Mints, *History of Banking Theory*, p. 29.
[40] Ibid., p. 9.
[41] Albert S. Bolles, *Practical Banking*, 7th ed. (New York: Homans Publishing Co., 1890), p. 71.

numbers of banks did not make loans in accord with the real-bills doctrine.

The real-bills doctrine implies that all bank loans should be short-term, and in general this seems to have been the case throughout the last part of the nineteenth century. Before the Civil War the average discount period for New York banks was about forty days.[42] Around the turn of the century most loans in bank portfolios ran for thirty, sixty, or ninety days. It was relatively rare to see loans longer than six months, and one year seemed to be the upper bound.[43] The average maturity was probably about sixty days. In 1913 the Comptroller of the Currency computed that 57 percent of all bank loans were made with maturities of less than ninety days.[44] Dunbar in his banking text set the upper bound for maturities of commercial loans at six-months,[45] although the length of loan maturities did fluctuate seasonally somewhat.[46] Were these short-term loans also self-liquidating? In 1876 the Comptroller of the Currency warned, ". . . Insist upon the payment of all paper at maturity, whether you need the money or not."[47] However, it appears that to a considerable extent commercial loans were not made to finance self-liquidating operations, but rather were used to meet needs for working capital, a view argued at great length by H. G. Moulton in his 1918 article, "Commercial Banking and Capital Formation."[48]

[42] J. S. Gibbons, *The Banks of New York, Their Dealers, the Clearing House, and the Panic of 1857* (New York: D. Appleton and Co., 1858), p. 200.

[43] Neil Jacoby and Raymond Saulnier, *Business Finance and Banking* (New York: National Bureau of Economic Research, 1947), p. 131.

[44] Ibid., p. 100. [45] Dunbar, *Chapters*, p. 29.

[46] In his study of Chicago banking, Dailey found that in preparation for peak credit demands in the fall, banks in the late summer were reluctant to loan as long as sixty days, and often refused to loan longer than thirty days. Dailey, "The Development of Banking," p. 499.

[47] Bolles, *Practical Banking*, p. 70.

[48] H. G. Moulton, "Commercial Banking and Capital Formation,

Contrary to the real-bills doctrine, commercial loans were by no means liquidated at maturity. It was estimated by "well-informed bankers" that at least 40 or 50 percent of unsecured loans in large cities were renewed at maturity.[49] Renewals were usually granted with the proviso that the customer pay off his or her loans entirely at least once a year. However, warnings were voiced that even these "clean-ups" were illusionary, because often they involved no more than a shifting of loans from the borrower's own bank to another bank for a season.[50]

The continuous renewal of commercial loans seems to indicate that many loans were not in fact self-liquidating as the real-bills doctrine required. Moulton estimated that at least 20 percent of noncollateral loans were used for financing fixed capital.[51] This practice of rolling over short-term loans to finance long-term investments was characteristic of continental banking, especially German, in the nineteenth century. The real-bills doctrine originated in England, where industrialization was a relatively gradual process which proceeded without any substantial utilization of the banking system for long-term financing.[52] On the other hand, Gerschenkron argues that in countries that industrialized relatively late pressures on the banking system for the mobilization of long-term financing were much greater, so he conceives this process of rolling over short-term loans for capital financing as a specific instrument of industrialization in a relatively backward country.[53]

I–IV," *Journal of Political Economy* (January–December 1918), pp. 484–508, 638–663, 705–731, 849–881.

[49] Ibid., p. 707.

[50] Joseph T. Talbert, "Commercial Credits," *Proceedings of the New York State Bankers' Association,* 1908, p. 84.

[51] Moulton, "Commercial Banking," p. 648.

[52] See Sidney Pollard, "Fixed Capital in the Industrial Revolution in Britain," *Journal of Economic History,* XXIV (September 1964), p. 308.

[53] Alexander Gerschenkron, *Economic Backwardness in Historical Perspective* (New York: Frederick A. Praeger, 1962), p. 14.

Another distinguishing characteristic of different types of credit instruments is the type of security backing them. Discounts are unsecured loans based on the general credit of the borrower. Loans, on the other hand, are generally secured by a pledge of some sort of collateral. The increasing importance of secured loans during the period was evidenced in the rising ratio of secured loans to total loans and discounts in national bank portfolios.[54]

As the value of many of the items used as collateral was subject to price fluctuations, loans were not made on the full value of the collateral. In New York and other large cities the market value of the collateral had to be 20 percent greater than the amount of the loan, whereas in other areas the required margin was only 10 percent.[55]

Secured loans may be divided into three categories—loans secured by stocks and bonds, loans secured by receivables, and merchandise loans. Call or brokers' loans were almost always secured loans, representing advances made to brokers by pledging stocks and bonds with the bank as collateral. Receivables could also be used as collateral, so that a merchant could use his customers' promissory notes as collateral for a direct loan rather than taking them to the bank and discounting them. Similarly, a firm might use its accounts receivable as collateral for a loan if it wanted funds immediately. A country bank could also offer the paper of its local customers as collateral for a loan to its city correspondent.

Merchandise loans are loans made upon the security of warehouse receipts, bills of lading, or other documents covering commodities. They are usually made for the purpose of financing the production, storage, and transportation of goods in accord with the real-bills doctrine. Warehouse loans are based upon commodities held by a warehouseman and represented by a warehouse receipt. Although apparently quite safe, such loans have some risk because of the possibility of depreciation in value or deterioration in quality of

[54] Jacoby and Saulnier, *Business Finance*, p. 100.
[55] Alcorn, *Duties and Liabilities*, p. 109.

the commodity while it is stored in the warehouse. A wide variety of commodities have served as collateral for warehouse loans, from grain in elevators and cotton in gins to fish and citrus fruits.[56]

Loans were also made on goods in transit, as well as in storage, with the bill of lading used as collateral. A bill of lading is a document from a railroad or other means of transportation acknowledging the receipt of goods for shipment. If the terms of the contract are cash upon receipt of the goods, the seller must wait several weeks until the goods are delivered before receiving payment. By using the bill of lading as collateral he can receive an advance from the bank upon his final sale. Thus the bank bridges the gap between the loading of the goods and their final delivery.

One other common form of collateral less in accord with the real-bills doctrine was real estate. Mortgage loans on real estate were prohibited to national banks until 1913, although, as discussed in Chapter II, other parts of the banking system, such as state banks and trust companies, as well as mortgage and life insurance companies, stepped into the market. Loans on real estate clearly did not originate in any commercial transaction, as did a bill of exchange. Real estate was considered poor collateral for commercial banks because of its illiquidity; it could not be easily converted into cash if the occasion arose.

In addition to types of security, loans may also be classified by maturities. Time loans, ones that were made at fixed rates of interest and ran for fixed time periods, constituted a majority of the loans and discount portfolios of both city and country banks.[57] In 1903 the Comptroller of the Currency reported the interest rates on loans of different maturi-

[56] Chester A. Phillips, *Bank Credit* (New York: Macmillan Company, 1920), p. 227.

[57] California and the Pacific Coast were exceptions to this generalization. In the East merchant promissory notes or bills of exchange had definite maturity dates, whereas on the Pacific Coast loans were often carried just as open accounts. As a result, banks there had a much higher proportion of demand loans without definite maturity dates in their portfolio than elsewhere. In California, as of June 30,

ties made by New York banks, which are presented in Table 6. Interest rates consistently rise with maturities, although from this information alone one cannot distinguish the strength of liquidity effect from the expectations effect in accounting for this term structure of interest rates.

Table 6

Interest Rates on Loans of Differing Maturities Held by New York Banks, 1903
(in percent)

	May	June	July	August	September	October
Time Loans:						
30 days	3¾–4	3½–5	3½–6	5–5½	4½–5½	4½–5½
60 days	3¾–4	3½–5	3½–6	5–5½	4½–5½	4½–5½
90 days	3¾–4	3½–5	3½–6	4½–5½	5–6	4¾–5½
4 months	4–4½	4½–5½	4¼–6	5–5½	5¼–6	4¾–5½
5 months	4–4½	4½–5½	4¼–6	5½–5¾	5½–6	4¾–5½
6 months	4½	5–5½	5–6	5½–6	5½–6	4¾–5½
7 months	—	5–6	5¼–5½	—	—	—
Commercial Paper:						
Double name, choice, 60–90 days	4½–5	4¾–5½	5–5¾	5¾–6	6	5½–6
Single name, prime, 4–6 months	4¾–5½	4¾–5½	5½–6	5¾–6½	6–6½	5½–6
Good, 4–6 months	5¼–6	5½–6	5¾–6½	6½–7	6½–7	6½–7

Source: U.S. Comptroller of the Currency, *Annual Report*, 1903. (Washington, D.C.: U.S. Government Printing Office), p. 13.

1914, demand loans constituted almost 70 percent of total loans, with little variation between city and country banks, whereas Oregon country banks held over 50 percent of loans as demand loans. In contrast, in New York demand loans, mostly call loans, were 36.3 percent of total loans; in other reserve cities, 29.5 percent; in country banks, 20.9 percent. Leroy Armstrong and J. O. Denny, *Financial California* (San Francisco: Coast Banker Publishing Co., 1916), p. 32.

Demand loans, on the other hand, run for no definite time period. They may be terminated at any time by either party; the lender may demand payment, or the borrower may make payments before it is demanded. The most common type of demand loan was the call loan, used for purchasing securities, which was another specifically American credit instrument, deviating from English practice and from the real-bills doctrine. The rate of interest on call loans might fluctuate with the market day by day, or, alternatively, it might be fixed in advance. Usually the interest rates on demand loans were lower than those on time loans because of their greater liquidity. The call loan rate, however, was also much more volatile than those on time loans, sometimes soaring to several hundred percent per annum in periods of financial stringency. Call loans were normally secured by collateral such as stocks and bonds and were regarded as a desirable secondary reserve because they were easily convertible into cash (in nonpanic periods). The center of the call loan market was, of course, in New York City. National banks there held between one-third and one-half of their loan portfolios in the form of call loans during the period and in addition purchased them for their out-of-town correspondent banks.

COUNTRY BANK LOANS

Country national banks in general had considerable difficulty in reconciling their loan and investment opportunities with the real-bills doctrine and the restrictions of the National Banking Act. The principal clientele of country banks were farmers in most areas, whereas the real bills doctrine, based on the experience of English banks in extending merchant credit, implied that sound loans must be based on commercial transactions. Just as country national banks found it difficult to comply with the provisions of the National Banking Act, which was directed more toward the financing of merchandising and commercial activities than toward providing agricultural credit, in many cases openly violating the prohibition on real estate lending, so also did they find it hard to follow the sound banking dictates of the real-bills doctrine.

On the whole, maturities of country bank loans were longer than those of city bank loans, and many could not be considered short-term. At the 1913 Federal Reserve Act hearings, the president of the Bank of Prescott, Arkansas, estimated that the ordinary length of their farmers' paper there was between three and nine months.[58] Similarly, in his study of rural banks in Minnesota, Russell Stevenson argued that the number of really liquid short-term loans that could be made in a rural community was small. He found that agricultural loans generally ran for nine months or more.[59]

Moreover, even if country bank loans were nominally short-term, their actual duration was substantially longer, because many were renewed rather than paid off at maturity. Phillips described the loans of country merchants as being characterized by renewals because of the habitual slowness of the merchants in making collections.[60] A country banker at the Missouri Bankers' Association convention in 1911 estimated that in an average month 65 percent of his maturing paper was renewed and only 35 percent paid off; he believed that in most rural areas the percentage paid off was even lower.[61] A banker from Quincy, Illinois, in 1916 complained about the illiquidity of many country bank local loans: "For though the good customer makes his note for but thirty days, he will renew at will until he is ready to pay. The only certainty about local loans is that in times of stress they will increase rather than be paid down."[62] Many of these

[58] Testimony of Thomas McRae, *Hearings on H.R. 7837 (S2639)*, p. 1281.

[59] Russell Stevenson, ed., *A Type Study of American Banking: Non-Metropolitan Banks in Minnesota* (Minneapolis: University of Minnesota Press, 1934), p. 12.

[60] Phillips, *Bank Credit*, p. 245.

[61] E. R. Gurney, "A Study in Liquidation," *Proceedings of the Missouri Bankers' Association*, 1911, p. 73.

[62] Crane, "Commercial Paper," p. 131.

loans were renewed not once but several times, so that a loan was often extended for many years.[63] Loans to farmers may have run even longer than loans to country merchants. In Kansas it was reported that fourteen years passed on a loan before the principal was repaid.[64] These often-renewed loans were known in the trade as "sleepers."[65]

One of the reasons the country banker had to endure such delays was, of course, that the extent of his market was relatively small and consequently notes could not always be selected from the most attractive class of customers. It was often claimed that the quality of collateral securing country loans was much poorer than that backing city loans. A Georgia country banker grumbled, "They [country bank borrowers] can get money on security that you city bankers would laugh at."[66] At the Federal Reserve Act hearings a New Orleans banker noted regional differences in the quality of collateral. The collateral in Southern and Western states, he argued, was on the average not as liquid as that in the New England and Eastern states,[67] which roughly amounts to a city-country division.

Bolles in fact asserted that collateral for loans by country banks was seldom received; personal responsibility, or trust, served as collateral instead.[68] The country banker may well have been long acquainted with a large number of his customers and familiar with their personal characteristics. Thus a man of known trustworthiness and responsibility might receive a loan significantly larger than one dictated by "sound" banking principles.[69] Several contemporary bankers, however, disputed the benignity of this system. At the 1914

[63] Moulton, "Commercial Banking," p. 706.

[64] E. N. Morrill, "Reminiscences of Banking in Kansas," *Proceedings of the Kansas Bankers' Association*, 1905, p. 55.

[65] Phillips, *Bank Credit*, p. 245.

[66] Address of C. T. Smith, *Proceedings of the Georgia Bankers' Association*, 1917, p. 119.

[67] Testimony of Sol Whitney, *Hearings on H.R. 7837*, p. 96.

[68] Bolles, *Practical Banking*, p. 144.

[69] Phillips, *Bank Credit*, p. 242.

Maryland Bankers' Association convention it was charged that country bank credit was in general extended haphazardly and unmethodically; country banks often were said not to conform to sound banking practices as evidenced by the fact that they hardly ever inquired about the purpose for which the borrowed money was to be used.[70]

The frequent renewals and poorer collateral of country bank loans, as well as the relatively illiquid loans on real estate security of state banks, should not necessarily be taken to indicate that country banks as a class were more unsound than city banks; the liabilities side of the balance sheet must also be considered. It was generally acknowledged that time deposits were a much larger fraction of total deposits for country banks than city banks. In the Comptroller of the Currency reports it is not possible to separate time from demand deposits, but in his study of rural Minnesota banking Stevenson calculated that about two-thirds of the deposits of country banks were time deposits. In contrast, the proportion of time deposits at city banks ranged between about 10 and 25 percent.[71] Consequently, if the liabilities of the country bank were primarily time deposits, it could afford to hold a relatively more illiquid loan portfolio than a city bank could.

One more difference existed between country and city loans: their size. In 1880 the Comptroller of the Currency published detailed information about the average size and size distribution of notes and bills discounted by national banks held on October 2, 1879. Table 7 presents the average size of loans in reserve cities; Table 8 reports the average loan size of country banks by region.

The higher average loan size for New England country banks was indicative of the higher level of industrial activity there. However, the average loan size among Southern, Midwestern, and Western country banks was substantially small-

[70] Claude Gilbert, "Country Credit Methods," *Proceedings of the Maryland Bankers' Association*, 1914, p. 50.

[71] Stevenson, *Type Study*, p. 12.

Table 7

Average Size of Loans of Reserve City National Banks,
October 2, 1879

	Average Size		Average Size
New York	$3,962	Milwaukee	$2,086
Boston	3,083	St. Louis	1,575
Philadelphia	1,688	Cincinnati	1,231
Pittsburgh	1,993	Cleveland	1,244
Chicago	2,244	Detroit	1,320
Baltimore	1,593	Louisville	1,007
		New Orleans	1,936

Source: U.S. Comptroller of the Currency, *Annual Report*, 1880
(Washington, D.C.: U.S. Government Printing Office, 1880),
p. 19.

Table 8

Average Size of Loans of Country National Banks,
October 2, 1879

States	Average Size
New England states	$1,563
Middle Atlantic states	1,176
Southern states	781
Western and Midwestern states	713

Source: U.S. Comptroller of the Currency, *Annual Report*, 1880
(Washington, D.C. U.S. Government Printing Office, 1880),
p. 90.

er than that of city banks. Administrative costs of a loan are
essentially fixed costs and independent of the size of the
loan. Thus average costs should be higher for country banks
than for city banks because of the smaller average size of
loans. The high cost of unit banking in the countryside has
been claimed to have been one of the principal factors responsible for higher rural interest rates; in reality, however,

cost differences could account for only a small fraction of observed interregional interest rate differentials.[72]

A number of city-country differences contributing to higher country loan rates have been presented here. Country loans were relatively illiquid because of frequent renewals and also in a number of cases may have had longer initial maturities; the collateral on average on country loans was poorer than that on city loans; costs were higher in country banks because the average loan size was smaller. Differences in risk on loans between regions will be discussed in Chapter VI. Other than accounting for risk, however, there is no way in which we are able to assess these qualitative differences between city and country loans, such as relative illiquidity and systematic differences in average maturities in order to determine what city-country differentials they imply. Nevertheless, it seems quite unlikely that such substantial changes in the liquidity or maturity of country loans occurred in the postbellum period as to account for the observed narrowing of interregional interest rate differentials.

COMMERCIAL PAPER

Commercial paper could be either single-name or double-name paper. Both types were unsecured promissory notes, the difference between them being that this paper was sold on the open market through a broker rather than discounted

[72] For an example of city-country cost differential argument, see J. Laurence Laughlin, ed., *Banking Reform* (Chicago: The National Citizens' League, 1912), p. 47. Estimates of cost functions of national banks indicate that the rapid growth of Western banks did allow them to exploit economies of scale. Average costs did fall twice as much in Western banks as compared with New England banks, but the narrowing cost differential was only 0.15 percentage points. In addition, this figure overstates the narrowing of interest rate differentials unless loan demand was completely elastic. It seems clear that narrowing cost differentials due to exploitation of economies of scale cannot explain a significant portion of the narrowing interest rate differentials. See John A. James, "Cost Functions of National Banks" (unpublished, 1974).

71

directly at a bank. The attributes of and market for commercial paper will be discussed in a section on the growth of the commercial paper market in Chapter V.

CREDIT DEPARTMENTS

One of the most important advances in bank operations in the late nineteenth century was the development of the credit department. The Importer's and Trader's National Bank of New York is credited with establishing the first one during the 1880s.[73] The concept did not capture the imagination of many bankers initially, but the Panic of 1893 proved to be a spur to development. In the period of recovery after the Panic, banks began requiring financial statements from borrowers in order to estimate the creditworthiness of the borrower.[74] In spite of the fact that by 1899 less than ten credit departments had been established, all of those in New York banks, the trend toward systematic investigations of the credit of potential borrowers was increasing. In 1899 a model credit department was set up for inspection at the convention of the American Bankers' Association, and after 1900 the number of credit departments grew rapidly.[75]

Objective criteria began to be employed in the analysis of creditworthiness. Balance sheet relationships, such as a proportion of 2 to 1 of quick assets to current liabilities,[76] began to be more important than just general good regard in the business world. The question of granting credit became more impersonal, and at the same time credit analysts became specialists and professionals. "The department must be manned by our most faithful, reliable, intelligent, tactful men, who must be capable of infinite pains, of inexhaustible patience, and of absolute loyalty. Their ears and eyes must

---

[73] Myers, *The New York Money Market*, p. 325.
[74] Westerfield, *Banking Principles*, p. 595.
[75] Myers, *The New York Money Market*, p. 325.
[76] Phillips, *Bank Credit*, p. 242.

be open to every contingency that no sign may go unheeded. They are compelled to walk in the ruts of routine and yet to be pathfinders constantly."[77]

The need for more careful and detailed examination of the financial records of prospective borrowers was primarily the result of the changing pattern of the finance of mercantile credit in the postbellum period. Loans were increasingly based on the general creditworthiness of the borrower, who issued a promissory note backed by no definite form of security, rather than on specific commercial transactions, as in a bill of exchange. Consequently, more satisfactory measures for determining financial soundness became important. Later in the postbellum period, the development of the open market in commercial paper heightened the need for objective evaluation procedures. The bank was confronted with notes from firms with which it was not personally acquainted. A more systematic, formalized method of credit investigation had to replace personal contact. Investigations of paper by its credit department became one of the principal services a city bank performed for its country correspondent banks.[78] The rapid growth of cities and thus of city banks made it more difficult to know each borrower personally, so some objective standards of creditworthiness needed to be established. In addition, Phillips argues that the rise of the corporation eliminated the personal element between borrower and creditor.[79] Balance sheets and solvency became more important in credit transactions than considerations of personal honor. Criteria for creditworthiness and methods of analyzing financial statements are discussed in great detail in Chester A. Phillips' *Bank Credit* and Ray Westerfield's *Banking Principles and Practice*.[80]

[77] J. G. Cannon, "Bank Credits," *Bankers' Magazine*, LXX (May 1905), p. 587.

[78] Phillips, *Bank Credit*, p. 148.

[79] Ibid., p. 151.

[80] Phillips, *Bank Credit*, Part II; Westerfield, *Banking Principles*, chap. 30.

National Bank Notes

Another important source of revenue for national banks was the issue of national bank notes. Two of the major purposes of the National Currency Act of 1863 were the establishment of a uniform national paper currency and, at the same time, a market for government bonds. The Act, amended in 1864, required every national bank to deposit government bonds amounting to at least one-third of its capital.[81] At the same time, national banks were allowed to issue national bank notes on the basis of government bonds held. The Act of March 3, 1865, limited note issue of national banks to 90 percent of the value of paid-in capital stock for banks with capital under $500,000 and to a lower percentage of capital for larger banks.[82] However, the Act of 1882 established the constraint as 90 percent of the market or par value, whichever was lower, of certain issues of U.S. bonds that the banks were required to purchase and deposit at the Treasury for collateral for the note issue.[83]

The multitude of varieties of state bank notes that characterized the antebellum stock of paper money disappeared after the tax on state bank notes was imposed in 1866. The great diversity of circulating state bank notes was replaced by a national currency backed by government bonds, even though it was still privately issued by the national bank system.[84] Even though it may not have been one of the prin-

[81] Charles F. Dunbar, *Laws of the United States Relating to Currency, Finance, and Banking* (Boston: Ginn and Co., 1897), p. 180.
[82] Ibid., p. 199.   [83] Ibid., p. 222.

[84] One area untouched by this development of a national paper currency was California, where gold coins rather than notes were used almost exclusively as currency during the late nineteenth century. During the Civil War, the bulk of U.S. gold available for circulation, about $25 million, was in California. It has been argued that the substantial discount at which greenbacks and notes sold there, because of the public's preference for gold, and hence the unfavorable exchange rate, retarded the inflow of capital and population from the East and thus California's economic development. Armstrong and Denny, *Financial California*, pp. 27–28.

cipal objectives of the Union, Alphonso Taft observed that "if the Civil War resulted in nothing else than providing the country with a uniform currency it would not have been fought in vain."[85]

One result of the new uniform currency system was that all national bank notes circulated at par throughout the country, no matter where they had been issued. In other words, a $5 national bank note issued by a Maine bank was still worth $5 in Michigan, in contrast to the antebellum period during which such a state bank note would ordinarily have sold at some discount because of the uncertainties of redemption. The Comptroller of the Currency mentioned the savings in discounts on circulating bank notes, usually 1 to 5 percent in the antebellum period, as one of the principal benefits of the national banking system, where all notes circulated at par, in his 1894 Report.[86] This elimination of risk discounts on nonlocal bank notes, of course, was not a result of the national nature of the new banking system at all. If all states had similarly enforced strict provisions as to the security behind state bank notes and limitations on their issue, risk discounts would have fallen in comparable fashion.

Another benefit of the system of national bank notes was the increase in welfare resulting from the use of paper rather than commodity, that is, gold, money. The social saving per year from the use of paper money equals the amount of paper money times the rate of return on alternative uses of the resources embodied in the gold money. However, estimates of these benefits for the antebellum period, in particular the social savings from notes issued by the Second Bank of the United States, are very small, about 0.15 percent of GNP.[87]

[85] A. Piatt Andrew, "The Crux of the Currency Question," *Yale Review*, n.s., II (July 1913), p. 609.

[86] U.S. Comptroller of the Currency, *Annual Report*, 1894, p. 30.

[87] Stanley Engerman, "A Note on the Economic Consequences of the Second Bank of the United States," *Journal of Political Economy*, LXXVIII (July/August 1970), pp. 727–728.

In addition, the shift in desired currency holdings between coin and national bank notes was much smaller in both magnitude and importance than the concurrent relative shift in public holdings of currency versus deposits.

The Act of March 3, 1865, also imposed an overall constraint on note issue, limiting the aggregate amount of notes issued to $300 million. The circulation was to be apportioned to banks in the various states, one-half according to state population and one-half according to existing banking capital, resources, and other considerations.[88] It soon became clear the $300 million limit would quickly be reached. Most of the first national banks had been organized in New England and the Middle Atlantic states, and banks in the Southern and Western states, organized later, found it impossible to obtain the quotas of note issue that they desired.

One attempt to deal with the imbalance of note issue was the Act of July 12, 1870, which raised the aggregate limit on notes in circulation and authorized a $54 million quota to be apportioned among states having less than their due proportion.[89] At a time when large sections of the country were agitating for more notes, New York banks were finding them hard to dispose of. They were not legal tender;[90] they

[88] Dunbar, *Laws of the United States*, p. 199.

[89] Ibid., pp. 202–203.

[90] Because national bank notes were not in fact legal tender, an interesting question arises as to their degree of substitutability with other forms of currency, such as specie or greenbacks. In particular, during periods of suspension of payments where did national bank notes stand? They were not legal tender and could not be counted in bank reserves; were they paid out to customers during suspensions, or were payments in notes suspended along with payments in specie? Sprague is very oblique about this subject, usually talking in terms of suspension of currency payments, without defining currency explicitly. There are some indications, however, that payments in notes as well as specie were suspended during panics. In a chart of currency premiums during the Panic of 1873, note is taken of a case when the premium on bank notes deviated from the quoted currency premium. In the Panic of 1893, premiums were regularly higher for small bills than for other kinds of money, but it is not clear whether these small

could not be counted as reserves and consequently could not be used for settling balances at the Clearing House. Many banks sold notes to brokers at a discount of 1/10 to 1/4 percent to have the brokers take the trouble of redeeming them. Interest-free loans for periods as long as two weeks were offered by a number of New York banks on the condition that the loans made in national bank notes be paid back in greenbacks.[91]

By 1873 the new limit was almost filled, and something had to be done. The Resumption Act of 1875 finally solved the problem by abolishing all the provisions limiting and apportioning the aggregate amount of notes to be issued.[92] Limits to the amount of national bank notes in circulation were further relaxed by the Gold Standard Act of March 13, 1900, which allowed banks to issue notes up to 100 percent of the amount of paid-in capital and of the par or market value of the government bonds.[93]

After the ceiling on note issue was removed in 1875, issuance of national bank notes did not explode; rather, the 1875 total of notes in circulation was not matched again until 1881. The amount of notes in circulation then actually declined in every year between 1882 and 1891. Such fluctuations in notes in circulation may be accounted for by variations in the profitability of note issue, which were caused primarily by fluctuations in the yield on government bonds.

---

bills referred to U.S. notes or national bank notes. Finally, in his discussion of the use of money substitutes during the Panic of 1893, national bank notes are never referred to as being a substitute, as opposed to being classed as actual currency. O. M. W. Sprague, *History of Crises under the National Banking System* (Washington, D.C.: U.S. Government Printing Office, 1910), pp. 57, 188, 198.

[91] Myers, *The New York Money Market*, p. 404.

[92] Dunbar, *Laws of the United States*, pp. 212–215.

[93] For those who may wish more thorough discussion of legislation pertaining to national bank note issue, it is available in almost excruciating detail. See, for example, *Report of the Monetary Commission of the Indianapolis Convention* (Chicago: University of Chicago Press, 1898), chap. 10.

However, the total amount of notes actually issued was quite low in proportion to the maximum allowable amount in the period before 1900. This is all the more curious in view of Cagan's calculations that note issue was quite profitable with the exception of the 1884–1891 period. Between 1892 and 1897, for example, note issue averaged a profit 3.3 percent above that on other bank assets,[94] but by 1900 only 28 percent of the maximum allowable amount of notes had actually been issued. The explanation for the relatively low issue of national bank notes is based on geographical differences in the relative profitability of note issue. In Southern and Western areas, where the demand for notes and currency was supposed to have been the greatest, few notes were issued above the minimum requirements. The high opportunity cost of note issue there, the local interest rate, made it unprofitable to do so. If the country bank there chose to issue notes, it would lose the high interest rate there on the difference between the market price of the security bond and 90 percent of par value.[95]

The original system made provision for redemption either over the counter of the issuing bank or in seventeen specified cities, whereas banks in those cities were required to redeem notes in New York. There was a growing demand to establish some central redemption point, which finally took the form of law in the Act of June 20, 1874, in which the Treasury became the sole redemption agency for all national bank notes. Cash no longer needed to be kept in bank vaults as reserve against circulation. Instead, national banks were required to maintain on deposit with the Treasury a fund equal to 5 percent of their outstanding circulation to be used in the redemption of their notes.[96]

[94] Phillip Cagan, *Determinants and Effects of Changes in the Stock of Money, 1875–1960* (New York: Columbia University Press, 1965), p. 88.

[95] For more detail, see John A. James, "The Conundrum of the Low Issue of National Bank Notes," *Journal of Political Economy*, LXXXIV (April 1976), pp. 359–367.

[96] Dunbar, *Laws of the United States*, pp. 210–214.

Usury Laws

Neither national nor state banks were free to maximize returns on their earning asset portfolio unconstrained by government regulations. Asset choices of national banks were restricted by the prohibition of mortgage loans until 1913 and by reserve requirements. Another constraint that affected the portfolio choice of both state and national banks was the usury law. Banks were constrained to make loans only at or below a certain interest rate ceiling. Was this constraint an effective one? Were banks actually restrained in their behavior so that they charged less than the market-clearing rate?

Usury laws have traditionally been one of the more ubiquitous forms of economic regulation. A history of usury laws subtitled "Fleecing the Small Borrower Being Stopped by the Government" is chronicled by the Comptroller of the Currency in the 1918 *Annual Report* in which the fall of Rome is attributed to the relaxation of laws against usury.[97] With the possible exception of the class of bankers, it was widely thought at the time that usury laws were necessary supports to commercial and social life. Indeed, in 1918 the Comptroller of the Currency himself observed, "States and communities in which literature presenting the most violent, dangerous, and incendiary forms of perverted socialism was most eagerly read and accepted were precisely those in which my reports showed that the interest charges to small borrowers were most extortionate."[98] In addition to the preservation of public order, usury laws also were considered supports of the public morality, finding ample justification in the scriptures. *Bankers' Magazine* at one point tried to argue that the Bible actually smiled on usury by citing the Parable of the Talents, which was taken as an injunction to make

[97] John S. Williams, "Usury and the Banks," Exhibit J in U.S. Comptroller of the Currency, *Annual Report*, 1918, pp. 204–210.
[98] Ibid., p. 205.

the most of one's wealth.[99] This alternative interpretation, however, seems to have made little impression on the public at large, and prohibitions against usury remained in effect in the great majority of the states.

A usury provision was explicitly included in the National Banking Act. No national bank could charge on any loan or discount, note, or bill of exchange a rate of interest higher than that fixed by the state law in which the bank operated. If no usury law existed in the state, the maximum legal interest rate was set at 7 percent per annum, which might be taken in advance. When interest above the maximum allowable was paid, the borrower could recover twice the interest paid. In addition, if the directors of a national bank could have been shown to have knowingly violated the usury laws, their charter could be revoked.[100]

The maximum interest rates fixed by state laws varied widely and, as the Comptroller of the Currency complained in 1872, seemed not to be governed "by any sound economical or business principles."[101] In the early 1870s the legal interest rate ranged from 12 percent in Minnesota and Virginia, to 10 percent in Illinois, Wisconsin, Missouri, and the District of Columbia, to 8 percent in Alabama and Ohio, down to 6 percent in Pennsylvania, Maryland, and Kentucky.[102] Severe usury laws in some states could influence the decision of whether to incorporate as a state or a national bank. In New York, for example, accepting interest above 7 percent could result in forfeiture of the entire loan plus a fine and imprisonment.[103] Table 9 presents the maximum legal rate of interest by state as of 1915. In some states a higher interest rate could be charged, if agreed upon between the parties, hence the special contract rate. The legal rate of interest ranged from 5 percent in Louisiana to 8 percent in several states, with most states establishing 6 percent as the maximum rate. However, in most states the special contract

[99] "The Morality of Usury," *Bankers' Magazine*, XXIV (June 1880), p. 957.
[100] U.S. Comptroller of the Currency, *Annual Report*, 1872, p. xxv.
[101] Ibid.   [102] Ibid.   [103] Ibid.

provisions allowed more leeway, with rates up to 12 percent allowed in several states, and in California, Colorado, Maine, and Massachusetts unlimited interest could be charged if agreed upon in writing.

Lance Davis has presented some evidence that the 6 per-

Table 9

Legal Rates of Interest by State, 1915

State	Legal Rate (%)	Special Contract Rate (%)	State	Legal Rate (%)	Special Contract Rate (%)
Alabama	8	8	Montana	8	12
Arizona	6	10	Nebraska	7	10
Arkansas	6	10	Nevada	7	12
California	7	Unlimited	New Hampshire	6	—
Colorado	8	Unlimited	New Jersey	6	—
Connecticut	6	12	New Mexico	6	12
Delaware	6	6	New York	6	—
D.C.	6	10	North Carolina	6	—
Florida	8	10	North Dakota	6	10
Georgia	7	8	Ohio	6	8
Idaho	7	12	Oklahoma	6	10
Illinois	5	7	Oregon	6	10
Indiana	6	8	Pennsylvania	6	—
Iowa	6	8	Rhode Island	6	—
Kansas	6	10	South Carolina	7	8
Kentucky	6	6	South Dakota	7	12
Louisiana	5	8	Tennessee	6	—
Maine	—	Unlimited	Texas	6	10
Maryland	6	6	Utah	8	12
Massachusetts	6	Unlimited	Vermont	6	—
Michigan	5	7	Virginia	6	6
Minnesota	6	10	West Virginia	6	6
Mississippi	6	8	Wisconsin	6	10
Missouri	6	8	Wyoming	8	12

Source: Exhibit T, "Legal Rates of Interest in Each State," U.S. Comptroller of the Currency, *Annual Report*, 1915 (Washington, D.C.: U.S. Government Printing Office, 1915), pp. 225–228.

cent interest ceiling in antebellum Massachusetts was actively enforced.[104] Presumably responding to some pressure, the American Bankers' Association periodically called for repeal of the usury laws.[105] Consequently, we might pose the question: Were the usury laws effective in limiting the rates of interest banks charged on loans? Or, put slightly differently, were the usury laws strictly enforced?

In 1871 the Comptroller of the Currency made it clear that he was sympathetic to the banks' opposition to usury laws. "While nothing will justify a bank for violating a provision of the law. . . ," he argued, "It is asserted by bank officers and admitted to be true, that local taxation is so high in some of the States as to make it impossible to lend money at legal rates without loss to the bank. . . ."[106] In 1872, he continued, "the Comptroller will not feel himself called upon to institute proceedings for the forfeiture of the charter of a bank for usurious transactions, when it is evident that the business of the association is conducted legitimately and safely in other respects."[107] Strict enforcement did not seem to be promised by the Comptroller of the Currency. Individual borrowers were able to file suit to recover usurious interest, but this did not seem to be an effective constraint either. Such suits were brought only rarely, because it was argued that the customer was often afraid of being blacklisted by the banks and thus being unable to borrow in the future.[108] In addition, at least as of 1894, every case in which national banks had been convicted of violation of

[104] Lance E. Davis, "The New England Textile Mills and the Capital Markets: A Study of Industrial Borrowing, 1840–1860," *Journal of Economic History*, XX (March 1960), pp. 1–30.

[105] See, for example, *Proceedings of the American Bankers' Association*, 1884, p. 10.

[106] U.S. Comptroller of the Currency, *Annual Report*, 1871, p. viii.

[107] U.S. Comptroller of the Currency, *Annual Report*, 1872, p. xxvi.

[108] U.S. Comptroller of the Currency, *Annual Report*, 1915, p. 31.

state usury laws, when appealed to the U.S. Supreme Court, had been reversed.[109]

Enforcement of these statutes both on the federal and state level did not appear to be either very vigorous or very successful. Indeed, as early as 1872 the Comptroller of the Currency observed that the usury laws were "so continually evaded that they have become obsolete."[110] Instead, "the rates of interest charged must correspond in some degree to the supply of money and to the demand."[111] The requiem for the observance of effectiveness of usury laws was pronounced by B. F. Clayton at the 1892 Iowa Bankers' Association convention, where he observed:

> . . . No legislative enactment will control the rate of interest in the commercial world. While politicians may arrogate to themselves great credit for the reduction of legal interest to 8 percent, while we should have an established legal rate of interest, and 8 percent is high enough, it will have no effect upon the commercial world. Money is worth what it will bring on the market. Rates of interest always have been and always will be governed by supply and demand, and the class of securities offered. . . .
>
> As far as business transactions are concerned, interest laws are a dead letter. . . . Located as they are in every business center and with sharp competition, it is the merest bosh to talk of a banking institution practicing extortion. They cannot do it and live. The day has come when such a bank would be driven out of business.[112]

How, in fact, did banks deal with usury laws? In his textbook, Westerfield observed that "usury laws are easily evaded by ingenious devices."[113] A perfectly legal way of getting

[109] Claudius B. Patten, *Practical Banking*, 5th ed. (New York: B. Rhodes and Co., 1894), p. 416.

[110] U.S. Comptroller of the Currency, *Annual Report*, 1872, p. xxv.

[111] Ibid., p. xxvi.

[112] B. F. Clayton, "The Banker and His Customer," *Proceedings of the Iowa Bankers' Association*, 1892, pp. 37–38.

[113] Westerfield, *Banking Principles*, p. 591.

above 7 percent was to take the discount in advance. However, few usurers were content with this small increment and turned to more lucrative methods. One common technique was requiring a borrower to maintain a "compensating balance" on deposit at the bank. He or she paid interest on the whole amount but could use only a percentage of it. Thus, the effective interest rate could be substantially higher than the stated rate. A contemporary banking textbook stated, "There is an unwritten law in banking that the borrower should keep on deposit one-quarter or thereabouts of the amount borrowed," and goes on to reveal that this practice "gives the bank a larger profit, for the borrower really has the use of but part of his loans, while he pays interest on the whole. It is a banking secret."[114] In 1874 Congressional hearings it was revealed that some banks loaned at the legal rate of 7 percent, with the understanding that 15 percent of the loan was to be left on deposit.[115] Another, more circumspect method involved chartering a bank and simultaneously establishing a private, unincorporated bank. Notes issued by the chartered bank were deposited with the private one and then relent at the market rate, rather than at the legal ceiling. This method was widely practiced in Chicago, for example, in the 1850s.[116]

In 1872 the Comptroller of the Currency found usurious practices to differ regionally. In Eastern cities balances equal to one-eighth or one-fourth of the amount borrowed were required to be kept on deposit; on the other hand, "the banks in the South and the West not infrequently charge the ruling rate without regard to the account of the customer."[117]

[114] Kniffin, *American Banking Practice*, p. 172.

[115] U.S. House, Committee on Banking and Currency, *Views Expressed before the Committee, 1874*, 43rd Congress, 2nd Session, 1874, p. 138.

[116] Rollin G. Thomas, "The Development of State Banks in Chicago" (unpublished Ph.D. dissertation, University of Chicago, 1930), pp. 44–45.

[117] U.S. Comptroller of the Currency, *Annual Report*, 1872, p. xxvi.

Where the general level of interest rates was higher, banks could be less circumspect.

Usury laws seem to have been openly violated almost universally. In 1915 the Comptroller of the Currency collected data from national banks on usurious loan charges and found that some national banks in nearly every part of the country and nearly all in some sections had been charging interest rates on loans that were not only illegal and usurious, but also "intolerable."[118] It was discovered that 1,247 national banks out of 7,600 total were openly charging interest rates illegal by state and federal statutes; more than twice that number were charging 10 percent or more on some loans.[119] Moreover, it was pointed out that many national banks had been charging these usurious rates for fifty years or more.[120]

Exhibits A–W in the 1915 *Annual Report* present the portfolios of usurious loans individually, citing amounts and interest rates, for some selected banks, and also include an address on "The Crimes of the Usurer in Oklahoma" by L. C. McNabb, whose arguments had made him "many implacable enemies among the bankers, who, his friends say, are now endeavoring to discredit him by the circulation of slanderous charges."[121] For example, a national bank in Texas charged from 8 to 166 percent interest between August 1, 1914, and November 27, 1914.[122] Three national banks in Oklahoma reported that the average rate of interest that they charged on all loans was 25, 36 and 40 percent, respectively, during the period September 2–November 10, 1915, with the highest rate ranging to 300 percent.[123] These examples are quite typical of those reported. It should be noted, furthermore, that these rates cited were in 1915, after a long period of decline in western interest rates.

[118] U.S. Comptroller of the Currency, *Annual Report*, 1915, p. 23.
[119] U.S. Comptroller of the Currency, *Annual Report*, 1918, p. 208.
[120] U.S. Comptroller of the Currency, *Annual Report*, 1915, p. 25.
[121] Ibid., p. 218.   [122] Ibid., pp. 149–161.
[123] Ibid., p. 217.

85

Table 10 presents the number of national banks by state charging usurious interest on some loans. The conclusion seems clear that the usury laws were widely and flagrantly disobeyed. To give a better picture of actual rates charged,

Table 10

Number of Banks by State Charging
Usurious Interest, September 2, 1915

State	Number	State	Number
Maine	—	Ohio	9
New Hampshire	2	Indiana	15
Vermont	5	Illinois	76
Massachusetts	—	Michigan	11
Rhode Island	—	Wisconsin	—
Connecticut	—	Minnesota	1
New York	—	Iowa	11
New Jersey	7	Missouri	26
Pennsylvania	—	Kansas	21
Delaware	—	Nebraska	1
Maryland	2	North Dakota	69
Virginia	42	South Dakota	—
West Virginia	43	Colorado	—
North Carolina	44	New Mexico	1
South Carolina	6	Arizona	13
Georgia	85	Utah	1
Florida	6	Wyoming	—
Alabama	60	Montana	1
Mississippi	4	Idaho	2
Louisiana	10	Nevada	—
Arkansas	8	California	—
Texas	168	Oregon	—
Tennessee	113	Washington	3
Kentucky	89	Oklahoma	287

States with blank entries had no effective usury constraint; any rate could be charged by special contract.

Source: Exhibit U, U.S. Comptroller of the Currency, *Annual Report*, 1915 (Washington, D.C.: U.S. Government Printing Office, 1915), p. 229.

because the legal ceiling varied from state to state, Table 11 lists the number of national banks by state for which the average interest rate on loans and discounts exceeded 10 percent. Unsurprisingly, most of these banks were concentrated in the West and, to a lesser extent, in the South.

Table 11

Number of Banks by State Charging an Average of 10 Percent or More on All Loans, September 2, 1915

State	Number	State	Number
Maine	—	Ohio	—
New Hampshire	—	Indiana	—
Vermont	—	Illinois	2
Massachusetts	—	Michigan	—
Rhode Island	—	Wisconsin	—
Connecticut	—	Minnesota	6
New York	—	Iowa	—
New Jersey	—	Missouri	2
Pennsylvania	—	Kansas	5
Delaware	—	Nebraska	18
Maryland	—	North Dakota	90
Virginia	—	South Dakota	25
West Virginia	—	Colorado	37
North Carolina	—	New Mexico	25
South Carolina	—	Arizona	—
Georgia	23	Utah	2
Florida	6	Wyoming	14
Alabama	21	Montana	38
Mississippi	—	Idaho	33
Louisiana	2	Nevada	1
Arkansas	17	California	13
Texas	317	Oregon	10
Tennessee	3	Washington	12
Kentucky	—	Oklahoma	300

Source: Exhibit V, U.S. Comptroller of the Currency, *Annual Report*, 1915 (Washington, D.C.: U.S. Government Printing Office, 1915), p. 230.

It seems fairly clear that, on average, usury laws were not an effective constraint on the banks, affecting their choice of earning assets. Usury laws seem to have been widely, openly, and commonly disobeyed. Similarly, for the antebellum period Rockoff has found that interstate differences in usury limits seem to have had no effect on the regional pattern of financial development.[124]

Nineteenth-century banks, especially country banks, have traditionally been pictured as being individual entities, operating in isolation, but in fact country banks had large numbers of connections through the correspondent banking system, as will be described in Chapter IV. The individual bank was commonly pictured as being subject to the real-bills doctrine in portfolio selection. In actuality, substantial numbers of loans were rolled over, so that rather than having a portfolio composed of actual short-term loans, the bank had a portfolio of loans with varying effective maturities. Usury laws were a government-imposed constraint on portfolio selection, but we have seen that it was not really a binding one. In spite of differing theoretical and legal constraints, then, nineteenth-century banks managed to operate in many ways like present-day ones. One can be misled about nineteenth-century bank operations by considering only the theoretical and legal framework in which they operated; the banks' responses to these constraints and the way in which they actually operated must also be taken into account.

[124] Hugh Rockoff, "Varieties of Banking and Regional Economic Development in the United States," *Journal of Economic History*, XXXV (March 1975), pp. 169–172.

CHAPTER IV

The Correspondent Banking System

DEFECTS OF THE BANKING SYSTEM AND THE APPEAL OF BRANCH BANKING

IN addition to its alleged failure in promoting economic stability, because of the unresponsiveness of the rate of national bank note issue to changes in the demand for credit, the postbellum banking system was also widely criticized for its inadequacy in promoting the transfer of capital, and hence economic growth. The problem with such a banking structure, it was often argued, was its lack of integration and coordination. Such a rationalized structure was impossible because of its heterogeneous character and large numbers of component banks—by 1900 the "banking system" was a patchwork of over 12,000 independent national, state, and private banks. The fundamental defect of the national banking system, according to J. Laurence Laughlin, professor of political economy at the University of Chicago, was the lack of cooperation between these independent institutions; indeed, it was not in any proper sense "a system" at all.[1] This system of independent banks, which inhibited coordination of the banking system, also resulted in "wide diffusion of reserves, extravagance in the use of banking resources, . . . inability to finance large operations with ease."[2] Chester A. Phillips pointed to the "absence of scientific coordination, so natural and so usual in countries relatively new"[3] in the American financial system.

[1] J. Laurence Laughlin, ed., *Banking Reform* (Chicago: The National Citizens' League, 1912), p. 12.

[2] Ibid., p. 199.

[3] Chester A. Phillips, "Introduction," in Walter H. Hull, ed., *Practical Problems in Banking and Currency* (New York: Macmillan Company, 1907), p. xxiii.

The principal reason for this proliferation of independent banks in the postbellum period was the system of unit banking established in the National Banking Acts. The question of branch banks does not seem to have been seriously considered in the debate before the passage of the National Banking Act, although in the Act of June 3, 1864, the following clause was inserted: "And its usual business shall be transacted at an office or banking house located in the place specified in its organization certificate."[4] Even though branch bank operations were not specifically prohibited, the implication to that effect is fairly clear, and in any case it had traditionally been held that what was not specifically authorized by the Act was prohibited. In 1892 a special act of Congress was required to allow Chicago national banks to establish branches at the Columbian Exposition.[5]

In the antebellum period the practice of branch banking was fairly widespread. In all, by 1860 in 13 states 39 branch banks were operating with 222 branches.[6] The passage of the National Banking Acts and the subsequent tax on state bank notes, however, firmly established the system of unit banking. Many of the state banks operating branches converted into unit national banks. A survey by the Comptroller of the Currency in 1896 found branch banking explicitly prohibited in only thirteen states, although in most other states there was no provision in the banking law for the establishment of branches and it was generally held in such states that opening branches was illegal.[7] Branch

---

[4] Shirley D. Southworth, *Branch Banking in the United States* (New York: McGraw-Hill Book Company, 1928), p. 12.

[5] Thomas P. Kane, *The Romance and Tragedy of Banking* (New York: The Bankers' Publishing Co., 1923), p. 205.

[6] For a more detailed examination of antebellum branch banking, see John M. Chapman and Ray B. Westerfield, *Branch Banking* (New York: Harper & Brothers, 1942), pp. 22–57.

[7] U.S. Comptroller of the Currency, *Annual Report*, 1896 (Washington, D.C.: U.S. Government Printing Office, 1896), p. 40; George E. Barnett, *State Banks and Trust Companies since the Passage of the*

banking for state banks and trust companies was definitely permitted in California, Delaware, Florida, Georgia, New York, Oregon, Rhode Island, Virginia, and Washington; it was allowed for trust companies only in Louisiana, Maine, and Massachusetts. Nevertheless, a survey of branch banks in 1901 revealed only forty-seven banks with a total of eighty-five branches in the entire country. New York had the largest number of branch banks, thirteen, with thirty-three branches.[8]

In any case, intrastate branch banking could be of only limited usefulness in the mobilization and transfer of capital from surplus to deficit areas. Over the course of the late nineteenth century, however, the advantages of an interstate branch banking system began to be discerned. Branch banks were argued to make more efficient use of reserves, "furnishing a much larger volume of loanable funds from the same amount of resources,"[9] to offer superior management, and also to be safer because of the opportunity for diversification of risk over wider areas.[10]

The greatest advantages of branch banking, however, were seen to be its implications for the interregional transfer of credit or short-term capital. Credit could be extended to remote areas. Branch banking would allow the establishment of branch offices in areas where the population was so small or sparse that an ordinary bank could not be supported, so that there would be no banking facilities at all available otherwise. In an address on the Scottish system of branch banks before the American Bankers' Association convention it was observed: "To one who has lived in Scotland the lack

National-Bank Act (Washington, D.C.: U.S. Government Printing Office, 1911), p. 135.

[8] U.S. Comptroller of the Currency, *Annual Report*, 1902, pp. 47–51.

[9] James B. Forgan, "Branch Banking," in Hull, *Practical Problems*, p. 253.

[10] O. M. W. Sprague, "Branch Banking in the United States," *Quarterly Journal of Economics*, XVII (February 1903), p. 243.

of banking facilities is very marked. This may sound strange, but I know of a great many villages in Wisconsin wholly destitute of banking privileges, while villages of equal size in Scotland would have one and perhaps two branch banks."[11] In his 1896 report the U.S. Comptroller of the Currency, J. H. Eckels, argued that the agitation for more currency was in reality an agitation for more credit facilities and that branch banking was the best solution, because it would provide more capital than any other method to the parts of the country needing it the most.[12]

Branch banking was recognized as an efficient mechanism for the interregional transfer of funds to capital-scarce areas, thereby eliminating interest rate differentials. In other words, "Under branch banking the mobility of capital is almost perfect."[13] Increasingly during the late nineteenth century foreign branch banking systems were studied, discussed, and favorably contrasted with the unit structure prevailing in the United States; the Canadian and Scottish systems were probably the most frequently cited. Sprague, for example, observed, "In Canada rates do not vary much more than one percent between different parts of the country," as opposed to the wide variation in the United States.[14] At the American Bankers' Association convention the Canadian system of branch banking was described or discussed in 1877, 1886, 1891, and 1893. The Comptroller of the Currency conducted a worldwide survey of branch banking by sending questionnaires to U.S. embassies in thirty-three countries in 1895; he discovered that "every country reporting allows the banks to maintain branch offices or banks" except the United States.[15]

The Indianapolis Monetary Commission, a nonpartisan

[11] *Proceedings of the American Bankers' Association*, 1902, p. 77.
[12] U.S. Comptroller of the Currency, *Annual Report*, 1896, pp. 103–105.
[13] Sprague, "Branch Banking," p. 245.
[14] Ibid., p. 246.
[15] U.S. Comptroller of the Currency, *Annual Report*, 1895, pp. 63–110.

group of businessmen charged with examining the state of the monetary system, recommended in 1898 the establishment of a branch banking system to promote "a larger supply and better distribution of loanable capital" and thus equalize regional interest rates.[16] R. M. Breckenridge, in an 1899 *Bankers' Magazine* article, argued that the effects of the National Banking Acts were especially severe on rural areas and that a branch banking system would alleviate and promote local interest rate convergence and stability.[17] The Comptroller of the Currency suggested legalizing limited branching several times during the 1880s and 1890s; for example, in 1896, in order to extend better credit facilities to rural areas, he recommended that national banks be permitted to establish branches in towns where there was no national bank and the population was under 1,000. In 1895, similarly, President Grover Cleveland argued that large banks be allowed to establish branches in smaller communities "as would serve the people."[18] Indeed, Sprague commented: "Upon few subjects has the consensus of opinion of both economists and financial writers been more general than upon the advantages of branch banking over a system of separate local banks. Its superiority in respect to safety, economy, the equalization of rates for loans, and the diffusion of banking facilities, cannot be questioned."[19]

Branch banking was not, however, universally endorsed. Country bankers, those who were most threatened by the prospect of competition from branch offices, strongly objected to it on economic and philosophical as well as on personal grounds. They charged that such a system would result in the monopolization of the banking system by a few large banks at the expense of the small-town bankers; the com-

[16] *Report of the Indianapolis Monetary Commission* (Chicago: University of Chicago Press, 1898), p. 386.

[17] R. M. Breckenridge, "Branch Banking and Discount Rates," *Bankers' Magazine*, LVIII (January 1899), pp. 38–52.

[18] Chapman and Westerfield, *Branch Banking*, p. 67.

[19] Sprague, "Branch Banking," p. 242.

petitive, unit banking system would be destroyed. Consequently, branch banking was seen to be "unpatriotic, unAmerican, unbusiness-like" in the eyes of the Kansas Bankers' Association.[20] Nevertheless, pressure for branch banking and the provision of increased credit in rural areas obtained some concessions in the Gold Standard Act of 1900, which lowered minimum capital requirements for national banks in small towns. After 1900 the movement for a branch banking system ebbed, and it was not until 1921 that national banks were allowed to open branches in states where branching was permitted.[21]

The branch banking movement represented a response to the unit structure of the postbellum banking system, which was seen to be inadequate in the provision of credit to rural areas and generally in the efficient transfer of capital across regions. Branch banking offered an integrated and coordinated system to achieve these ends, in contrast with the uncoordinated structure of the then-existing system of unit banks. In the words of the Indianapolis Monetary Commission: "Nowhere save in the United States is there such a multitude of small and unconnected institutions. There is, perhaps, no more striking characteristic of the banking system of the United States than the immense number of banks of low capitalization, and the absence of institutions of large capital with branches."[22]

Such discussions of the defects of the banking system almost always focused on the national banking system. To be sure, relatively high minimum capital requirements undoubtedly limited the number of national banks established in small towns and rural areas. R. M. Breckenridge argued in his *Bankers' Magazine* article, for example, that the dearth of rural banking facilities was primarily the result of the national banking system, through the tax on state bank notes and the high capital requirements; this position has been

[20] Thornton Cooke, "Branch Banking for the West and South," *Quarterly Journal of Economics,* XVIII (November 1903), p. 112.

[21] Chapman and Westerfield, *Branch Banking,* p. 4.

[22] *Report of the Indianapolis Monetary Commission,* p. 376.

restated in more recent times by Richard Sylla.[23] However, alternatives to national banks existed in the form of state and private banks. State banks generally were subject to lower capital requirements than national banks, and private banks were bound by no requirements at all. As will be shown in Chapter VI, it was state and private banks that provided the bulk of banking services to small towns. Just because small and rural communities were deprived of the services of national banks, this did not mean that they were deprived of all banking services. However, the roles of state and private banks were virtually ignored in the debate, which centered on the structure of the national banking system.[24]

The unit structure of the banking system and its fragmentation into an "immense" number of small banks was similarly taken as evidence of the lack of integration or coordination among the numerous independent banks. A study of only the legal unit banking structure, however, leads to an erroneous picture of the nature of the short-term capital market. Rural banks were not isolated and unconnected entities; rather, they were part of a widespread and intricate network linking city and country banks known as the correspondent banking system, which facilitated the flow of capital between regions. Even though banks were legally separate and distinct entities, it did not mean that they were unconnected or that mechanisms for the transfer of funds did not exist.

FUNCTIONS OF THE CORRESPONDENT BANKING SYSTEM

The system of correspondent banking developed quite early in the United States. Before the Civil War interior

[23] Richard Sylla, "Federal Policy, Banking Market Structure, and Capital Mobilization in the United States, 1863–1913," *Journal of Economic History*, XXIX (December 1969), pp. 657–686.

[24] One exception to this neglect of state banks was Cooke's article, which argued that the experience of states with very low capital requirements had been unsatisfactory and that a branch banking system instead was needed to extend credit to very small communities. Cooke, "Branch Banking," pp. 100–102.

bankers began to deposit funds in leading trade centers, especially New York City; these deposits were referred to as bankers' balances. Because there was a constant flow of funds and goods between New York and the interior, most interior bankers found it convenient to maintain some funds on deposit in New York. As New York exchange usually sold at a premium, balances in New York were more valuable to the interior banker than balances at home.[25]

The flow of funds due to domestic trade resulted in a large number of state bank notes passing through New York. To facilitate redemption, many interior banks maintained balances with a city correspondent.[26] In addition to the demands of trade and the maintenance of a redemption fund, funds were also drawn to New York by the practice of paying interest on bankers' balances. "Idle" balances could be deposited with a city correspondent and thereby earn a return. The practice of paying interest on deposits seems to have developed as a competitive technique among New York banks to attract depositors, although the payment of interest on deposits was not a general practice in the antebellum period and many banks did not pay interest. Rates on bankers' balances paid in the antebellum period ranged between 3 and 6 percent.[27] After the Civil War rates generally declined from the "steady rate" of 4 percent then prevailing[28] to 2 percent, where the rate paid on bankers' balances stabilized for the remainder of the postbellum period. Moreover, more and more New York banks switched to the explicit payment of interest rates during the period. The payment of interest on bankers' balances in New York in the postbellum period is discussed in more detail in Appendix B.

[25] Margaret G. Myers, *The New York Money Market, Volume I: Origins and Development* (New York: Columbia University Press, 1931), p. 103.

[26] Ibid., p. 105.   [27] Ibid., p. 122.

[28] Don Dailey, "The Development of Banking in Chicago before 1890" (unpublished Ph.D. dissertation, Northwestern University, 1934), p. 428.

New York state banks were the first to accumulate balances in New York banks. By 1835 one-eighth of total assets of New York country banks were held as bankers' balances in New York City.[29] The practice spread to other Eastern and Midwestern, and eventually Southern, states, so that by 1850 almost 600 of the 700 incorporated banks in the United States kept balances in New York,[30] and also began to be institutionalized as states began to allow New York balances to be counted as bank reserves, thus recognizing the already existing informal practice. In Ohio, for example, after 1851 one-half of the 30 percent reserve requirement might be kept on deposit in New York or some other Eastern city; in 1858 Massachusetts began to allow bankers' balances to be counted as reserves.[31]

In Chicago bankers' balances began to accumulate also, although the process began later and was more gradual than that in New York. Only in the 1850s did the deposits of country banks begin to accumulate in Chicago banks.[32] However, holdings of country bank balances in Chicago did not really increase rapidly until the passage of the National Banking Act. By 1868, 75 to 80 percent of country national banks in Illinois, Iowa, and Wisconsin maintained accounts in Chicago.[33]

The reserve system established by the National Banking Act in effect gave legal sanction to this system of bank interrelationships that had developed in the antebellum period. The 1863 Act required every national bank to hold a 25 percent reserve in lawful money against notes and deposits. Country banks, however, were required to hold only two-fifths of that, 10 percent, in their vaults. The remaining portion of the reserve requirement could be held on deposit with a national bank in any of nine cities—Boston, New York, Philadelphia, Baltimore, Cincinnati, New Orleans, Providence, Chicago,

[29] Myers, *The New York Money Market*, p. 108.
[30] Ibid., p. 115.   [31] Ibid., p. 107.
[32] Dailey, "The Development of Banking," p. 183.
[33] Ibid., p. 363.

and St. Louis.[34] Lawful money for fulfilling the reserve requirement included U.S. notes, specie, gold and silver certificates, and clearing-house certificates.

The National Banking Act of 1864 amended the original Act and established the three-tiered structure of banking relationships that existed for the remainder of the period. New York was designated the central reserve city in which all national banks were required to maintain a 25 percent reserve in lawful money against deposits and note circulation; later, the Act of June 20, 1874, abolished the required reserve held against note circulation, replacing it with a redemption fund on deposit with the Treasury.[35] Eighteen other cities were designated reserve cities.[36] Their national banks were required to maintain 25 percent reserves also, but only half had to be held in lawful money. The other half could be held as deposits in New York banks. The remaining national banks were classed as country banks, which were required to maintain only 15 percent reserves, of which three-fifths, 9 percent, could be held as deposits in reserve or central reserve cities.

This "pyramiding" of reserves or concentration of country bank balances in reserve and central reserve cities was thus sanctioned by the establishment of the national banking system. Indeed, Margaret Myers computed that if the National Banking Act had been in effect in 1860, $17,564,000 would have been held as bankers' balances in New York, while at that time $17,287,000 was actually held as net

[34] Myers, *The New York Money Market*, p. 219.

[35] After 1887, whenever three-quarters of the national banks in a city of over 200,000 population requested it, the Comptroller of the Currency could designate that city as a central reserve city. Chicago and St. Louis became central reserve cities in 1887.

[36] After 1887, whenever three-quarters of the national banks in a city of over 50,000 population requested it, the Comptroller of the Currency could designate that city as a reserve city. By 1913, the beginning of the Federal Reserve period, the number of reserve cities had increased to 47.

bankers' balances there.[37] So the establishment of the national banking system did not so much promote the concentration of balances in New York and other reserve cities as recognize the existing pattern of the allocation of funds. However, required reserves did not serve the same function as voluntarily held reserves because they could not be used to meet shortfalls, so after the initial adjustment period country banks held balances in New York substantially in excess of the required reserve level.

Country banks maintained accounts with one or more reserve agents in one or more reserve or central reserve cities; reserve city banks, in turn, maintained accounts with one or more reserve agents in the central reserve cities. These city reserve agents were generally known as city correspondents. Very close ties developed between city banks and their country correspondents, with city banks performing a number of useful services for their country bank depositors. One of the original purposes of maintaining city balances was the facilitation of trade. City accounts were maintained primarily to provide a source of New York or Boston exchange, for example, for its country customers. By keeping balances in reserve cities, a country bank could easily provide customers with domestic exchange.

Another important function of the correspondent banking system was the facilitation of out-of-town collections. If, for example, a country bank had a note, acceptance, or bond coming due in New York, or for that matter, a check drawn on a New York bank, the country bank would send the item to its city correspondent in New York, which would act as the country bank's agent in its collection. These items, when added to the country bank's New York account, represented both a lawful reserve and a source of New York exchange, which usually sold at a premium. The arrangement was a reciprocal one also; the country bank in turn would collect items due in its area for its city correspondent. In general,

[37] Myers, *The New York Money Market*, p. 229.

the larger the account maintained with its city correspondent, the more collection items the country bank was given to collect in its home city. Often the country bank exacted profitable rates of exchange on items sent for collection by its New York correspondents.[38]

The growth in the use and acceptability of checks in the postbellum period, as well as the degree of competition among New York banks, however, by the mid-1880s resulted in New York banks collecting out-of-town as well as New York items for their country correspondents. In 1884 the president of the East River National Bank complained, "Remittances from the country that used to be sent in drafts on New York or in money are now sent in checks drawn on banks situated from Maine to Texas, which have to be sent back for collection to those places. . . . So far as New York is concerned the usage has assumed its present dimensions from the habit into which country correspondents have fallen of remitting in checks."[39] Competition, however, prevented each New York bank from insisting on remittances in the form of New York drafts. Indeed, in addition to just accepting country checks, competitive pressures ultimately forced New York banks to absorb the collection charges rather than passing them on to their correspondents, notwithstanding a resolution passed by the New York Clearing House Association calling on members to charge for the collection of country checks.[40]

The increasing number of country checks received in New York was one indication of the general expansion in the use of demand deposits. Checks had originally been intended for use in local transactions; for transmitting funds at a distance a draft on a bank in that locality or on New York was used, for which there was a "reasonable charge." A banker at the

[38] L. H. Langston, *Practical Bank Operation* (New York: Ronald Press Co., 1921), p. 100.

[39] Address of Charles Jenkins, *Proceedings of the American Bankers' Association*, 1884, p. 57.

[40] Address of A. W. Blye, *Proceedings of the American Bankers' Association*, 1885, p. 136.

1885 American Bankers' Association convention grumbled, "Twenty-five years ago no one would have thought of liquidating a payment in Boston, Philadelphia, or Chicago by use of a check upon a bank, located in his own town or at least adding to the amount to be paid a fair and proper amount for collection."[41] It was recognized that as long as there was no "concert of action" among banks, collection charges could not be "in practice thrown back upon the customers or upon the drawers of the various items."[42] As a result, uniform collection charges were often suggested because of the "obvious necessity of cooperation and uniformity, to avoid the cutting of rates, unhealthy competition and the like on the part of banks located in the same place."[43] Such efforts enjoyed no success in New York, but did prevail in some other cities.[44]

The correspondent system thus furnished an efficient means for both city and country banks to make out-of-town collections. Moreover, the city correspondent made available to its country clients some of the advantages of large-scale operations. Even though credit departments began to be established in city banks during this period, most country banks were too small to support one. Consequently, the city bank acted in effect as a financial advisor to its country correspondents, answering credit inquiries through its own credit department.[45] One of the primary reasons that country banks were interested in the creditworthiness of firms outside

[41] Ibid., p. 135.

[42] C. W. Hammond, "Clearings of Country Collections," *Proceedings of the American Bankers' Association*, 1890, p. 107.

[43] Address of Col. R. M. Nelson, *Proceedings of the American Bankers' Association*, 1885, p. 101.

[44] For example, in San Francisco, at least in the 1870s and 1880s, collection charges were strictly enforced. A Tacoma banker observed in 1890, "Competition is not always the life of trade. . . . We are not in the West for our health. As bankers we proposed to make some money on collections as well as on deposits and loans." Leroy Anderson and J. O. Denny, *Financial California* (San Francisco: Coast Banker Publishing Co., 1916), p. 129; *Proceedings of the American Bankers' Association*, 1890, p. 114.

[45] Chester A. Phillips, *Bank Credit* (New York: Macmillan Company, 1920), p. 148.

the region was for the purchase of commercial paper. New York correspondents in addition served as agents for country banks in the purchase and sale of commercial paper, bonds, and other securities in the New York market. Thus, country banks even in remote areas had easy access to the New York money market through their correspondents. The contemporary literature contains a number of references to country banks, even in rural Kansas, Nebraska, and South Dakota, purchasing commercial paper in the New York market through their city correspondents.[46] In turn, the country banks provided information to their city correspondents about potential borrowers or commercial paper issuers located in their area.

Another important function of correspondent banks was serving as a source of funds for country banks, either through interbank loans or through the rediscounting of notes held by the country bank. This function will be discussed in greater detail later with regard to its role in the interregional transfer of funds in Chapter V.

Besides serving as sources of funds, city correspondent banks also functioned as repositories of funds for country banks. The payment of interest on deposits attracted funds to reserve cities in excess of the amount required for normal business purposes. At the time these were known as "surplus funds," which country banks sent to the cities to earn interest. Indeed, less than half the bankers' balances represented part of the legal reserve.[47] The remainder constituted a liquid part

[46] See, for example, C. L. Brokaw, "A Study in Bank Investments," *Proceedings of the Kansas Bankers' Association*, 1908, pp. 37–48; J. H. Case, "The Desirability of Commercial Paper as a Bank Investment," *Proceedings of the New Jersey Bankers' Association*, 1912, p. 41; Noble Crandall, "Commercial Paper," *Proceedings of the Nebraska Bankers' Association*, 1903, p. 189; N. E. Franklin, "Commercial Paper," *Proceedings of the South Dakota Bankers' Association*, 1912, p. 127.

[47] Leonard L. Watkins, *Bankers' Balances* (Chicago: A. W. Shaw Co., 1929), p. 80.

of the country banks' secondary reserve, easily convertible into cash (except for perhaps in occasional panics), which offered a positive rate of return, usually 2 percent over the period,[48] as opposed to vault cash, which earned nothing.

Because at least a part of total bankers' balances was fairly volatile, the city correspondent was rather reluctant to loan out much of these funds on time. Rather, in New York much of the bankers' balances on deposit there were invested in the call loan market. Because call loans could be called at any time, they represented a very liquid investment that at the same time enabled city banks to meet demands for withdrawals of bankers' balances fairly easily. National banks were required to report to the Comptroller of the Currency once a year the amount of demand loans on collateral security, which we may take as the volume of all call loans on securities collateral. Between 1868 and 1878 call loans consisted of about one-third of total loans of New York national banks; in the period 1879–1904 the growth rate of call loans was much more rapid, and call loans averaged almost one-half of total loans, although after 1904 the proportion of call loans declined and by 1913 it was about one-third again.[49]

The volume of call loans moved closely with the volume of bankers' balances in New York. The upward trend in call loans was matched by one in bankers' balances. Only after 1904 did they diverge when call loans declined while bankers' balances continued to increase at a reduced rate, probably due to the declines in security prices.[50] Except for the period following 1904, call loans amounted to approximately 75 percent of bankers' balances, just the ratio that would have existed if all bankers' balances had been loaned on call except for the 25 percent reserve requirement. Peaks and

[48] The stability of the 2 percent rate on bankers' balances in New York is documented in Appendix B.

[49] Myers, *The New York Money Market*, pp. 270–271.

[50] Ibid., p. 270.

troughs in the call loans series and the bankers' balances almost always coincided in timing. In only nine out of forty-three years did the series move in opposite directions.[51]

Another service provided by city banks was making loans directly for their country correspondents. Thus, the city banks would loan its country correspondent's funds directly on the call market for them, usually exacting ⅛ to ¼ percent interest in compensation.[52] Thirty New York banks and trust companies reported to the Pujo Committee figures for bankers' balances held and call loans made on the banks' own accounts and for correspondents during the period 1908–1912. In those data there was an inverse relationship between bankers' balances and call loans for correspondents.[53] Apparently, when the call rate was high, country banks would invest in the call loan market directly; when the call rate was low, country funds were invested in bankers' balances.

EXTENT OF THE CORRESPONDENT BANKING SYSTEM

Concentration of funds in reserve cities continued, encouraged or at least sanctioned by the national banking system, in the postbellum period. Table 12 shows net bankers' balances, that is, due from banks less due to banks, held on deposit in reserve city and central reserve city banks by country national banks at ten-year intervals between 1870 and 1900. The absolute amounts of correspondent balances held by country banks in every region rise over time; in addition, the percentage figures are highest in every region at the last date, 1900. Thus, with the exception of 1890, country banks on average devoted an increasingly larger percentage of their total asset portfolio to correspondent balances.

[51] Ibid., p. 271.

[52] William H. Kniffin, *American Banking Practice* (New York: McGraw-Hill Book Company, 1921), p. 187.

[53] Myers, *The New York Money Market*, p. 269.

Table 12

Bankers' Net Balances[a] of Country National Banks,
Due from Other Banks, 1870–1900

Year	New England	Middle Atlantic	South	East North Central	West North Central	Mountain-Pacific
			($ million)			
1870	16.4	17.4	2.3	8.8	2.6	0.6
1880	16.4	29.1	6.8	20.6	5.2	3.9
1890	17.3	35.5	14.1	26.5	12.4	11.3
1900	23.9	69.3	69.3	58.9	23.7	28.0
		(as percent of total assets)				
1870	6.1	6.7	6.1	6.9	9.0	16.7
1880	5.0	9.4	7.6	10.0	8.7	15.4
1890	5.0	8.4	6.2	9.0	6.7	8.2
1900	5.8	11.2	10.1	13.5	10.9	18.3

[a] Values for each region are the sum of "due from national banks," "due from state banks," and "due from reserve agents," less the sum of "due to national banks," "due to state banks," "due to trust companies," and "due to reserve agents," for each state, summed over the states in the region, averaged arithmetically over the five reported call dates for each year. These entries represent assets of country banks.

Source: Richard Sylla, "The United States, 1863–1913," in Rondo Cameron, ed., *Banking and Economic Development* (New York: Oxford University Press, 1972), p. 252. Reprinted with the permission of Oxford University Press.

Bankers' balances held in reserve cities represented not only the correspondent deposits of country national banks, but also those of state banks, trust companies, and private banks; they were liabilities of reserve city banks and assets of the latter group of banks. Net bankers' balances, "due to banks" less "due from banks" in this case because these funds are on balance liabilities of reserve city banks, held by reserve city banks are presented in Table 13 for the period 1870–1900. The trend seems to be toward increasing concentration of bankers' balances in reserve cities. One exception is the East North Central region, because Chicago and

Table 13

Bankers' Net Balances[a] of Reserve City National Banks,
Due to Other Banks, 1870–1900

Year	New England	Middle Atlantic	South	East North Central	West North Central	Mountain-Pacific
($ million)						
1870	4.4	0.5	0.2	2.8	−0.2	—
1880	8.1	4.2	1.2	11.5	3.9	0.3
1890	11.7	5.5	2.9	4.1	8.2	0.5
1900	27.5	38.7	1.9	13.1	21.3	1.7
(as percent of total assets)						
1870	3.1	0.3	−2.6	4.2	1.0	7.3
1880	4.3	2.1	4.7	11.1	2.6	6.3
1890	5.4	2.0	6.9	3.9	13.4	6.3
1900	10.2	7.7	3.0	6.0	15.1	3.8

[a] See note to Table 12. These figures are derived by subtracting the "due from . . ." items from the "due to . . ." items. These entries represent net liabilities of reserve city banks.

Source: Richard Sylla, "The United States, 1863–1913," in Rondo Cameron, ed., *Banking and Economic Development* (New York: Oxford University Press, 1972), p. 253. Reprinted with the permission of Oxford University Press.

St. Louis were reclassified as central reserve cities during this period. Bankers' balances held increased in absolute amounts and also in most cases as a percentage of total assets.

The concentration of deposits becomes evident as the apex of the pyramid of reserves, the central reserve cities. In Table 14 are presented the holdings of bankers' balances in central reserve cities. The flow of correspondent deposits into central reserve cities is clear. Between 1870 and 1900 holdings of bankers' balances as a percentage of total assets of New York banks doubled. By the end of the period, 1900, deposits from interior banks amounted to one-third of total assets in New York national banks; for Chicago and St. Louis banks this proportion approached one-fourth.

The dominant position of New York in the correspondent banking system is even more apparent in Table 15, which shows the relative concentration of national bank correspondent deposits in reserve and central reserve city banks as of November 10, 1915. More than 43 percent of the total amount of bankers' balances of national banks in the United

Table 14

Bankers' Net Balances[a] of Central Reserve City Banks,
Due to Other Banks, 1870–1900

Year	New York	Chicago	St. Louis
	($ million)		
1870	65.9		
1880	101.8		
1890	140.6	28.5	6.6
1900	339.3	60.0	21.2
	(as percent of total assets)		
1870	16.4		
1880	22.1		
1890	27.1	22.3	16.9
1900	33.7	24.1	23.0

[a] See notes to Table 12 and 13.

Source: Richard Sylla, "The United States, 1863–1913," in Rondo Cameron, ed., *Banking and Economic Development* (New York: Oxford University Press, 1972), p. 254. Reprinted with the permission of Oxford University Press.

States were held in New York national banks. New York's closest rival, Chicago, held only 11 percent of total national bank correspondent deposits. National banks in every region except the Western states held more correspondent balances in New York than in any other reserve city, including the regional financial center, such as, for example, Chicago in the Midwest or San Francisco in the Pacific states.

An examination of the number of correspondent accounts also indicates the dominant position of New York. In an 1890 study the Comptroller of the Currency found that New

Table 15

Bankers' Balances Held by National Banks,
November 10, 1915

(in percent)

Deposits Held by National Banks in:	New England	East	Depositing Banks Located in: South	Midwest	West	Pacific	United States
New York City	47.23	64.15	35.14	30.66	14.80	30.74	43.27
Chicago	2.94	3.90	4.57	24.91	11.93	10.79	11.25
St. Louis	0.48	0.48	8.17	6.22	4.00	1.39	3.32
Boston	35.65	2.30	0.66	2.79	0.59	1.68	5.16
Philadelphia	8.80	15.07	4.44	3.70	0.49	1.56	7.83
Richmond	0.02	0.13	5.51	0.07	—	—	0.56
Atlanta	0.14	0.04	1.51	0.01	—	—	0.16
Dallas	—	—	3.09	—	0.22	—	0.29
Cleveland	0.08	0.45	0.34	5.58	0.08	0.22	1.84
Minneapolis	—	—	—	3.24	10.58	0.69	1.83
Kansas City	—	0.01	2.46	2.44	17.79	0.88	2.41
San Francisco	0.01	0.03	0.05	0.15	0.69	26.71	2.66
Other reserve cities	4.06	12.97	34.00	20.16	38.76	25.29	19.34
Total	100.00	100.00	100.00	100.00	100.00	100.00	100.00

Source: U.S. Comptroller of the Currency, *Annual Report*, 1915, Vol. I (Washington, D.C.: U.S. Government Printing Office, 1915), pp. 12–13.

York national banks held balances from 94 percent of all national banks, while Chicago national banks maintained accounts from 31 percent.[54] Table 16 presents the number of out-of-town accounts held by ten selected New York banks in 1913, which totals 15,483 accounts for these banks alone. If we make the crude assumption that this figure represents total New York correspondent accounts and that each out-

Table 16

Number of Correspondent Accounts Held by
New York Banks, 1913

Name	No. of Out-of-Town Depositors
Bankers Trust Co.	237
National Bank of Commerce	1,671
Chase National Bank	3,103
First National Bank	579
Guaranty Trust Co.	182
Hanover National Bank	4,074
Liberty National Bank	312
Mechanics Metals National Bank	1,010
National City Bank	1,889
National Park Bank	2,426
Total	15,483

Source: B. H. Beckhart and J. G. Smith, *The New York Money Market: Volume II, Sources and Movements of Funds* (New York: Columbia University Press, 1932), p. 156. Reprinted with the permission of Columbia University Press.

of-town bank maintained only one correspondent account in New York, then at least 60 percent of all commercial banks in existence in 1913 held New York accounts.

The position of New York as the apex of the pyramid of concentration of bankers' balances should not, however, be taken to indicate that such deposits were unimportant in

[54] U.S. Comptroller of the Currency, *Annual Report*, 1890, p. 20.

other cities. In several other reserve cities deposits of bankers' balances represented a major source of funds to local banks and presumably had significant influences on the local money market, a fact obscured by the predominance of the New York money market in terms of absolute size. For instance, around the turn of the century in Chicago and Kansas City, bankers' balances constituted on average about one-half of total deposits of national banks; in St. Louis the percentage was slightly less. In other reserve cities, such as Boston, Detroit, Cleveland, Minneapolis, and so forth, the ratio of bankers' balances to total deposits was around one-third. The president of the Continental and Commercial National Bank of Chicago in 1913 claimed, perhaps somewhat exaggeratedly, "We have about 5,000 correspondents located in every state in the Union, and at the present time we are carrying a little over $100,000,000 in balances of those banks."[55]

In spite of the great concentration of accounts of interior correspondent banks in New York, there seems to be no evidence that the New York market was a noncompetitive one or that a "Money Trust" in fact existed.[56] The stability of the 2 percent rate paid on bankers' balances in New York even in times of severe downward pressure on interest rates, as described in Appendix B, and the abolition of charges to correspondents for collecting country checks in spite of efforts to maintain them are both evidences of the working of a competitive market. In addition, around the turn of the century correspondent accounts began to be "openly and ostentatiously" solicited by circulars, letters, and even traveling representatives of city banks.[57] Such competition for

[55] Testimony of George M. Reynolds, in U.S. Senate Banking and Currency Committee, *Hearings on H.R. 7837 (S2639)*, 63rd Congress, 1st Session, p. 237.

[56] U.S. House Subcommittee on Banking and Currency, *Money Trust Investigation*, 62nd Congress, 3rd Session.

[57] Fritz Redlich, *The Molding of American Banking: Men and Ideas* (New York: Johnson Reprint Co., 1968), p. 177.

correspondents allowed country banks some bargaining power *vis-à-vis* the much larger city bank. A city banker told the American Bankers' Association convention, "We love the country bankers, but they are the masters of the situation. We dance at their music and pay the piper."[58] It may be somewhat overstated to argue as Redlich does that "in many cases the country correspondents *de facto* controlled the city banks";[59] but in any case it is clear that there was essentially a competitive market among New York banks for correspondent deposits. Even though the number of New York banks holding bankers' balances was small relative to the number of country banks, there were enough banks in New York in competition for correspondent deposits to constitute a quite competitive market structure.

Tables 15 and 16 convey some sense of the wide expanse of the correspondent system and the extent to which Western and Eastern banks were linked together. For example, in the Federal Reserve Act hearings in 1913 a bank in Hattiesburg, Mississippi, not a financial center of the South, was noted to be maintaining deposits in New York, St. Louis, Chicago, and New Orleans.[60]

In Table 17 the dispersion of correspondent accounts maintained by banks in some selected states for a slightly later date for which data are available, 1925, is presented. Once again, the links between the interior of the country and New York are quite extensive. In Georgia 600 out of 655 total banks maintained accounts in New York; in Kansas over half the banks maintained balances in New York banks. In addition to the interregional links revealed in this compendium of correspondent accounts, a well-developed structure of intraregional relationships is also exhibited. Within states such as Georgia, Illinois, or Kansas banks appear to be closely linked. The system of correspondent balances seems to have promoted a highly interrelated or interdependent banking structure both within a region and across regions.

[58] Ibid. [59] Ibid., p. 193.
[60] *Hearings on H.R. 7837*, p. 1514.

EVALUATIONS OF THE CORRESPONDENT BANKING SYSTEM

The postbellum banking system was widely criticized because of its unit banking structure and prohibition of branch banking, which impeded coordination or cooperation among banks; on the other hand, the link that did exist among banks in the form of the correspondent banking system was also continuously and severely criticized over the period.

One evil that it was said to have promoted was the maintenance of fictitious reserves, so that actual available reserves were much less than legally required reserves; because float was customarily included, a check in the process of collection might serve double, or even triple, duty as a legal reserve. The size of this float was estimated at between $300 million and $500 million.[61] Country banks usually counted their gross deposits with their correspondents in computing their reserve balance, but only their net deposits, subtracting off items in the process of collection, in calculating the reserve required,[62] thus overstating their actual reserves.

The most frequent criticisms, however, of the correspondent system were the assertions of the drain of funds from West to East and, the other side of the coin, the concentration of balances in New York. The culprit behind this movement of funds was oftentimes identified as the payment of interest on bankers' balances, which, for example, was periodically condemned by the Comptroller of the Currency in such years as 1873,[63] 1890,[64] and 1900[65] and was frequently excoriated in articles appearing in *Bankers' Magazine.*[66] A

[61] Ray Westerfield, *Banking Principles and Practice* (New York: Ronald Press Co., 1924), p. 330.

[62] Ibid.

[63] U.S. Comptroller of the Currency, *Annual Report*, 1873, p. xxxi.

[64] U.S. Comptroller of the Currency, *Annual Report*, 1890, pp. 11–12.

[65] U.S. Comptroller of the Currency, *Annual Report*, 1900, p. xxv.

[66] See, for example, "Interest on Country Deposits," *Bankers' Magazine*, XXXIX (December 1884), pp. 414–415.

more outspoken witness appearing before an 1874 Congressional committee heaped abuse upon "the system of paying interest on deposits by the national banks which draws nearly all the surplus money of the country banks of the United States to New York City and it is there used for the purposes of speculation and extortion. . . ."[67]

O. M. W. Sprague, professor at Harvard University and student of banking crises, was one of the most important of many writers who emphasized the undesirable consequences of the concentration of funds in New York through the payment of interest on bankers' balances.[68] One disadvantage of this practice to Sprague was that the interest-paying banks were unable to maintain large reserves and at the same time realize a profit on the use of the funds they attracted.[69] Con-

[67] U.S. House Committee on Banking and Currency, *Views Expressed before the Committee*, 1874, 43rd Congress, 2nd Session, 1874, p. 124.

[68] Margaret Myers, on the other hand, argues that the payment of interest alone did not draw balances to New York. In 1873 and again in 1886 it was noted that only about half of New York banks explicitly paid interest on correspondent deposits. However, the remaining banks performed services for correspondents in lieu of interest payments, and by 1891 most of the banks had begun the explicit payment of interest. Moreover, she holds that if the payment of interest had been the chief reason for the flow of deposits to New York, periods of low rates should be marked by low balances, but in fact the reverse is true. Of course, one should not look at the rate on bankers' balances alone, but rather one should consider the opportunity cost of funds. The flow of funds into bankers' balances should be a function of the differential between the local loan rate and the rate on bankers' balances, not just of the rate on bankers' balances alone. Indeed, the Comptroller of the Currency noted that the "marked slackening of demand for money in the interior of the country" in the summer of 1899 led to a large flow of funds to be invested in bankers' balances in Eastern cities. Myers, *The New York Money Market*, p. 249, 250; U.S. Comptroller of the Currency, *Annual Report*, 1900, p. xxv.

[69] O. M. W. Sprague, *History of Crises under the National Banking System* (Washington, D.C.: U.S. Government Printing Office, 1910), p. 21.

Table 17

Distribution of Correspondent Banks as Reported
by Banks in Selected States, 1925

State	Total No. of Banks	Within the State		Outside the State	
		Cities in Which Correspondents Are Reported	No. of Banks Reporting	Cities in Which Correspondents Are Reported	No. of Banks Reporting
Georgia	665	Atlanta	435	New York	600
		Savannah	205	Philadelphia	26
		Macon	155	Baltimore	22
		Augusta	50	Chattanooga	22
		Athens	16	Chicago	20
		Valdosta	14	Boston	14
		Americus	7	Richmond	7
		Dublin	7	Cincinnati	2
		Albany	5		
		Tipton	5		
Illinois	1,896	Chicago	1,705	New York	832
		Peoria	126	St. Louis	534
		Quincy	61	Indianapolis	43
		Joliet	56	Boston	27
		Decatur	48	Philadelphia	21
		Bloomington	43	Evanston, Ill.	20

Table 17 *Continued*

	City	Number	City	Number
	Springfield	31	Milwaukee	16
	Galesburg	20	Clinton, Ia.	14
	Freeport	17	Cedar Rapids, Ia.	8
	Kankakee	17	Cleveland	5
	Mt. Vernon	16	San Francisco	5
	Rockford	16	Cincinnati	4
	Champaign	15	Pittsburgh	4
	Danville	13	Dubuque, Ia.	2
	Rock Island	12	Los Angeles	2
	Monmouth	11	New Orleans	2
	Monticello	10	Terre Haute	2
	Cairo	9	Vincennes, In.	2
	Aurora	8		
	Jacksonville	8		
	Mattoon	8		
	Elgin	7		
	Ottawa	7		
	Alton	6		
	Centralia	5		
Kansas 1,293	Kansas City	1,222	New York	699
	Wichita	137	Chicago	155
	Topeka	56	St. Joseph	118
	Hutchinson	52	Independence, Mo.	22
	Atchison	36	Omaha	9
	Leavenworth	31	Boston	6
	Salina	27	Pueblo	4

Table 17 Continued

		Within the State		Outside the State	
State	Total No. of Banks	Cities in Which Correspondents Are Reported	No. of Banks Reporting	Cities in Which Correspondents Are Reported	No. of Banks Reporting
		Emporia	14	Denver	3
		Ottawa	10	Philadelphia	3
		Great Bend	9		
		Clay Centre	7		
		Lawrence	7		
		Concordia	6		
		Winfield	6		
		Paola	5		
Massachusetts	429	Boston	392	New York	207
		Worcester	14	Philadelphia	87
		Springfield	8	Albany	46
				Chicago	34
				Buffalo	2
				St. Louis	2
				San Francisco	2
Ohio	1,101	Cleveland	509	New York	934
		Cincinnati	320	Chicago	163
		Columbus	158	Pittsburgh	152
		Toledo	111	Philadelphia	44
		Akron	8	Boston	18

Table 17 *Continued*

		Dayton	7	St. Louis	6
		Fostoria	6	Wheeling	6
		Tiffin	6	Ft. Wayne, In.	4
		Lima	5	Baltimore	3
Pennsylvania	1,602	Philadelphia	1,095	New York	1,356
		Pittsburgh	622	Chicago	82
		Scranton	28	Baltimore	51
		Lancaster	10	Boston	32
		Reading	9	St. Louis	17
		Harrisburg	7	Cleveland	14
				San Francisco	5
				Buffalo	3
				Washington	3
				Syracuse	2
				Wilmington	2
California	644	San Francisco	485	New York	515
		Los Angeles	261	Chicago	217
		Sacramento	38	Boston	20
		Oakland	12	Philadelphia	17
		San Diego	7	Kansas City	4
		Eureka	5	St. Louis	4
				Omaha	3
				Denver	2
				Seattle	2

Source: Leonard L. Watkins, *Bankers' Balances* (Chicago: A. W. Shaw Co., 1929), pp. 408–411.

sequently, the New York banks felt compelled to loan out as much of the bankers' balances that they received as they could and kept only about the minimum required reserve; almost all of New York bankers' balances were loaned on the call loan market.[70]

Call loans, payable on demand, were the most liquid asset in which the bank could invest. Under ordinary circumstances the New York bank could easily meet its country correspondent's demand for funds by demanding payment of call loans outstanding. New York banks, where most correspondent balances were concentrated, were in a much more liquid position than banks in other reserve cities, where the call loan market was not so well developed. Even Chicago lacked a highly developed call loan market, and a relatively high percentage of bankers' balances on deposit there was devoted to ordinary commercial uses instead of being invested in demand loans.[71] Such an arrangement between city and country banks was clearly of mutual advantage. Country

[70] Similar arguments about the risky uses to which funds had to be put to turn a profit and the uncertainty of withdrawals of deposits attracted by the payment of interest were also offered frequently against the payment of interest on regular demand deposits. That practice also had its origins in the antebellum period, having been adopted by Chicago banks, for example, to attract new depositors in the 1840s and 1850s. Again, competition for deposits led to the continuance of the practice in the face of repeated disparagement. The ex-superintendent of the New York State Banking Department warned in 1905, "The payment of interest on commercial deposits by discount banks is the greatest menace in banking today. I do not believe that there is a conservative banker in the country today who does not in his heart depreciate the practice of paying interest on these deposits, and who would not do away with it if he could see his way clear to do so without largely reducing his volume of business." Dailey, "The Development of Banking," p. 184; U.S. Comptroller of the Currency, *Annual Report*, 1890, pp. 11–12; Albert H. Cox, Jr., "Regulation of Interest Rates on Bank Deposits," *Michigan Business Studies*, XVII, no. 4 (1966); Frederick D. Kilburn, "Payment of Interest by Discount Banks upon Commercial Deposits," in Hull, *Practical Problems*, p. 78.

[71] Watkins, *Bankers' Balances*, p. 354.

banks acquired a very liquid secondary reserve asset that earned a return; city banks could profitably reinvest the bankers' balances in the call market, although, of course, at any given time the profit realized depended on the prevailing call rate. In 1913 the president of the Continental and Commercial Bank of Chicago estimated the average net profit on bankers' balances to be 0.5 percent,[72] although such a figure seems to be on the low side.

In the case of a period of financial stringency or panic, country banks usually wished to recall some or all of their correspondent deposits. New York banks, carrying few excess reserves, would ordinarily call in call loans to meet the country banks' demands. However, although security loans are callable by a single bank, they are not callable by all banks at the same time without producing a fall in stock values so severe as to cause widespread bankruptcy. Consequently, a decline in bankers' balances produced a decline in reserves, and a suspension of payments of New York banks was often the result. Put more elegantly, "The payment of interest exercised an attraction for loose funds from interior banks and forced New York banks to sail farther from shore to show a profit. It was under these circumstances that sudden squalls brought about stringency and even panics."[73] This criticism, however, somewhat missed the point. Profit-maximizing banks should, for a given degree of risk, maximize the returns on their asset portfolio. It makes no difference what the source of the funds was as long as the probability of withdrawal was about the same; in a general panic there seems to be no reason to believe that withdrawal demands of banks should differ from those of the public at large. Moreover, even if banks had not paid interest on bankers' balances, there is no reason that they should not have loaned funds on the call market if call loans were an attractive asset.

In any case, Sprague argued that the concentration of

[72] *Hearings on H.R. 7837*, p. 242.
[73] Watkins, *Bankers' Balances*, p. 7.

119

funds in New York under the national banking system made New York the focal point for financial pressures during panics. In each of the banking crises under the national banking system—in 1873, 1884, 1890, 1893, and 1907—the withdrawal of deposits by country banks played a role. In the 1873 Panic, bankers' balances in New York banks declined by 39 percent between September 13 and October 15 and was almost equivalent to the decline in reserves.[74] As a result, New York banks were forced to adopt a partial suspension of payments, and when country banks were no longer able to withdraw their correspondent balances, many of them were forced to suspend also. Thus, the correspondent banking system appeared to act to some degree as the transmission mechanism of the panic to the rest of the country.

The Panics of 1884, of 1890, and of 1893 were all marked by withdrawals of funds from New York by country banks, thereby increasing the pressures on New York banks. In the Panic of 1907, the last serious one under the national banking system, over $100 million on net was shipped from New York to the interior between late October and early December.[75] Once again in 1907 suspension in New York led to suspension by banks in the interior. Sprague did not see this succession of panics during the late nineteenth and early twentieth century as the result of greed or mismanagement, but rather as the natural outcome of the pyramiding of reserves under the national banking system. Country banks only tried to strengthen their reserves in a time of stringency, but this concentrated pressures on New York banks through the loss of reserves.[76]

Contemporary writers, such as Sprague, were quite criti-

[74] According to Myers, such a fall in reserves often represented actual shipment of funds to the interior, whereas a fall in individual deposits often represented loan repayments and hence no loss in reserves. However, this distinction seems somewhat artificial. Myers *The New York Money Market*, p. 409.

[75] Sprague, *History of Crises*, p. 285.

[76] Ibid., pp. 306–307.

cal of the structure of the correspondent banking system. The pyramiding of reserves that it promoted was alleged to make it susceptible to panics. This view, however, confuses the issues of the elasticity of supply of funds and the role of the correspondent banking system. One of the frequent criticisms of the national banking system was the inelasticity of the currency. The unresponsiveness of note issue was largely an irrelevant issue, because currency was becoming a smaller and smaller percentage of the money supply. However, the fact that there was no way to expand the money stock in times of panics to meet the increased demands was important. The supply of reserves could not be increased in times of financial stringency. If the demand for reserves increased during panics, there was no lender of last resort to increase the supply. This was the basic problem of the national banking system, not the drain of reserves to country correspondents, which was only a transfer within the banking system.

Banks, both state and national, were prohibited from interstate operations, and the correspondent banking system represented a response to this constraint. When a bank faced the problem of dealing interregionally within the United States, there were in effect three possibilities.

First, it could do so within the bank, but that was illegal because interstate branch banking was prohibited. One alternative institutional arrangement that allowed close, essentially internalized, coordination among unit banks that developed in the postbellum period was the organization of groups of "chains" of banks owned by the same persons. The system of chain banking began in the 1880s, but did not experience substantial growth until around the turn of the century. By 1902 A. B. Hepburn, former Comptroller of the Currency, noted the growth of chain banking and also of bank holding companies.[77] W. S. Witham of Atlanta, for example, by that date had started twenty-six banks, of each of which he was president.[78] Chain banking was most prevalent

[77] Redlich, *Molding*, p. 201.
[78] Forgan, "Branch Banking," p. 261.

121

in the Midwest,[79] but the practice had expanded such that an investigation of the relationship between the National City Company, a bank stock holding company, and its parent company, National City Bank, in 1911 revealed that 300 other banks had similar arrangements.[80] Nevertheless, in relation to the banking system as a whole, the extent and influence of chain banking systems were quite limited in the postbellum period. Such formalized ties were by far the exception rather than the rule.

Second, faced with the problem of dealing interregionally, the bank could do so within a market, which is reflected in the development of the commercial paper market, to be discussed in some detail in Chapter V. Finally, the bank could do so through relationships with other banks. This third method is the correspondent banking system, which may be viewed as an institutional development to circumvent the prohibition of interstate banking. Correspondent banking thus served as a substitute for branch banking. Fritz Redlich noted disparagingly of the postbellum banking system that "what little coherence existed among them [unit banks] was brought about by clearing houses, correspondent relationships. . . ."[81] In fact, substantial coherence resulted from the links of the correspondent banking system. It was a very effective means of mobilizing funds, of linking banks interregionally, and for providing channels for flows of funds between regions. "The network of bank connections spreads all over the country, weaving the banks together into a harmonious system, unorganized by law, but held together by the binding force of service."[82]

The correspondent banking system, then, was a means of internalizing some interregional operations. This is evidenced in the reciprocal arrangements for collections between city and country banks. Country banks derived benefits from

[79] Redlich, *Molding*, p. 201; Cooke, "Branch Banking," pp. 107–108.
[80] Laughlin, *Banking Reform*, pp. 204–205.
[81] Redlich, *Molding*, p. 175.
[82] Kniffin, *American Banking Practice*, p. 4.

large-scale operations in the services of a credit department, as well as in the opportunity to participate directly, through their correspondents, in the New York money markets, such as the call loan market, the bond market, and the commercial paper market. On the other hand, the interregional ties of the country banks were also valuable to city banks. Westerfield points out that through their country correspondents city banks "established national connections and got into contact with innumerable areas, customers, and lines of business . . . in every part of the United States."[83] Contrary to assertions that the correspondent system developed as a result of the "weakness of the smaller banks and their necessary recourse to others in times of special strain,"[84] the system was one of mutual advantage, allowing both city and country banks to extend their operations interregionally.

The development of correspondent banking, then, represented a nonmarket response to the prohibition of interstate or interregional banking. It was in effect an institutional development to facilitate the flow of funds between regions. As we have seen in the distribution of bank correspondents in Table 17, the correspondent banking system was a far-reaching and complex structure, linking both areas within a region and different regions together through the mechanism of bankers' balances. The system of bankers' balances and the structure of the correspondent banking system were potentially quite efficient means of mobilizing funds and concentrating them in a national funds market, the New York money market. However, from examining the structure alone, we cannot determine how successful the system actually was in mobilizing funds. The performance of the market in terms of interest rate movements must be considered in addition to market structure in order to assess its efficiency, which will be done in Chapter VI.

Richard Sylla has argued that the national banking system was a very effective structure for transferring funds from agriculture into industrial and commercial activities and

---

[83] Westerfield, *Banking Principles*, pp. 325–326.
[84] Laughlin, *Banking Reform*, p. 208.

from West to East.[85] Just because bankers' balances were accumulated in New York, however, does not necessarily mean that the funds remained there. Rather, New York may well have functioned as a national financial intermediary. Some of the funds concentrated in the, in effect, national money market in New York may have been sent back to the West in the short-term market through direct commercial loans or the purchase of commercial paper issued by Western firms. More important, however, was the function of the call loan market. Call loans represented a way of transferring funds from the short-term market, bankers' balances, into the long-term one to finance capital expenditures through the purchase of equity. Securities purchased on the basis of call loans could have been issued or sold by any firm or anyone, anywhere. There is no reason to believe that these funds would have remained in New York, especially in view of the rapid expansion of manufacturing in the Midwest. The correspondent banking system, then, was an efficient means of concentrating funds in a national market and of transferring capital from the short-term to the long-term market to facilitate industrial financing; it does not follow, however, that it necessarily resulted in a net flow of funds from West to East.

Instead of a fragmented, segmented capital market in the United States, with substantial interregional barriers to the flow of funds, the correspondent banking system was a quite sophisticated structure promoting interregional flows. Banks quite far apart had a very rapid means of communication available, the telegraph. As early as the Panic of 1857, the news of financial distress was carried "with the speed of lightning to every part of the land"[86] by telegraph, resulting

[85] Richard Sylla, "The United States, 1863–1913," in Rondo Cameron, ed., *Banking and Economic Development* (New York: Oxford University Press, 1972), p. 254.

[86] J. S. Gibbons, *The Banks of New York, Their Dealers, the Clearing House, and the Panic of 1857* (New York: D. Appleton and Co., 1858), p. 357.

in a withdrawal of bankers' balances by country banks. Similarly, in 1873 New York banks received urgent demands for funds by telegraph from correspondents in all parts of the country.[87] Banks in different sections of the country, rather than being isolated, were closely linked together in an interdependent system. There is no reason to believe that regions were isolated from each other and that funds did not flow among them.

FINANCIAL FLOWS

In the previous sections the mechanism that allowed interregional flows of funds was described; here the magnitude and direction of interregional capital flows under the national banking system will be estimated. The direction of seasonal flows will be considered first, and then the more general questions of the size and direction of short and long-term capital flows will be taken up.

The contemporary view of seasonal transfers of specie was well known and widely accepted. The cause of the seasonal transfers was variations in agricultural demand for funds. In periods of slack agricultural activity, such as the winter and summer, demand for credit from country banks was low. A Nebraska banker observed that in the western part of the state where cattle were important, there was a "plethora of money in banks in late fall and early winter";[88] similarly, in North Dakota the slack period of demand ran from October to May.[89] "Idle" funds also accumulated in the summer, between planting and harvest times. The country banks, therefore, were faced with finding employment for "surplus" funds during these slack seasons.

One solution was investment in commercial paper, the

[87] Sprague, *History of Crises*, pp. 43–44.

[88] E. Royse, "The Critical Season in Banking in Nebraska," *Proceedings of the Nebraska Bankers' Association*, 1903, p. 364.

[89] E. M. Stevens, "Commercial Paper," *Proceedings of the North Dakota Bankers' Association*, 1903, p. 31.

market for which was expanding rapidly during the late nineteenth century. Paper could be purchased with particular maturity dates, so that funds would be freed before local loan demand increased again. This will be discussed in greater detail in Chapter V. However, the most frequent and most important form of employment for these "surplus funds" was as bankers' balances in correspondent banks. They offered country banks a very liquid asset, which also yielded a return. Thus, in periods of slack demand in the countryside, winter and summer, country banks sent surplus funds in the form of bankers' balances to city banks, especially to New York, to earn interest when they could not be profitably employed locally. On the other hand, in periods of high agricultural demand for credit, such as spring, the planting season, and fall, the harvesting and crop-moving season, the funds on deposit in city banks were withdrawn by the country banks to meet the increased local demand for loans.

Consequently, city banks, especially those in New York where deposits of bankers' balances were concentrated, experienced pronounced seasonal flows of funds to and from the countryside. In periods of slack demand in the interior, such as winter and summer, funds flowed into New York from the countryside; in periods of strong agricultural demand for credit such as the spring and especially the fall, funds flowed out of New York to meet credit demands in the interior. Thus, the direction of the flow of short-term funds was from West to East during the winter and summer and from East to West in the fall and spring through the channel of bankers' balances.

In the fall when country banks withdrew funds from the city to finance crop-moving activities, the effects were especially severe. Many financial observers, the most noted of whom was O. M. W. Sprague, identified the fall decrease in correspondent deposits in New York banks as resulting in an actual flow of currency from East to West.[90] Consequent-

[90] See, for example, O. M. W. Sprague, *History of Crises*, p. 33.

ly, New York banks, as a whole, lost reserves in the fall and were forced to contract. Because bankers' balances were usually loaned out on the call loan market, the withdrawal of funds from New York led to very high call rates there every fall. As a rule, then, the New York money market experienced a period of financial stringency and rising interest rates in the fall as a result of the withdrawal of correspondent deposits by country banks.

This autumn period of tightness was regarded as one of the most serious consequences of the structure of the correspondent banking system and thus the national banking system. The concentration of bankers' balances in New York led to the concentration of financial pressures in the fall there also. During those months the strain put on the banking system made it extremely vulnerable to any additional demands. Thus, Sprague observed, "With few exceptions all our crises, panics, and periods of more severe monetary stringency have occurred in the autumn, when the western banks, through the sale of cereal crops, were in a position to withdraw large sums of money from the East."[91]

C. A. E. Goodhart in his book, *The New York Money Market and the Finance of Trade, 1900–1913*, takes exception to this widely held picture. Goodhart argues that the central flaw in the accepted analysis is that it explained cash movements between regions entirely in terms of capital movements and ignored the balance of trade between New York and the interior. In the fall, during the harvest season, New York ran a large balance-of-trade deficit with the interior, so the interior banks should have been more liquid than the country banks.[92]

These variations in liquidity positions between New York and the interior banks should have been reflected in interest rates. If the countryside ran a balance-of-trade surplus in

[91] Ibid., p. 127.
[92] C. A. E. Goodhart, *The New York Money Market and the Finance of Trade, 1900–1913* (Cambridge, Mass.: Harvard University Press, 1969), p. 79.

the fall against the East (or New York), so that there was a cash flow into the interior, there should have been a rise not only in the demand for funds in the interior, but also in the supply. As a result, the liquidity position of the country banks should have remained roughly constant, and so should have interest rates. On the other hand, when New York was running a balance-of-trade surplus against the interior, liquidity was accumulating in New York banks relative to country banks. It follows, therefore, that New York rates in the summer should have been low relative to those in the interior.[93]

These interest-rate differentials between New York and the interior in turn should induce a capital flow. In the fall there should be a short-term capital inflow from the interior into New York to take advantage of the higher interest rates. In the summer, because interest rates in New York are low relative to those in the countryside, there should be a capital outflow from New York. Thus, in Goodhart's hypothesis seasonal fluctuations in the balance of trade cause New York interest rates to rise, both absolutely and relative to those in the countryside, in the autumn and to decline in the summer. This pattern of interest rate fluctuations induces a capital inflow into New York in the fall and an outflow from New York in the summer.[94]

Goodhart's hypothesis, then, implies interregional capital flows in exactly the opposite directions from those in the traditional explanation. In the fall if the countryside ran a strong balance-of-trade surplus with New York there had to be either a net cash flow from East to West or else an export of capital from West to East to balance the account. Goodhart emphasizes the latter effect by arguing that, in the autumn, funds were attracted to New York to take advantage of the call loan rates, which were high relative to interior interest rates; on the other hand, the traditional hypothesis emphasized the former effect, that there was a net cash flow

[93] Ibid., p. 95.　　　　　　　　[94] Ibid., p. 96.

from East to West primarily through reductions in bankers' balances in New York. Similarly, in the summer, if the interior ran a balance-of-trade deficit, there must have been a net cash flow into New York or export of capital from East to West; the traditional hypothesis focuses on the former, and Goodhart, on the latter.

The crucial deficiency in the traditional theory, according to Goodhart's hypothesis, therefore, is its explanation of cash movements entirely in terms of capital movements, ignoring the much stronger influences of the interregional balance of trade. To support the theory, Goodhart presents two types of evidence. He argues that interior interest rates were very stable relative to New York rates, so that New York rates were relatively high in the autumn and low in the summer, and in addition that the seasonal variation in bankers' balances held in New York was neither sufficiently large nor of the correct timing to support the traditional hypothesis.[95] First the Goodhart argument itself and then the evidence that is presented in support of it will be assessed.

In Goodhart's analysis, seasonal net flows between regions are confused with equilibrating forces. He does not prove that capital flows move in the opposite direction from the traditional or Sprague theory; he in effect only shows that there are compensating or equilibrating forces at work brought about by seasonal changes in the interregional balance of trade, and then they are confused with the total net flow. In the process that Goodhart describes, the interior runs a balance-of-trade surplus and drains reserves from New York; this in turn causes New York rates to rise relative to those in the interior and the fund flow is reversed. In this sequence, the traditional drain of funds from the East is admitted. A rise in the New York interest rate in the fall may have moderated the outflow, but one certainly could not conclude that the direction of the net flow was reversed. Moreover, after the harvest, funds did become relatively abundant in the countryside, due to some combination of an

95 Ibid., p. 126

increase in supply and decrease in demand, and they were in fact attracted back into New York, but that occurred in the winter, not in the fall.

Consider the chart of New York money market rates by month in Figure 6. If funds had flowed into New York in the fall from the interior, attracted by high rates in the call market, there should have been a gradual decline in the call rate over the autumn or at least a retardation in its rise. In Figure 6 there is no evidence of either of these effects. The seasonal peak was usually reached in November, late in the fall, and there seems to be no trace of a retardation in the rate of increase over the fall.

Similarly, Goodhart argues that short-term capital was flowing out of New York in the summer. If this had been the case, there should have been gradually rising interest rates over the summer. However, in Figure 6 that is not observed; instead rates remain quite low over the summer and show no general upward trend.

First of all, then, the hypothesis is not convincing in its attempt to argue that there would be seasonal capital inflows into New York in the fall. Now let us turn to the evidence that Goodhart presents in support of the theory. For interest rates he relies on rates reported in *Dun's Review* during the period. Much of the argument rests on the astounding stability of those interest rates in interior cities. For example, the interest rate in Kansas City remained virtually stable during the 1906–1910 time period,[96] apparently insensitive to any influences including variations in seasonal demands. In general, the volatility of local money markets seemed to decrease as their distance from New York increased. The New York market was the most volatile, the call loan market in particular. Local markets, ranked in decreasing order of volatility, were New York, Boston, Philadelphia, Chicago, Montreal, St. Louis, Detroit, and Kansas City.[97] Thus, the money markets in interior cities were quite stable, while the

[96] Ibid., p. 91.   [97] Ibid., pp. 87–88.

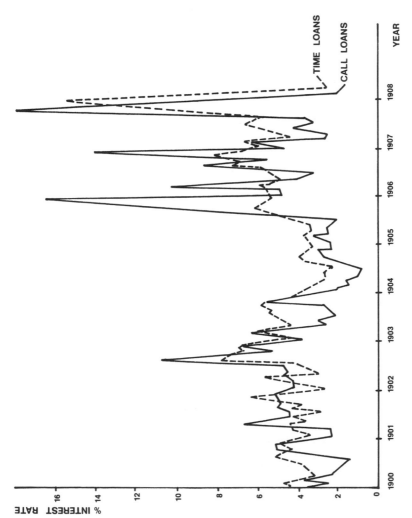

Figure 6. New York Call Loan and Time Loan Rates, 1900–1908.

market in New York was quite unstable. In the fall, then, New York rates rose over the stable interior rates, eliciting a capital inflow into New York; in the summer, New York rates fell below the imperturbable interior rates, causing a capital outflow from New York. Thus, the stability of interior interest rates is a crucial part of Goodhart's argument.[98]

The rather questionable reliability of these interest rates is discussed in Appendix A. First of all, it is not clear what they represent. Moreover, the manner in which they were collected is not known; indeed, it is not known whether they were collected systematically at all. Because the figures were collected by correspondents, some of them may have reported the same number week after week to save effort. Besides, if we are interested in interest rate differentials between the countryside and New York due to seasonal shifts in the agricultural demand for credit, we should be looking at rate fluctuations of country banks, which were the ones supposedly withdrawing funds in the fall to meet home demand. The proportion of bankers' balances to total deposits was actually higher in Chicago, St. Louis, and Kansas City banks than in New York ones, and the ratio in a number of other reserve cities was only slightly lower. Banks in those cities should have been subject to the same withdrawal demands from country banks as New York banks were. The stability of such reported rates in the face of this makes them seem quite implausible.

Thin markets have been traditionally thought to be more volatile and unstable, producing a wider range of variation

[98] The interest rates calculated in Appendix A show very distinct patterns of seasonality in contrast with Goodhart's figures. The range of seasonal variation in Eastern cities of average loan rates is quite small, whereas in the Plains states interest rates vary about 1 percentage point and several Southern states show a range of seasonal variation of around 2 percentage points. Moreover, these seasonal components are underestimates, because the computed rates are semi-annual averages. Not only the period of high fall rates, but also the low winter rates are included in the averaged figure. So the actual seasonal variation should be substantially higher than our estimates.

in observed rates than more developed markets with larger numbers of buyers and sellers. However, Goodhart's data show just the opposite. How does he explain this anomaly? The first explanation that is considered is that thinner markets are less anonymous and rely more on direct dealings between lender and borrower. Thus, banks may wish to keep rates high, even in slack periods, by loaning excess funds in Eastern markets; and on the other hand, when squeezed for liquidity, they may refuse loans rather than raise rates.[99] So, to maintain good customer relations local loan rates are held below the free-market rate in times of stringency; in similar fashion, to reap high profits, local rates are set above free-market rates in periods of slackness. One necessary condition for such a policy is an oligopolistic local market structure among interior banks. In the cities the rate stability of which Goodhart is trying to explain, such as Chicago, St. Louis, or Kansas City, there were a relatively large number of banks, and the market was probably much closer to a competitive one than to an oligopolistic one. In Chicago, for example, in 1890 thirty-five state and national banks alone were operating, not counting private banks.[100] Goodhart himself rejects this first explanation.

Instead, Goodhart offers the explanations discussed earlier, that interior money markets were more stable because there was less variation in the liquidity positions of interior banks. Thus, in the fall when the balance of trade favors the interior, there is a rise in both the demand for and the supply of funds in the countryside, while New York banks are drained of reserves, resulting in a rise in New York interest rates relative to those in the interior. It has been argued, however, that this process requires a capital outflow from the East, the opposite direction of that which Goodhart is arguing. His hypothesis claims only that in turn there will be an equilibrating flow back into New York, a statement with which the traditional explanation is in accord—however, it

[99] Goodhart, *The New York Money Market*, pp. 92–93.
[100] Dailey, "The Development of Banking," pp. 309, 413.

comes during the winter months rather than the fall. Thus, the data used to support the assertion of the stability of interior rates are questionable in themselves, and the explanation offered to account for their anomalous nature is unsatisfactory.

The other body of evidence employed to support the Goodhart hypothesis is a set of estimates of seasonal flows of bankers' balances on deposit in New York during the period 1900–1913.[101] In brief, Goodhart argues that seasonal fluctuations in bankers' balances were relatively small in relation to the total and that most of the fall decrease in bankers' balances did not leave New York, but rather was channeled into the call loan market to take advantage of the high rates, especially after 1908.[102] Consequently, there was real-

[101] Reestimates of the seasonal fluctuations in bankers' balances, obtained by regressing first differences of levels of New York bankers' balances on five dummies, representing the five call dates, over the same time period, turned out to be significantly different from Goodhart's calculations. The magnitude of the seasonal variation was larger than that in the Goodhart figures, and also they were in the directions predicted by the traditional theory for both national and non-national banks. Moreover, the same pattern holds for bankers' balances in Chicago and St. Louis, where call markets were much less developed, so a fall decrease in bankers' balances most certainly represents a drain of reserves. See John A. James, "The Evolution of the National Money Market, 1888–1911" (unpublished Ph.D. dissertation, MIT, 1974), pp. 221–231.

[102] Goodhart distinguishes between bankers' balances of national and non-national banks, arguing that state bank and trust companies, because of lower reserve requirements, most likely held balances in relatively nearby banks as secondary reserves. Thus, state banks and trust companies holding New York balances were likely to be New York banks themselves. To examine the influence on interregional flows, then, he had only to look at seasonal fluctuations in bankers' balances of national banks, which he found to be very small. Consequently, variations in New York bankers' balances were said to have had little influence on interregional cash flows.

The correspondent banking system has been shown to have been an extensive and well-integrated network of interrelationships among banks, which antedated the national banking system. Banks maintained correspondents because they performed useful services for

ly no fall drain of reserves to the interior from New York after all.

The argument appears convincing, but its generality is limited because the period chosen, 1900–1913, does not seem to be representative of the postbellum period. Looking ahead for a moment to Figure 8, we see not only that between 1907 and 1913 New York did experience continual cash inflows with the exception of minor outflows in the autumns of 1908 and 1909, but also that this sustained cash inflow was atypical; this direction of net flows does not appear to follow the pattern of earlier years at all. The inference, then, that country balances in New York actually increased in the fall is drawn from a set of years in which New York was running a sustained balance-of-payments surplus with the interior, a period that does not appear to be typical of earlier years, and as a result the net flow of funds during that period should not be inferred to represent usual patterns of financial flows under the national banking system.

Additional evidence of the unrepresentativeness of the 1900–1913 period chosen by Goodhart may be found in the observations of Thornton Cooke, who in a 1903 article contrasted the present financial situation in the Midwest with what it had been only a few years earlier. By 1903, "Western banks have not only handled the crops without borrowing in the East—an unprecedented feat,—but they are now lending

---

them, and there is no reason to believe that these services were not also useful to state banks. The large number of correspondent accounts held in New York, as shown in Table 16, cannot be accounted for by national banks and New York state banks alone. In addition, as noted in Chapter II, states permitted correspondent deposits to be counted as some specified percentage of required reserve, which created the same incentives to hold bankers' balances, or even stronger ones, that the National Banking Act did. So, contrary to Goodhart, variations in non-national banks' holdings of bankers' balances cannot be ruled out for not representing interregional flows. Goodhart, *The New York Money Market*, pp. 97–99; Barnett, *State Banks and Trust Companies*, pp. 120–121.

to the East on the New York Stock Exchange."[103] Clearly, the implication is that the new circumstance was exceptional; in the past crop moving must have required transfers of funds from the East.

Even if bankers' balances had not flowed out of New York in the fall, as Sprague asserts, it does not mean that reserves necessarily flowed into New York in the autumn. The crucial factor is the interregional balance of trade. If New York runs a strong balance-of-trade deficit against the interior in the fall, New York must either import capital, as Goodhart argues, or be drained of specie. Looking ahead, in Table 19 we see that cash did actually flow out of New York in the fall, even if not entirely through the channel of bankers' balances.[104]

The Goodhart hypothesis regarding the direction of seasonal interregional capital flows, therefore, is suspect at several points. First of all, the net direction of flows is confused with compensating or equilibrating flows. Moreover, the evidence on which the theory is based, the constancy of interior interest rates and the shifting of bankers' balances into the call market, is also questionable, the interest rates because they appear to be unreliable and the bankers' balances figures because they seemed to be based on unrepresentative years. Sprague may well have overemphasized the role of withdrawals of bankers' balances and neglected the changes in

[103] Cooke, "Branch Banking," p. 97.

[104] One indicator of the direction of interregional flows of funds should be the domestic exchange rates. If funds were moving on net from New York to the interior in the fall, New York exchange should have been at a discount in the interior. The results for the latter part of Goodhart's period, however, are ambiguous. Weekly quotations for New York exchange in major cities appeared in *Bradstreet's*. Over the last years of the decade of the 1900s, New York exchange sold at a discount in the fall, as we would expect, in cities such as Chicago, St. Louis, St. Paul, and Fort Worth but, on the other hand, New York exchange remained at a premium in Kansas City and Omaha. We have seen, however, that this time was one of sustained cash inflows into New York, so perhaps it is not the period for such a test of exchange rates.

the interregional balance of trade in accounting for the annual fall drain of funds from New York, but there is no reason to believe that the flow direction was in fact reversed, so that there was a fall inflow into New York, as Goodhart concludes.

Now the magnitude and direction of net interregional flows will be examined. How large were long-term capital flows, and did they indeed move from low-interest-rate areas to high-interest-rate areas? Many contemporary sources noted and complained about the apparent net flow of short-term capital from West to East, from high-interest-rate areas, on the whole, to low-interest-rate areas. Did money in fact flow naturally from West to East "like water flows downhill"?[105] Sylla emphasizes the concentration of reserves in New York, implicitly assuming a flow of specie from West to East; Lance Davis, on the other hand, emphasizes the breaking down of the barriers to capital mobility and the transfer of short-term capital into high-interest-rate areas, that is, from East to West.

Unfortunately, these questions cannot be answered with precision, but some suggestive inferences may be drawn. Some information is available about net cash flows into and out of New York. The balance of trade is not directly observable, but if we make some assumptions about its direction, given net cash flows and some information about long-term capital flows, we may infer at least some bounds on the short-term capital flows.

There are two data sources for net cash flows from New York. E. J. Kemmerer, in a report for the National Monetary Commission, *Seasonal Variation in the Relative Demand for Money and Capital in the United States*, attempted to collect data on interregional cash flows for the period 1905–1908, but was not very successful. He sent out a questionnaire to all cities of population 50,000 or more in 1907, of which there were ninety-one with a total population of 20,984,-

[105] Testimony of John T. M. Johnston, *Hearings on H.R. 7837 (S2639)*, p. 113.

278.[106] Out of those he received usable reports from clearing houses in thirty-two cities. The original sample certainly seriously underestimated the banking facilities in each region and hence the size of the regional flows; the actual sample, even smaller, is of no use in judging interregional flows. We cannot examine net cash flows from the East, but data were collected from the New York Clearing House, so we can examine net flows into and out of New York. Banks that were not members of the Clearing House were not included, but they constituted only a small part of the total. The N.M.C. statistics also excluded flows between New York City banks and New York state country banks; but this too is not a significant disadvantage because we are interested primarily in net cash flows between New York and the West.

The *Commercial and Financial Chronicle*, on the other hand, reported weekly statistics for net cash flows into and out of New York. Unfortunately, the magnitudes of this series and the N.M.C. series differed substantially. Goodhart has pointed out that during the period 1896–1913 the *Chronicle's* series put the net cash inflow into New York at around $2355.4 million, a sum greater than total individual deposits of all New York banks on June 30, 1914.[107] This fact would seem to indicate that the N.M.C. series may be the more reliable. However, movements of the two series are actually quite similar; the principal difference between them lies in the levels.

The longer, unadulterated *Commercial and Financial Chronicle* series cannot be used to represent net cash movements, but because the series are highly correlated, a corrected one can be constructed. The N.M.C. series was regressed on quarterly values of the *CFC* series for 1905–1908 and an index of business activity, the residuals from a

---

[106] E. J. Kemmerer, *Seasonal Variations in the Relative Demand for Money and Capital in the United States* (Washington, D.C.: U.S. Government Printing Office, 1910), p. 53.

[107] Goodhart, *The New York Money Market*, p. 184.

regression of quarterly bank clearings outside New York City on a time trend.[108] The plots of the actual and fitted series are presented in Figure 7. The correspondence between the two series is quite close. The fitted values were then extrapolated to cover the period 1896–1913 and plotted in Figure 8. The sum of the net cash flows for the entire 1896–1913 period turns out to be a substantial inflow of +511.93 million. However, much of the total is accounted for by the strong, sustained, positive net cash flows in 1911–1913, which amounted to +362.73 million. The total net cash flow into New York for 1896–1910 was +4.64 million; for 1900–1910, +75.65 million. The trend is clear in Table 18, the net cash flow into New York becomes more and more positive over time.

Table 18

Net Cash Flows into and out of New York City
($ million)

Time Period	Net Cash Flow
1896–1899	−71.01
1900–1905	−22.07
1906–1910	+97.72
1911–1913	+507.29

From the computed series of net cash flows the seasonal components in cash flows into and out of New York may be estimated. Net cash flows from New York were regressed on

[108] Bank clearings outside of New York City were employed as a business cycle proxy because, on the whole, they represented transactions in goods and services, as opposed to New York bank clearings, which were tainted by a large number of transactions involving stocks and other financial assets. The residuals are used as a variable because the time trend in the growth of bank clearings had to be removed to get a cyclical index. Geoffrey Moore, ed., *Business Cycle Indicators,* Vol. II (Princeton, N.J.: Princeton University Press, 1961).

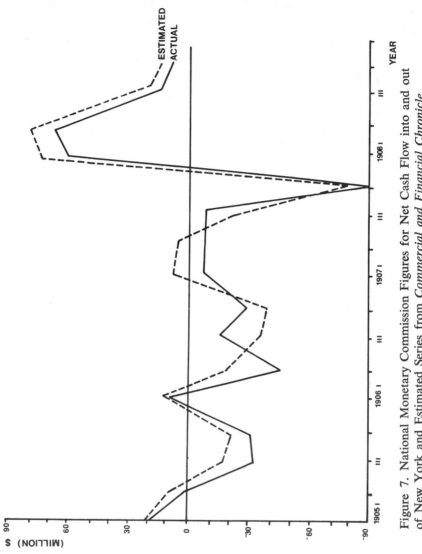

Figure 7. National Monetary Commission Figures for Net Cash Flow into and out of New York and Estimated Series from *Commercial and Financial Chronicle* Reports.

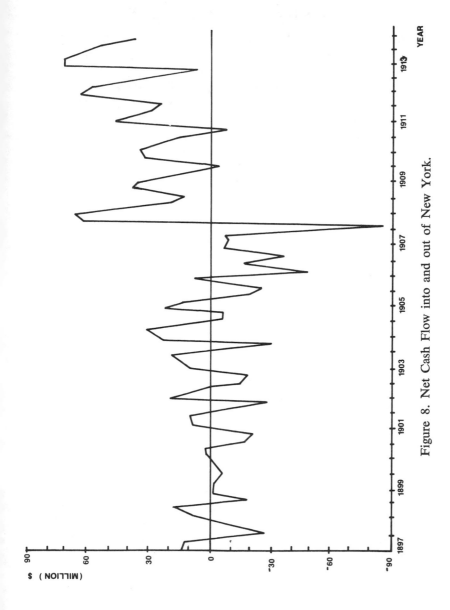

Figure 8. Net Cash Flow into and out of New York.

four seasonal dummies. The results are reported in Table 19. It is clear from these results that there was a definite and sizable net cash outflow from New York in the fall in the earlier period, contrary to Goodhart's assertion. A comparison of the 1905–1910 period with the 1896–1899 and 1900–1904 periods in Figure 8 as well as the many observations during the late nineteenth century in virtual unanimity about the fall drain of reserves from New York into the interior all

Table 19

Seasonal Variation in Net Cash Flows from New York
($ million)

Time Period	Winter	Spring	Summer	Fall
1896–1899	+4.15	+5.86	−17.94	−9.83
1900–1904	+11.19	+13.23	−7.65	−19.78
1905–1910	+24.83	+14.83	+.80	−25.78
1896–1913	+21.37	+19.19	+.38	−12.50

support the contention that the time period chosen by Goodhart was unrepresentative of the entire period. An Eastern balance-of-trade deficit was not compensated for by a short-term capital flow into New York as Goodhart suggested. Instead there was a cash flow out of New York in the fall, except for the 1905–1913 period. Furthermore, Goodhart himself found that flows from Canadian banks did not respond to changes in New York call rates as his theory forecasted.[109]

The pattern of cash flows derived here poses a number of questions. How are the increases in net cash inflows into New York during the period and especially the extraordinarily large ones for 1911–1913 to be explained? Are they part of a new trend or only an anomaly? The fall outflow of

[109] This failure was attributed to the oligopolistic structure of the Canadian banking system. Goodhart, *The New York Money Market*, pp. 139–156.

cash is certainly in evidence in Table 19; however, in the spring there are sizable cash inflows and in the summer moderate net cash outflows, neither of which are explained by the traditional hypothesis.

Contemporary evidence on the size of long-term interregional flows is extremely scarce. An 1879 *Bankers' Magazine* estimate of the amount of loans in the West made by New England runs to about $100 million,[110] with most Eastern capital at that time loaned in the West in the form of bonds or mortgages.[111] To get a more systematic picture of long-term capital flows, Easterlin's estimates of nonagricultural capital located in each region and the amount owned by the residents of each region for the dates 1880, 1900, and 1919–1921 are employed.[112] Between any two dates the change in capital located in the region represents the net amount of nonagricultural investment in the region; similarly, the change in the amount of capital owned represents the amount of savings over the period by residents of the area. The difference, then, between investment in the region and savings by its residents during the period equals the net capital flow into or out of the region,[113] a positive figure signifying net capital imports into the region, a negative number representing net capital exports. These estimates of capital flows give an impression of smaller total movements of capital than actually occurred to the extent that there were intraregional capital flows from cities to the countryside, and that interregional investment went into agriculture rather than industry. This effect, then, will undoubtedly bias downward the estimates of capital imports in agricultural regions,

[110] *Bankers' Magazine*, October 1879.

[111] Testimony of Mr. McArthur, *Investigation by a Select Committee of the House of Representatives Relative to the Causes of the General Depression in Labor and Business, etc.*, House Miscellaneous Documents No. 29, 45th Congress, 3rd Session, p. 170.

[112] Everett S. Lee et al., *Population Redistribution and Economic Growth*, Vol. I (Philadelphia: American Philosophical Society, 1957), pp. 728–737.

[113] Lee, *Population Redistribution*, Vol. III, p. 179.

such as the South and Midwest. Total net flows for two periods, calculated by interpolation, are presented in Table 20.[114]

Table 20

Estimates of Net Interregional Long-Term Capital Flows
($ millions)

Region	1900–1910	1897–1913
East	−9,509	−12,830
South	+3,536	+4,751
Midwest	+5,929	+7,595
West	−293	+492

+ represents imports; − represents exports.

Source: Computed from Richard A. Easterlin, "State Income Estimates," in Everett S. Lee et al., *Population Redistribution and Economic Growth*, Vol. I (Philadelphia: American Philosophical Society, 1957), pp. 728–737.

[114] Easterlin's estimates of regional wealth were in current prices, so the long-term capital flows in Table 20 are in current prices. However, if we wish to examine changes in the magnitude of these flows over time, we must convert them into real terms, especially in view of the inflation around World War I, which leads to a serious overestimate of the growth in the capital stock between 1900 and 1920. Consequently, Easterlin's estimates of the capital stock in 1880, 1900, and 1919–1921 were converted into real terms, in 1900 prices, and then long-term interregional flows were calculated in real terms. Total interregional net flows in dollars and also as a percentage of 1900 real total regional wealth for the period 1880–1920 are presented in Table 21. We may examine these flows in somewhat greater detail

Table 21

Real Interregional Long-Term Capital Flows, 1880–1920
(in $ million, 1900 prices)

Section	Total Net Flow	As Percent of 1900 Total Wealth
East	−8617	−20.89
South	+3571	+25.21
Midwest	+5213	+12.77
West	+222	+2.10

These figures appear to be plausible ones. As expected, the East was a capital exporter, and the magnitude of the outflow is such that it could have been generated by Eastern savers,[115] although most probably at least part of that total

---

by calculating net long-term flows for the six regions outlined by the Comptroller of the Currency. Also, we may compare the size of real flows during 1890–1900 with ones during 1900–1910. Table 22 presents long-term flows during 1890–1900.

Table 22

Real Interregional Long-Term Capital Flows
(in $ million, 1900 prices)

Region	1890–1900 (as percent of 1895)		1900–1910 (as percent of 1905)	
	Total Net Flow	Total Real Wealth	Total Net Flow	Total Real Wealth
I	−478	−5.74%	−520	−5.31%
II	−1954	−7.18	−1356	−4.11
III	+475	+3.88	+1310	+8.01
IV	+937	+3.11	+820	+2.20
V	+1011	+13.76	+37	+0.37
VI	+88	+1.53	−180	−2.13

We find in both periods that New England and the Middle Atlantic states were strong capital exporters. Also, Region IV, the Midwest, was a fairly steady capital importer in both periods. However, the South, Region III, which was a substantial capital importer in the 1890–1900 period, became a very strong importer after 1900, net imports almost doubling in 1900–1910. On the other hand, Region V, the Great Plains and Mountain states, was a strong importer before 1900, imports amounting to almost 15 percent of total regional wealth over the decade; but after 1900 they fall almost to zero. Strangely, the Pacific states switched from capital importer to capital exporter after the turn of the century.

[115] Department of Commerce estimates of average national income during the 1902–1906 period is $24.2 billion, and national saving averaged something over $3 billion. Assuming that the Eastern states generated about 50 percent of national saving, because they had about 50 percent of national income, then the East produced about $1.5 billion of savings per year and exported something less than two-thirds of it. U.S. Bureau of the Census, *Historical Statistics*

145

represents Western short-term capital inflows that were re-exported as long-term capital with New York acting as the financial intermediary. The South and Midwest, on the other hand, were long-term capital importers. It is somewhat surprising that the West was virtually in balance, but a state-by-state analysis of the Western region reveals that capital did flow from the low-interest-rate state, California, to the other high-interest-rate states within the region.[116] Thus, in the long-term capital market, capital did flow from capital-abundant regions, as indicated by lower interest rates, to capital-scarce regions, as indicated by higher interest rates.

For the nonce, let us assume that New York represents the East. New York, as we have seen, during the 1900–1910 decade had a net cash flow with the rest of the country that was virtually even. If long-term capital was flowing out at an average rate of about $1 billion per year, the balance of trade plus short-term capital movements must then sum up to about $9.5 billion (our estimate) for the decade. Goodhart asserted that the interregional balance of trade was about zero.[117] This could not be true if those funds remained in New York, because it would have meant an inflow of over $9 billion of short-term capital into New York during the decade, or almost $1 billion per year. In 1909 the total assets of all New York City banks, national and non-national, were only $4,345 million.[118] It is a feasible figure, however, if New York functioned as a financial intermediary.

If the net cash flow out of New York during 1900–1910 is approximately in balance, then the interregional overall bal-

---

(Washington, D.C.: U.S. Government Printing Office, 1961), pp. 139, 155; Richard Easterlin, "Regional Income Trends, 1840–1950," in Seymour Harris, ed., *American Economic History* (New York: McGraw-Hill Book Company, 1961), p. 535.

[116] Lance Davis, "The Investment Market, 1870–1914: The Evolution of a National Market," *Journal of Economic History*, XXV (September 1965), p. 388.

[117] Goodhart, *The New York Money Market*, p. 79.

[118] Ibid., p. 11.

ance of payments must be about zero over the period. Because there was a long-term capital outflow from the East of about $1 billion per year, to balance the accounts, unless the East ran a very large interregional trade surplus with the West of about $1 billion per year during 1900–1910, the East must have imported short-term capital from the West.[119] This result is consistent with the functioning of New York as a financial intermediary, the locus of the national money market, linking Western saving and investment by borrowing short and lending long. This process would have concentrated bankers' balances in New York through the correspondent banking system, even if capital moved from New York to the West through mortgage lending or the purchase of equities. Thus we can reconcile the observations of contemporaries that money (specie) moved to New York "like water flowing downhill," as money flows to financial centers with the movement of capital from capital-abundant areas, the East, to capital-scarce areas, the West, if New York functioned as national financial intermediary.[120] As we noted

[119] It should be noted that including consideration of foreign trade here does not change our conclusions. During the 1900–1910 decade the United States ran a persistent balance-of-payments surplus, importing slightly over $700 million of gold as a result. Let us make the extreme assumption that New York functioned only as an intermediary in foreign trade, so that the specie flowed straight through New York to the West. If this had been the case, domestic net cash flows into New York would have been at most +$700 million if total cash flows had been in balance. This change makes little difference; the Eastern balance-of-trade surplus may have been larger or the short-term capital inflow into New York smaller by an average of $70 million per year, which is a small correction in relation to the Eastern long-term capital outflow of about $1 billion per year. U.S. Bureau of the Census, *Historical Statistics*, p. 564.

[120] On the other hand, in Jeffrey Williamson's model of late nineteenth-century American development there is a reversal of the net capital outflow from the East around the mid-1880s. From 1885 to 1910 the net flow moves from Midwest to East. Our figures show instead the East to have been a long-term capital exporter during 1900–1910, while the Midwest was a long-term capital importer. If New York functioned as a financial intermediary, then the Midwest

147

in the previous section, the concentration of bankers' balances in New York does not mean that those funds remained there.

It appears, then, that probably on net short-term capital was moving from West to East. If this were the case, then an erosion of barriers to interregional capital mobility and consequently an increased supply of short-term capital in the West from the East does not seem to be a satisfactory explanation of the narrowing interregional short-term interest rate differentials; short-term funds on balance were moving in the opposite direction. Consequently, reducing barriers to interregional capital mobility does not appear to have been a crucial factor in reducing short-term interest-rate differentials. In fact, the findings thus far are still consistent with the existence of a perfect capital market, with there having been no significant barriers to interregional capital mobility. The explanations for the narrowing short-term interest rate differentials will be examined in detail in Chapter VI.

The interregional balance of trade has to be known before the direction of short-term flows can be definitely identified, and unfortunately it is not. However, if the annual Eastern surplus in the balance of trade during the 1900–1910 period was not enormous, less than $1 billion per year, then short-term capital on net must have moved from West to East. This result is consistent with the observations of many contemporaries on the concentration of balances in New York. The smaller the Eastern balance of trade surplus was, the more New York functioned as a national financial intermediary, and thus the more of the incoming short-term funds were transferred back to the West. This chapter has focused on the flow of interregional funds from West to East; Chapter V will examine the other aspect of the interregional short-term capital market, methods of transferring funds from East to West.

---

was also a total net capital importer. Jeffrey G. Williamson, *Late Nineteenth-Century American Development* (Cambridge: Cambridge University Press, 1974), p. 132.

Methods of Interregional Transfers of Funds

INTERBANK BORROWING

IN Chapter IV it was shown that the correspondent banking system was quite effective in transferring short-term funds from West to East and concentrating them in an essentially national market, the New York money market. The task of transferring balances from East to West was a more difficult one, because it was a process of diffusing rather than concentrating funds, but the structure of the correspondent banking system facilitated the flow of funds in that direction also. Interbank borrowing was one of the means by which funds in the correspondent banking system were transferred from areas of relative financial ease to areas of financial stringency, on the whole from East to West and South and from city banks to country banks, representing an offset to the accumulation of bankers' balances in New York City. The pattern of borrowing had a large seasonal component in that country banks in agricultural areas often faced shortages of funds because of the increased demand for credit during crop-harvesting and crop-moving periods. One method of obtaining additional funds was borrowing from city banks. Similarly, during panics country banks might borrow from larger city banks to meet demands for liquidity.

One of the principal services of city correspondents was the provision of loans to their country correspondents. The absence of an established rediscount market made the existence of a dependable source of funds in times of local stringency very important to an average bank because of the feeling of security it provided.[1] In hearings on the Federal

[1] Leonard L. Watkins, *Bankers' Balances* (Chicago: A. W. Shaw Co., 1929), p. 153.

149

Reserve Act, Festus J. Wade, president of the Mercantile Trust Co. of St. Louis, observed that country banks knew their city correspondent would take care of them and that was one of the principal reasons why they kept deposits there. Large city banks, he noted, frequently made loans to country correspondents of from $1,000 up to $50,000.[2]

The maintenance of correspondent accounts, then, was quite important to country banks, because a bank ordinarily could borrow only from a city bank with which it carried an account.[3] General arrangements for borrowing were usually established at the time a correspondent account was opened. The normal procedure involved a credit investigation of the depositing bank before the account was accepted.[4] The line of credit extended to the depositing bank, as in the case of individual depositors, depended on the average balance on deposit in the correspondent account. In New York the practice developed that borrowings could not exceed four or five times the average balance on deposit by the bank, thus "standardizing" the competition for country correspondents.[5]

Interest rates charged on borrowings varied fairly widely, but 6 percent seems to have been the most common rate in the pre-Federal Reserve period,[6] so it would have cost a country bank 4 percent on net to borrow to establish a bankers' balance account. The relatively high rate may be accounted for by the fact that most borrowings occurred in the fall when the demand for money, and, consequently,

---

[2] Testimony of Festus J. Wade, U.S. Senate, Banking and Currency Committee, *Hearings on H.R. 7837 (S2639)*, 63rd Congress, 1st Session, p. 129.

[3] Thomas Conway and Ernest Patterson, *The Operation of the New Bank Act* (Philadelphia: J. B. Lippincott Co., 1914), p. 95.

[4] The process is described in detail in Chester A. Phillips, *Bank Credit* (New York: Macmillan Company, 1920), pp. 256–258.

[5] Conway and Patterson, *Operation of the New Bank Act*, p. 95.

[6] Oliver C. Lockhart, "The Development of Interbank Borrowing in the National System, 1869–1914, I," *Journal of Political Economy*, XXIX (March 1921), p. 157.

interest rates were also high. In panic periods, the rates ranged much higher—up to 12 percent for rediscounts during the Panic of 1893.[7] Laughlin asserted that in times of emergency the rediscount rate in New York rose to 100 or 150 percent.[8] Other factors, of course, also influenced the borrowing rate. If the borrowing bank wanted merely to increase its deposits, loans could be made at a lower interest rate than if it wanted to withdraw the funds from the city,[9] most probably because funds withdrawn to the interior were usually desired to be in lawful money, the removal of which reduced the city bank's legal reserve holding.[10]

Thus, the provision of facilities for interbank borrowing was one of the principal services provided by city banks to their country correspondents, although it will be seen that it was more important to Southern banks than to Western banks. Just as the existence of the correspondent banking system antedated the establishment of the national banking system, interbank borrowing was a recognized practice at least as early as the establishment of the national banking system.[11]

Interbank borrowing occurred in a number of forms, but only the two principal means were reported by the Comptroller of the Currency. One method was rediscounting paper of customers of the borrowing bank, which appeared in balance sheets as "notes and bills rediscounted." The other principal method was loaning on the note of a borrowing bank. The bank's notes were backed by collateral such as stocks and bonds or customer loans; borrowings of this type appeared in the balance sheet as "bills payable." However, banks sometimes borrowed through overdrafts on correspond-

[7] O. M. W. Sprague, *History of Crises under the National Banking System* (Washington, D.C.: U.S. Government Printing Office, 1910), p. 419.

[8] J. Laurence Laughlin, ed., *Banking Reform* (Chicago: National Citizens' League, 1912), p. 337.

[9] Lockhart, "Development of Interbank Borrowing," p. 159.

[10] Ibid., pp. 159–160.

[11] Ibid., p. 139.

ent accounts.[12] City banks also made loans to country banks in exchange for certificates of deposit. Another method employed was the purchase of bonds or other securities by the "lending" bank with the understanding that they would be resold to the "borrowing" bank sometime in the future.[13]

The common form of interbank loan was in the form of bills payable, in which the bank issued its own note, generally secured by collateral. The greater part of the collateral offered was usually notes held by the bank or some of the bank's bills receivable. The amount of collateral required was a function both of its quality and the credit rating of the bank, with the margin of collateral over the face value of the loan running from 10 or 20 percent to as high as 100 percent.[14] This margin of security was the primary reason why city bankers preferred to lend on the direct obligation of the borrowing bank.[15]

The other principal form of interbank borrowing, rediscounting, involved the borrowing bank endorsing some of its customers' notes and sending them to its city correspondent. The city bank then purchased the customer's note from its country correspondent; it rediscounted it. So the process was essentially the reselling of loans and discounts in the country bank's portfolio to its city correspondent. Rediscounting was, on average, less popular than lending on the bank's own note secured by collateral. If the bank's note had been unsecured there would have been little difference between the bank's note and a rediscounted note. During the postbellum period bills payable usually constituted the larger part of interbank borrowings.[16]

[12] Ibid., p. 142.

[13] Phillips, *Bank Credit*, p. 253.

[14] Ibid., p. 255; Lockhart, "Development of Interbank Borrowing," p. 151.

[15] Lockhart, "Development of Interbank Borrowing," p. 151.

[16] From 1870 to 1882 bills payable composed the greater part of total interbank borrowing. However, in the decade after 1882 the relationship reversed and rediscounts exceeded direct loans; after 1893 a reversal took place once again. After that date the proportion

Another explanation for the popularity of direct interbank borrowing relative to that of rediscounting was that the borrowing bank's customers often looked with great displeasure upon the sale of their notes to another bank. Farmers in particular were supposedly highly averse to this practice, and country bankers often cited this fact as a principal reason why they preferred to borrow through bills payable rather than rediscounting.[17] To avoid revealing the rediscount, the notes were often endorsed in pencil and then erased when the note was returned for payment; the lending bank was similarly requested not to place its endorsement on it.[18]

Rediscounting and other forms of interbank borrowing were looked upon with disfavor because they were regarded as a sign of weakness by the bank. There seemed to be a rather general belief that a borrowing bank was bordering on insolvency and would be unable to accommodate its customers.[19] As a result, many banks tried to conceal the extent of interbank borrowing. This tendency toward concealment was also promoted by a provision of the National Banking Act. Except for circulating notes, deposits, drafts upon deposits with correspondents, and liabilities to stockholders for dividends and reserve profits, "no association shall at any time be indebted, or any way liable, to an amount exceeding its capital stock. . . ."[20] This limitation on the size

---

of rediscounts to total interbank borrowings declined steadily to about one-sixth of the total, as compared with 44 percent in 1869–1882, and 72 percent in 1882–1892. There is no apparent reason for this wide variation in the relative use of rediscounts, which is all the more strange because of the abruptness of the reversals. Lockhart, "Development of Interbank Borrowing," pp. 153, 154.

[17] Conway and Patterson, *Operation of the New Bank Act*, pp. 109–110.

[18] Lockhart, "Development of Interbank Borrowing," p. 152; L. H. Langston, *Practical Bank Operation* (New York: Ronald Press Co., 1921), pp. 271–272.

[19] Lockhart, "Development of Interbank Borrowing," pp. 145–146.

[20] Ibid., p. 147.

of interbank loans provided an additional inducement to conceal them. On the other hand, it should be noted that this prejudice against interbank borrowing did not extend to the lending banks. It was the experience of many New York banks that loans to correspondents were among their safest investments.[21]

Borrowing banks devised several techniques to conceal interbank borrowing, some of which have already been noted. "Borrowing" banks might sell bonds or other securities to a "lending" bank with the understanding that they would be repurchased at a later date. Besides its covert character, this method had the advantage of allowing the borrowing bank to secure an advance equal to the full value of its securities, whereas a direct loan would have ordinarily required a margin of collateral above the face value of the loan.[22] Similarly, loans could be concealed by borrowing banks issuing certificates of deposits to the lending banks. City correspondents might advance funds to country banks by allowing them to overdraw their correspondent account, thus concealing the interbank transfer of funds.

Borrowings could be hidden in the balance sheet in the entry "other liabilities," because interbank borrowings could be entered as part of "money borrowed in different forms," although this figure had been small for many years.[23] Probably the most common method of concealment was the use of personal credit by the officers or director of the borrowing bank. In a loan transaction the borrowing bank might be charged by the lender in a special account and credited by writing up its bankers' balance account, so the borrowing bank reported the loan as "due from banks."[24] In a similar fashion, bank officers might obtain a loan on their own notes, but with the bank's endorsement or guarantee. Yet another form of subterfuge involved the bank selling some of its bills receivable to its officers, who in turn rediscounted them or pledged them as collateral for a loan from another bank.

All of these methods, varying in their degrees of ingenuity,

[21] Ibid., p. 146.
[22] Ibid., 144–145.
[23] Ibid., pp. 142–143.
[24] Ibid., pp. 143–144.

were employed to conceal the actual level of interbank borrowing. Therefore, the Comptroller of the Currency figures for rediscounts and bills payable certainly understate the true extent of interbank borrowing. It was established by a "former government official" that at the fourth call date of 1913 (August 9), secret borrowings of national banks amounted to between $50 and $100 million.[25] Reported borrowings at that call date were slightly over $100 million, so the reported figure could understate the actual amount of borrowing by as much as 100 percent.

In view of the stigma attached to interbank borrowing during the postbellum period, it should not be surprising that a well-developed national rediscount market did not evolve. A combination of customer preferences and national bank regulations prevented a secondary market in notes and discounts from developing, but the correspondent banking system served as a substitute. Rediscounting was confined to transactions between correspondents, but nevertheless, interregional transfers of funds between banks were possible. A speaker at the 1903 Nebraska Bankers' Association convention argued that the unpopularity of rediscounting bank paper was an obstacle in bringing about interregional equilibrium and concluded that it was not used to such an extent as to make it an important factor in the interregional flow of funds.[26] Breckenridge also discounted rediscounting as an effective method for promoting interregional transfers.[27]

In order to assess its role in the interregional capital market, the extent and distribution of interbank borrowing will be examined. In the early period from 1869 to 1882, total reported borrowings,[28] that is, bills payable plus re-

[25] Ibid., p. 145.

[26] C. F. Bentley, "Commercial Paper as an Investment for Country Banks," *Proceedings of the Nebraska Bankers' Association*, 1903, p. 178.

[27] R. M. Breckenridge, "Discount Rates in the United States," *Political Science Quarterly*, XIII (March 1898), p. 139.

[28] It should be noted that all of the following figures cited are reported borrowings, which, as we have seen, may significantly underestimate total actual borrowings.

discounts, were not large and did not fluctuate widely, averaging under $9 million per year. In the decade 1883–1892, during which rediscounts became much more significant, total borrowings increased somewhat, averaging about $16.5 million per year. From 1893 to 1906 borrowings fluctuated substantially, ranging above $50 million in the summer of 1893 and averaging $24.5 million. In the period after 1906 up to 1914, borrowings rose dramatically, so that at each call date during the period they exceeded the 1893–1906 average. From 1906 to 1914 total borrowings averaged $61 million. The substantial increase in borrowings in this later period was attributed to the necessities of the Panic of 1907 and to the gradual deterioration of the prejudice against interbank borrowing because of the influence of the campaign for banking reform centering on the provision of facilities for rediscount.[29] The growing regard for the practice of rediscounting is evidenced in the rediscount powers given the Federal Reserve banks and the importance attached to them initially.

Central reserve city banks, unsurprisingly, borrowed very little from other banks. Such borrowing would have been inconsistent with their position as banks of deposit for other banks. Reported borrowings by central reserve city banks formed only about 10 percent of total borrowings in the fall of 1902.[30] Reserve city banks were in a slightly different position than those in central reserve cities in that they were usually closer to agricultural regions and thus subject to wider fluctuations in demand. Reserve city borrowings ranged between one-twelfth and one-third of total borrowings and averaged about 18 percent of the total.[31]

As one might expect, country banks, subject to wider seasonal fluctuations in the demand for funds, were the largest borrowers. Between 1900 and 1914, country banks were responsible for 80 percent of total borrowing, ranging up to 91 percent in March and June 1911. In the late nine-

[29] Lockhart, "Development of Interbank Borrowing," pp. 223–225.
[30] Ibid., p. 225.   [31] Ibid., p. 226.

teenth century, the percentage accounted for by country banks was only slightly smaller.[32]

To get an idea of the relative importance of interbank loans, consider Table 23, in which interbank borrowing is

Table 23

Rediscounts and Bills Payable as Percentage of
Due from Banks,[a] 1910–1914
(yearly average of five call dates)

Year	All Banks	All Natl. Banks	Country Banks	State Banks and Trust Companies
1910	5.98%	5.57%	8.77%	8.30%
1911	4.90	4.48	7.29	7.08
1912	5.01	4.60	7.34	7.33
1913	6.52	5.98	9.05	9.61
1914	9.26	8.90	13.43	11.37

[a] Represents assets of banks—"Due from . . ." items. See note to Table 12.

Source: Computed from Leonard L. Watkins, *Bankers' Balances* (Chicago: A. W. Shaw Co., 1929), pp. 156–157.

presented as a percentage of bankers' balances held by various classes of banks on a yearly average; for example, borrowings by country banks are shown as a percentage of "due from banks" which are assets of country banks. Information about borrowings of state banks and trust companies is available only after 1910, so the table covers the period 1910–1914. Because the reported figures for rediscounts and bills payable probably significantly understate the actual amount of interbank borrowing, it is virtually impossible to form an accurate picture of the actual extent of borrowing. However, applying our previous estimate that borrowings were understated by reported figures something less than

[32] Ibid.

100 percent, we see that interbank borrowing for both country banks and state banks, which seem to be of similar orders of magnitude, may have amounted to almost 20 percent of their bankers' balances deposited with city correspondents.

Table 23 shows the average level of borrowing over the year, which gives an idea of the average net flows among banks resulting from interbank borrowings. However, one of the most distinctive characteristics of interbank borrowing was its seasonal nature. The demand for money increased substantially during the fall crop-harvesting and crop-moving season. Country bank borrowings usually increased over the year and in fact did peak in the fall; the seasonal pattern of reserve city borrowing was very similar.[33]

The demand for interbank borrowing greatly increased during panics. Even though city banks themselves were pressed for funds, interbank borrowings did rise. The difficulty of borrowing, however, was reflected in the interest rates charged, which, as we have noted, increased substan-

---

[33] Country bank borrowings reached their maximum in the fall at the fourth call, when on average more than one-quarter of total borrowings took place. Country bank borrowings were the highest on the fourth call every year between 1900 and 1914 except for 1905 and 1907, when the fourth call came in August; country borrowings were the lowest on the first call in eleven of those years. The general pattern of country bank borrowings shows a rising trend over the year, with 14.2 and 14.3 percent of total borrowings occurring at the first two call dates and 27.0 and 25.0 percent taking place at the fourth and fifth calls.

The seasonal pattern of reserve city borrowing is very similar. The first and second calls accounted for 15.0 and 13.0 percent of total borrowings respectively, whereas the last two dates represented 25.1 and 30.1 percent. To the extent that reserve city banks were located in agricultural areas or held substantial amounts of bankers' balances of country banks, they were subject to the same pressures as country banks. The peak at the fifth call rather than the fourth as for country banks may be explained by the fact that city banks, instead of country banks, were often called upon to finance crop moving, as opposed to harvesting. Lockhart, "Development of Interbank Borrowing," pp. 230–231; Watkins, *Bankers' Balances*, p. 159.

tially during panics. In the 1890 Panic borrowings, reflected in the fifth call, were 5 percent above the 1883–1892 average. Similarly, in the Panic of 1893, borrowings exceeded the seasonal average by 9 percent; and again in the 1907 Panic, fifth call borrowings greatly exceeded the average.[34] So the correspondent banking system did provide some assistance to distressed banks in panics, contrary to the complaint of the National Monetary Commission that there was no cooperation of any kind among banks outside of clearing house cities in times of panics.[35]

In addition to the variation of borrowings over time, in a study of the interregional capital market the geographical distribution of interbank borrowing should also be considered. The principal source of funds was, of course, New York. The size of the market and the relatively favorable terms that could be obtained there made it attractive to bankers from all parts of the country. New York banks made about one-third of the total interbank loans; central reserve city banks in Chicago and St. Louis were also important sources of funds, providing about one-fourth of total borrowings. Thus, central reserve city banks as a whole provided about 60 percent of the funds for borrowing while holding substantially less than half of total bankers' balances.[36] In Table 24 we see that interbank loans made up a fairly large proportion of total loans in central reserve cities—more than 6 percent in New York, more than 8 percent in Chicago, and more than 13 percent in St. Louis.

Table 24 presents the amount of interbank lending by banks in selected cities in 1914. One surprising fact the table reveals is the importance of interbank loans in several cities. In Southern cities interbank loans averaged around 20 percent of bankers' balances on deposit there, which were liabilities of the city banks; in Kansas City interbank loans

[34] Lockhart, "Development of Interbank Borrowing," p. 233.

[35] U.S. National Monetary Commission, *Report* (Washington, D.C.: U.S. Government Printing Office, 1911), p. 7.

[36] Lockhart, "Development of Interbank Borrowing," p. 236.

Table 24

Interbank Loans of Reserve City Banks,
January 13, 1914
($1,000)

Loans to All Banks on Rediscounts or Bills Payable, by Banks in:		Interbank Loans as Percentage of Bankers' Balances on Deposit	Interbank Loans as Percentage of Total Loans
East			
Boston	$ 3,696	3.80%	1.93%
New York	59,107	7.96	6.36
Philadelphia	6,859	3.95	3.09
Albany	276	0.70	1.25
Baltimore	2,621	8.04	4.40
Pittsburgh	710	0.89	0.54
South			
New Orleans	1,134	15.70	5.76
Richmond	1,629	14.85	4.40
Atlanta	893	20.12	3.55
Dallas	1,386	22.21	7.11
Houston	1,866	14.79	7.89
Louisville	2,205	18.76	8.34
Midwest			
Chicago	25,664	9.20	8.54
St. Louis	14,271	15.79	13.74
Cleveland	1,164	3.17	1.97
Cincinnati	1,956	6.00	3.74
Minneapolis	2,621	8.37	4.48
Omaha	5,769	31.12	18.41
Kansas City	18,844	34.36	28.10
West			
San Francisco	3,296	7.19	2.94
Los Angeles	1,375	8.44	2.87
Portland	572	6.79	2.67
Seattle	603	8.02	2.46

Source: U.S. Comptroller of the Currency, *Annual Report*, 1914, Vol. I (Washington, D.C.: U.S. Government Printing Office, 1914), p. 144.

constituted almost 30 percent of the total loan and discount portfolio. On the other hand, some cities, such as Pittsburgh and Albany, and to a lesser extent Boston, Philadelphia, and Cleveland, showed very small amounts of interbank loans. These intercity variations are revealing of the different functions performed by correspondents in various cities. In some cities, such as Albany or Pittsburgh, for example, city correspondents primarily provided services of collection and exchange, whereas in others granting loans was relatively important.

The size of some of the interbank loan figures, such as in the South and Great Plains, suggests that in addition to its role in interregional transfers, the effect of interbank borrowing in transferring funds from city to country banks within a region cannot be ignored. Even towns as small as Marion, Indiana, were local centers of interbank lending.[37]

To give an indication of the extent of interregional transfers of funds resulting from borrowing, Table 25 presents the distribution of interbank borrowings during the period 1897–1914. The striking thing in Table 25 is the fact that the

Table 25

Percentage Distribution of Interbank Borrowing, 1897–1914

Region	Percentage
New England	8.6
East	19.0
South	48.9
Midwest	12.2
West	7.0
Pacific	4.3

Source: Oliver C. Lockhart, "The Development of Interbank Borrowing in the National System, 1869–1914, II," *Journal of Political Economy*, XXIX (March 1921), p. 227. Reprinted with the permission of the *Journal of Political Economy*.

[37] Ibid., p. 237.

South, which had significantly fewer banks per capita than any other region, accounted for almost half of total borrowings. The story is the same when the number of borrowing banks is examined. On September 4, 1904, about 43 percent of Southern national banks were engaged in interbank borrowing as compared with 18 percent of all national banks. In November 1904, the ratio of borrowings to "due from banks" was almost 15 percent for Southern banks and less than 6 percent for all country banks. By December 31, 1914, the ratio was 42 percent for Southern banks and 18 percent for all country banks.[38] For the whole period, Southern banks borrowed almost as much as all other national banks combined. Comparing Tables 24 and 25, we see that whereas almost 50 percent of total interbank loans went to the South, less than 10 percent of interbank loans were generated by Southern city banks; so, unambiguously interbank borrowing represented a strong interregional inflow of funds into the South.

One explanation that has been offered for the heavy borrowing in the South has emphasized the marked seasonal nature of cotton growing. The strain in the fall would be much more pronounced in "one-crop" areas such as the cotton South than in other agricultural areas with diversified crops maturing successively. The difficulty of utilizing banking resources adequate to meet peak demands in the other seasons led to an undersupply of banking facilities and thus substantial borrowing.[39] In the Midwest, however, particular areas were concentrated in wheat or corn, but there was no "undersupply" of banking resources and extensive interbank borrowing there. The relative "undersupply" of local banking facilities in the South as compared with the Midwest might have been due to higher risk, but it was risk associated with cotton production rather than with one-crop agriculture itself. Cotton prices in the postbellum period had sizable year-to-year fluctuations and appeared to be essentially ran-

---

[38] Watkins, *Bankers' Balances*, pp. 157–158.
[39] Lockhart, "Development of Interbank Borrowing," p. 277.

dom, whereas wheat prices had a fairly strong element of autocorrelation, that is, next year's wheat prices could be fairly accurately predicted from this year's prices.[40]

Lance Davis rejects interbank borrowing as a mechanism for substantial interregional capital transfers by pointing to Breckenridge's estimate that over 1892–1897 interbank loans averaged only about 1.5 percent of total loans and discounts.[41] This assertion may be substantially correct in the aggregate, but not necessarily so for specific regions, the South in particular. Consider Table 26. Interbank borrowing

Table 26

Range of Interbank Borrowing as Percentage
of Loans and Discounts, 1892–1897

Region	Low Period	High Period
New England	1.13%	1.50%
East	0.42	0.53
South	2.69	8.00
Midwest	1.25	1.50
Mountain	3.00	3.38
Pacific	2.00	2.45

Source: R. M. Breckenridge, "Discount Rates in the United States," *Political Science Quarterly*, XIII (March, 1898), p. 137.

by Breckenridge's calculations supplied up to 8 percent of the funds for total Southern loans and discounts. If the understatement involved in that figure is considered, it would not seem unlikely that on average more than 10 percent of Southern loan funds were borrowed from other banks, a

[40] Thomas F. Cooley and Stephen De Canio, "Varying-Parameter Supply Functions and the Sources of Economic Distress in American Agriculture, 1866–1914," NBER Working Paper No. 57 (September 1974), pp. 28–29.

[41] Lance Davis, "The Investment Market, 1870–1914: The Evolution of a National Market," *Journal of Economic History*, XXV (September 1965), p. 371.

fairly substantial figure. Table 26 does indicate that, on balance, higher-interest-rate areas tended to borrow more than lower-interest-rate areas, with Western banks borrowing about 5 percent of total loans and discounts from other banks, roughly correcting for understatement.

Davis's observation that banks in general seemed to use rediscounting just to meet seasonal and panic demands[42] does not necessarily detract from their importance as a mechanism for promoting capital market integration. In times of financial stringency even a small inflow of funds through rediscounting may have had significant effects on local interest rates, thereby promoting interregional interest-rate convergence. In addition, even though interbank borrowings were not a substantial impact in particular areas, such as the South, where they did represent an important link between Southern banks and banks in other regions.

Because a formal rediscount market did not develop under the national banking system, the correspondent banking system allowed interbank borrowings between correspondents. The system thus promoted interregional transfers of funds and increased the elasticity of supply of funds in regions during periods of stringency. These interbank borrowing relationships that developed between correspondents served as a substitute for a branch banking system in the interregional movement of funds.

Direct Interregional Lending

Another method of transferring funds between regions was direct lending, that is, a bank loaning to a borrower in another part of the country. Even in a world of perfect information the administrative cost of a loan would increase with distance. However, in a world of imperfect knowledge the lending bank must also take the information costs involved in interregional lending into account in addition to

[42] Ibid.

the higher return it might expect.[43] The correspondent banking system was also a means of reducing such information costs. One of the mutual services provided between correspondents was the furnishing of credit information about borrowers located within each bank's area.

Tables 27 and 28 convey some idea of the extent of interregional lending. Table 27 presents the geographical distribution of domestic loans made by reserve city and central reserve city banks as of November 10, 1915. Table 28 shows the distribution of loans made by national banks in all cities of population greater than 75,000 as of December 27, 1916. The higher interest rates were in a region, the less likely banks in that region were to loan interregionally. A very large part of the loans of Southern and Western banks were concentrated in their own regions. In contrast, in Table 27, almost 30 percent of Eastern reserve city national bank loans were made interregionally. There did seem to be a flow of funds into high-interest areas. For example, in both tables the South appears to have attracted substantial amounts of funds from every other region except for the Pacific states. On November 10, 1915, 49 percent of all loans in the South made by reserve city banks were made by banks outside the South.[44] To be sure, this probably overstates the proportion of interregional borrowing in the total amount of Southern loans outstanding, because we are confining ourselves to reserve city banks. Country banks most likely engaged in much less interregional borrowing and lending, so if all loans made in the South are considered, instead of just those by reserve city banks, the interregional component should be smaller.

[43] The decision is actually still more complicated, because the bank is a diversifier and must consider the covariance between the interregional loan and local loans. If they are only weakly correlated, the bank may be willing to accept a lower rate of return on distant loans.

[44] U.S. Comptroller of the Currency, *Annual Report*, 1915, Vol. I (Washington, D.C.: U.S. Government Printing Office, 1915), pp. 18–19.

Table 27

Geographical Distribution of Loans Arranged According to Location of Borrowers Made by National Banks in Reserve Cities and Central Reserve Cities,[a] November 10, 1915

(in percent)

Reserve Cities in	New England	East	South	Midwest	West	Pacific	Total United States
New England	70.65	13.99	3.48	10.22	0.94	0.69	100.00
East	3.92	78.68	8.03	7.63	0.82	0.89	100.00
South	0	0.38	98.81	0.57	0.22	0.01	100.00
Midwest	1.40	4.47	6.11	80.36	6.38	1.26	100.00
West	0.43	1.67	3.14	6.24	87.73	0.76	100.00
Pacific	0.41	1.33	0.55	3.26	0.52	93.94	100.00

[a] Distribution of domestic loans.

Source: U.S. Comptroller of the Currency, *Annual Report*, 1915, Vol. I (Washington, D.C.: U.S. Government Printing Office, 1915), pp. 18–19.

Table 28

Geographical Distribution of Loans Arranged According to Location of Borrowers Made by National Banks in All Cities of over 75,000 Population,[a] December 27, 1916

(in percent)

Region	New England	East	South	Midwest	West	Pacific	Total United States
New England	77.42	9.78	2.71	8.96	0.56	0.53	100.00
East	3.55	80.72	6.36	8.01	0.74	0.59	100.00
South	0.08	2.61	95.53	1.49	0.22	0.03	100.00
Midwest	1.69	5.54	5.23	81.35	5.26	0.91	100.00
West	0.73	3.63	4.13	8.99	81.45	0.99	100.00
Pacific	1.33	5.75	0.78	5.07	1.35	85.68	100.00

[a] Domestic loans only.

Source: U.S. Comptroller of the Currency, *Annual Report*, 1917, Vol. I (Washington, D.C.: U.S. Government Printing Office, 1917), pp. 206–207.

As one example of the interregional lending of a city bank, we find in 1913 the Mercantile Trust Co. of St. Louis lending in Seattle and Portland and all through Kansas, Oklahoma, and Texas.[45] However, because of the concentration of bankers' balances in New York, it would be especially interesting to see the amount of interregional lending done by New York banks. Table 29 presents a breakdown of the

Table 29

Loans of Thirty Largest New York Bank and Trust
Companies, September 24, 1913

Brokers' loans	
Made for banks outside of New York	$174,945,900
Made on own account	264,383,800
Loans and discounts made to borrowers in	
Eastern states (ME, NH, VT, MA, RI, CT, NY, NJ, PA, MD, DC, DL)	617,830,800
Southern states (VA, WV, NC, SC, GA, FL, AL, MS, LA, KY, TN, TX, AR)	174,140,500
Western states (OH, IN, IL, MI, WI, MN, IA, MO, ND, SD, NB, KA, MT, WY, CO, OK, NM, WA, OR, CA, ID, UT, AZ, NV)	167,720,600
Foreign countries	2,898,800
	$1,226,974,500

Source: U.S. Senate, Committee on Banking and Currency, *Hearings on H.R. 7837 (S2639)*, 63rd Congress, 1st Session, pp. 2772–2776.

loans of the thirty largest New York banks and trust companies on September 24, 1913, collected for the hearings on the Federal Reserve Act. More than 28 percent of total loans went directly to banks or individual borrowers outside the Eastern states. However, the ultimate destination of funds from brokers' loans is not known, because they could very

[45] Wade, *Hearings on H.R. 7837*, p. 133.

well have been used to pay someone outside of New York. Consequently, the 28 percent may be regarded as a lower bound for the interregional flow of loans out of New York. If brokers' loans are neglected and only loans and discounts made to banks or individual borrowers are considered, then loans outside the Eastern states account for 36 percent of total loans of these banks.

To get a better idea of the distribution of these loans, consider Table 30, which shows the geographical distribution of

Table 30

Distribution of Non-Stock Exchange Loans of the National
City Bank of New York, November 25, 1913
(in percent)

Region	To Banks	To Others	Total
East	1.16	52.57	53.73
New England	—	3.12	3.12
South	9.68	7.47	17.15
Midwest	2.23	18.72	20.95
West	0.65	0.62	1.27
Pacific	0.65	1.42	2.07
Foreign	—	—	1.65
Total	14.37	83.92	100.00

Source: Thomas Conway and Ernest Patterson, *The Operation of the New Bank Act* (Philadelphia: J. B. Lippincott Co., 1914), p. 292. Reprinted with the permission of J. B. Lippincott Co.

non-stock exchange loans of the National City Bank of New York on November 25, 1913, as reported to the Pujo Committee investigation. Almost half of the non-stock exchange loans of the National City Bank loans were to borrowers outside the Eastern states. In addition, 70 percent of those loans made outside the East were to individual borrowers rather than to other banks. Thus, interregional lending rep-

169

resented a substantial part of loans made by New York banks, and the majority of them were made directly to individual borrowers rather than to banks.

The amount of interregional lending offset to some extent the concentration of correspondent balances in New York. In early 1914 interregional loans of all forms represented about 30 percent of the total loan portfolio of New York national banks, but still amounted to only 36 percent of correspondent balances on deposit in New York,[46] a result consistent with the tentative conclusion in Chapter IV that there must have been on balance an inflow of short-term funds into New York, from West to East. Nevertheless, interregional lending may have had a significant impact on particular regions, such as the South, where we have seen that a substantial amount of total loans, at least in reserve cities, was provided by outside sources.

INTERREGIONAL HOLDINGS OF BANK STOCK

Funds were transferred from East to West within the structure of the correspondent banking system through interbank lending and by direct interregional lending, but Eastern capital also was invested directly in Western banks by buying stock. Eastern purchases of Western bank shares, then, represented an interregional transfer of funds that increased the capital stock of Western banks and thus enabled them to expand their loan portfolio.

The Comptroller of the Currency in 1889 noted the importance of these interregional holdings of bank stock. He estimated that the average of interest rates then prevailing, having in view all classes of loans and the entire country, was about only one-third of the rate prevailing thirty years earlier,[47] an indication of the disequilibrium of the antebel-

[46] U.S. Comptroller of the Currency, *Annual Report*, 1914, Vol. I, pp. 143–144.

[47] U.S. Comptroller of the Currency, *Annual Report*, 1889, p. 12.

lum interregional capital market. One of the principal factors responsible for this remarkable diminution in interest rates, he argued, was the national banking system, which facilitated direct interregional investment in bank stock. Investors were said to be more reluctant to put their funds into state banks at a distance because of the variation in regulations from state to state and the consequent difficulty in deciphering and keeping up with the multitude of different restrictions. Regulations of the national banking system, on the other hand, were uniform across the country and thus supposedly reduced the information costs in interregional investment considerably. "Eastern capitalists have been induced to become stockholders in associations located in the sparsely settled States, where no other form of investment could tempt them."[48] If state banks yielded higher returns on average, they may well have been more attractive investments in spite of the higher information costs associated with them. Unfortunately, no figures on the amount of interregional investment in state banks are available in order to make a comparison of the degree of interregional investment in state and national banks.

Tables 31 and 32 present out-of-state holdings of bank stock as a percentage of total shares in areas between 1887 and 1897 for country and reserve city national banks. Out-of-state holdings of bank stock were quite high in several high-interest-rate areas. Over one-third of country bank stock in Division 8, the Western states, was held by out-of-state investors. Similarly, in Division 6, roughly the Great Plains states, around one-quarter of country bank stock and more than one-third of reserve city stock was held by outsiders. Large amounts of shares of Southern country and reserve city banks were also held by outside investors.

The trend in Western and Southern country banks toward greater amounts of outside ownership is clear. Figures for the geographical distribution of bank stock in 1876 are avail-

[48] Ibid.

able,[49] but they are not directly comparable to the figures in Tables 31 and 32 because the 1876 data do not separate country from reserve city banks. Nevertheless, in a region such as the Pacific states where there were few reserve cities (San Francisco), the longer-term trend in bank ownership can be approximated. From 1876 to 1897 out-of-state holdings of Western states bank shares rose from somewhat over 9 percent to over one-third. Eastern capital did seem to be moving westward.

To be sure, however, one must be guarded in interpreting these out-of-state holdings of bank stock as being equivalent to interregional transfers. Breckenridge argued that only under the most favorable possible construction could the stockholdings of nonstate residents in Southern and Western banks be interpreted as investments exclusively of Northern and Eastern capital.[50] A large amount of those out-of-state-held shares were most probably held by people living in nearby states, so that they represented intraregional rather than interregional transfers of funds.

Interstate branch banking was the most direct method of extending control over banking resources across regions, but, of course, it was prohibited. The purchase of stock in several different banks offered another alternative means to the same end. Such a practice could certainly have been carried on by individual investors. However, toward the end of the nineteenth century it began to become more formalized in chain banking systems in which a holding company, such as the National City Company, associated with the National City Bank, purchased stock in a large number of state and national banks.[51]

Breckenridge dismissed the importance of interregional holdings of bank stock as a means of facilitating interregional transfers. He pointed to the fact that in 1897 nonresident

[49] U.S. Comptroller of the Currency, *Annual Report*, 1886, pp. xxviii–xxix.

[50] Breckenridge, "Discount Rates," pp. 135–136.

[51] Laughlin, *Banking Reform*, pp. 204–207.

Table 31

Percentage of National Bank Shares Held outside
the State—Country Banks
(par value $100)

Year	Div. 1	Div. 2	Div. 3	Div. 4	Div. 5	Div. 6	Div. 7	Div. 8
1887	7.67	5.43	15.89	12.83	7.04	23.09	12.02	35.05
1888	8.26	6.39	15.27	14.07	7.67	25.50	11.06	36.00
1889	9.23	6.43	14.62	15.88	8.42	29.08	14.33	36.72
1897	8.06	6.89	14.20	16.42	9.27	24.92	20.57	39.95

Division 1—Maine, New Hampshire, Vermont, Massachusetts, Rhode Island, Connecticut; Division 2—New York, New Jersey, Pennsylvania; Division 3—Delaware, Maryland, District of Columbia, Virginia, West Virginia; Division 4—North Carolina, South Carolina, Georgia, Florida, Alabama, Mississippi, Louisiana, Texas, Arkansas, Tennessee, Kentucky; Division 5—Ohio, Indiana, Illinois, Michigan, Wisconsin; Division 6—Iowa, Minnesota, Missouri, Kansas, Nebraska; Division 7—Colorado, Nevada, California, Oregon; Division 8—North Dakota, South Dakota, Idaho, Montana, New Mexico, Arizona, Utah, Wyoming, Washington, Oklahoma, Indian Territory.

Source: U.S. Comptroller of the Currency, *Annual Report* (Washington, D.C.: U.S. Government Printing Office), 1887, pp. 62–65; 1888, pp. 44–47; 1889, pp. 174–177; 1897, pp. 347–349.

Table 32

Percentage of National Bank Shares
Held outside the State—
Reserve City Banks
(par value $100)

Year	Div. 1	Div. 2	Div. 3	Div. 4	Div. 5	Div. 6	Div. 7 (SF)
1887	6.65	20.84	6.34	19.47	10.62	36.73	34.07
1888	7.35	22.38	6.18	19.29	11.10	43.87	4.44
1889	7.91	22.52	6.81	20.35	12.96	43.74	8.68
1897	6.75	20.15	6.43	22.08	13.44	30.89	8.40

Source: See Table 31.

holdings of bank stock were equal to 14.7 percent of total loans and discounts of Western national banks and 14.4 percent of total loans and discounts for Pacific banks.[52] Contrary to Breckenridge, these percentages appear to be quite substantial, although they are somewhat smaller for the South. Nevertheless, in the Western region funds for about 15 percent of total loans and discounts were provided from sources outside the state through purchases of bank stock. This method of transferring funds, it may be noted, altered the local banking market structure in an area, whereas the previous two methods did not. Did purchases of this size have relatively large or small effects on interest rates? Once more the distinction between structure and performance must be emphasized. By examining structures facilitating interregional flows of short-term capital and the quantities of funds involved, one cannot say directly what effects they will have; the performance of the market has to be assessed also.

THE COMMERCIAL PAPER MARKET

The commercial paper market represented another important mechanism promoting the interregional flow of funds. However, unlike the rediscount and interbank borrowing markets, which operated within the structure of the correspondent banking system, the commercial paper market was essentially an open, impersonal market. During the late nineteenth and early twentieth centuries the open market in short-term paper expanded rapidly both in volume and in geographical extent. Such growth was the result of outward shifts in both the supply and demand schedules for the new credit instrument.

First we shall consider the supply-side effects. Why were firms willing to offer their paper or notes on the open market rather than just confining their borrowing to local

[52] Breckenridge, "Discount Rates," p. 136.

sources? One reason may have been that local banks were unable to meet the firms' demands for funds because of legal restrictions on lending. The National Banking Act limited loans to a single borrower to one-tenth of the capital and surplus of the bank; similar, but less stringent, provisions were in effect in a number of states. Especially with the growth of large-scale industry in the postbellum period, increasing numbers of firms may have found it difficult to obtain adequate financing from local banks. As a result, they had to go elsewhere, and one of the sources to which they turned was the open market.

A more important motivation for open-market borrowing most probably was the desire to escape the monopoly power, and hence high interest rates, of local banks. In small towns, the market for banking services was limited, so that only a relatively few local banks could be supported. Such a concentrated market structure gave local banks some degree of monopoly power and hence allowed them to extract a premium on local loans above what the open-market, competitive rate on such a loan would have been. The commercial paper market therefore offered the local firm an opportunity to escape the local banking monopoly by selling its note on the open market to a bank in another area. Consequently, the spread of the commercial paper market may have been instrumental in the erosion of local monopoly and thus the decline of local interest rates. A speaker at the 1916 American Bankers' Association convention complained that after a borrower had received an offer of funds at some rate, "which might be far lower than was fair owing to conditions in that locality," he reports it to his local banker and "forces the banker to meet his wishes from the fear of losing his deposit."[53] A. O. Greef attributed much of the growth of the commercial paper market in the period before the Federal Reserve system to the fact that a large

[53] Thomas P. Beal, Jr., "Effect of Increased Operations of Note Brokers upon the Earnings of Commercial Banks," *Proceedings of the American Bankers' Association*, 1916, p. 500.

number of firms in the South and West could borrow much more cheaply on the open market than with their local banks.[54] As a result, the amount of open-market borrowing increased substantially.

On the demand side, commercial banks, which were by far the major purchasers of commercial paper, desired to hold open-market paper in their asset portfolios for several reasons. For one thing, commercial paper made a very good secondary reserve asset. Speakers at a number of state banking conventions during the period strongly advocated the use of commercial paper as a secondary reserve. A banker from Quincy, Illinois, observed in 1916: "My record extending over twelve years shows an average discount rate [on commercial paper] of 4.88 percent. But the loss in earnings between 4.88 and the average local rate is more apparent than real, for had it not been for the possession of this readily available second reserve, larger cash reserves would have been kept idle."[55] One of the chief virtues of commercial paper in this role was its liquidity in the older meaning, referring to an asset actually being paid off in cash at its maturity date. Normal loans were often rather illiquid, often being renewed several times before finally being repaid. "To a considerable degree in the average bank they [local loans] are a fixed asset."[56] On the other hand, commercial paper was never extended and was always paid off at maturity. Because there was not a formal rediscount market in the United States before the establishment of the Federal Reserve system, commercial paper was not always instantly convertible into cash at any moment before its maturity

[54] Albert O. Greef, *The Commercial Paper House in the United States* (Cambridge, Mass.: Harvard University Press, 1938), p. 55.

[55] F. W. Crane, "Commercial Paper Purchased from Brokers," *Proceedings of the Illinois Bankers' Association*, 1916, p. 132. See also N. E. Franklin, "Commercial Paper," *Proceedings of the South Dakota Bankers' Association*, 1912, p. 126; G. A. Rogers, "Loaning Money," *Proceedings of the Kansas Bankers' Association*, 1905, p. 139.

[56] Crane, "Commercial Paper," p. 132.

date, but in most cases city banks stood ready to rediscount paper of their country correspondents. To be sure, C. A. Phillips has noted quite correctly that the liquidity of commercial paper with respect to an individual bank does not imply that it is liquid for the system as a whole, because the paper can be reissued after maturity and just shifted from one bank to another,[57] but this objection has little relevance to its value in an individual bank's portfolio. Commercial paper was a short-term repository of funds which paid a fairly high interest rate and actually paid off at maturity, and thus was a desirable secondary reserve asset.

The attraction of commercial paper as an earning asset in the bank's portfolio was especially strong to country banks. Banks in agricultural areas were subject to strong seasonal fluctuations in the demand for funds. The peak demands came at planting and harvest time, and in the interim the demand was relatively slack. These seasonal "surplus funds," as they were known, were traditionally channelled into bankers' balances, but commercial paper, as it spread across the country, came to be an increasingly attractive alternative. It generally offered a higher yield than bankers' balances did, making it also attractive relative to holding idle balances, needless to say. In addition, commercial paper of varying maturity dates could be purchased, so that idle funds could be invested in paper for exactly the duration of the period of slack demand. For example, if a banker knew that there would be a substantial withdrawal of deposits or an increase in the demand for loans four months in the future, he or she could buy paper maturing in four months, thus keeping funds fully employed but available when they would be needed. On the other hand, local loans, if often renewed or extended, would not fulfill this criterion. C. B. Hazelwood of the Union Trust Company of Chicago argued the advantages of commercial paper in spreading out seasonal loan fluctuations. He observed: "Almost without exception the brokers state that the purchases

[57] Phillips, *Bank Credit*, p. 273.

177

are made in the spring and early summer, thus bringing maturities in the fall. I find that practically no paper is sold to banks in this state during the fall months."[58]

Commercial paper was essentially a discount or promissory note of a borrower put up for sale on the open market. Therefore, like ordinary discounts, it was exclusively a short-term instrument in line, at least superficially, with the real-bills doctrine. Maturity dates on commercial paper usually ranged between two and nine months. Some paper carried maturity dates up to twelve or eighteen months, but only relatively few firms borrowed on the open market with paper longer than six months, and few banks were willing to buy paper with longer maturities.[59] The preferred periods were four, five, or six months, and six months was by far the most common duration.[60] With such a range of short-term maturities, banks found it quite easy to select commercial paper of appropriate duration to cover their slack demand periods which matured as the time loan demand increased.

It was also argued that the prohibition of lending on real estate to national banks severely limited their lending opportunities, resulting in the accumulation of additional "surplus funds." According to the president of the Des Moines National Bank in 1910, Iowa national banks were "driven" into the commercial paper field to find employment for their excess balances which could not be employed locally,[61] although the exercise of local monopoly power through restricting local lending might have been an additional motive.

[58] C. B. Hazelwood, "Commercial Paper as a Secondary Reserve for West Virginia Banks," *Proceedings of the West Virginia Bankers' Association*, 1913, p. 84.

[59] Roy A. Foulke, *The Commercial Paper Market* (New York: The Bankers Publishing Co., 1931), p. 152.

[60] Greef, *The Commercial Paper House*, p. 231.

[61] George E. Barnett, *State Banks and Trust Companies since the Passage of the National-Bank Act* (Washington, D.C.: U.S. Government Printing Office, 1911), pp. 107–108.

In any case, whatever the motivation, commercial paper increasingly served as an outlet for "surplus funds" of country banks. In an 1887 address at the American Bankers' Association it was observed that country bankers in the Midwest—Illinois, Iowa, Michigan, Wisconsin, Indiana—were investing their unemployed funds in commercial paper in greatly increasing amounts.[62] At banking conventions in North Dakota and Nebraska in 1903 and in Michigan in 1904 the practice of investing surplus funds of country banks in commercial paper was noted and it was implied to have been going on for several years.[63] All in all, one contemporary banker concluded, "Commercial paper offers the best outlet for the investment of surplus funds available at the present time."[64]

Another important motive for holding commercial paper was diversification. A country bank located in an agricultural area could inject little variety into its loan portfolio. The fortunes of the great part of its borrowers were tied directly or indirectly to the state of agriculture in its region. By buying commercial paper, the bank could acquire obligations of firms in different industries or in different parts of the country which might be prosperous even though local conditions were depressed. By adding loans to the portfolio that were only weakly related to or independent of local loans, the country banker could thus reduce the risk of his or her loan portfolio. As Phillips observed, more elegantly,

[62] W. H. Baker, "Commercial Paper," *Proceedings of the American Bankers' Association*, 1887, p. 45.

[63] Noble Crandall, "Commercial Paper," *Proceedings of the Nebraska Bankers' Association*, 1903, p. 188; H. P. Hilliard, untitled address, *Proceedings of the Michigan Bankers' Association*, 1904, p. 69; E. Royse, "The Critical Season in Banking in Nebraska," *Proceedings of the Nebraska Bankers' Association*, 1903, p. 365; E. M. Stevens, "Commercial Paper," *Proceedings of the North Dakota Bankers' Association*, 1903, p. 31.

[64] James K. Lynch, "Banking in Theory and Practice," *Proceedings of the Arizona Bankers' Association*, 1910, p. 35.

179

"It is a 'strong anchor to windward' to have a part of the banks' funds invested in quarters not affected by the depression at home."[65]

Portfolio diversification could be achieved by purchasing paper from different regions or different industries, which were relatively insulated from local business fluctuations. For example, a bank in cattle country could purchase notes from firms other than cattle companies, and so on. Country bankers were increasingly urged to take advantage of commercial paper in reducing risk. In 1908 a speaker at the Oregon Bankers' Association convention, for instance, stressed the benefits of geographical diversification of bank assets.[66] It seemed to be a common practice to select at least some commercial paper issued by firms in different industries from those of local customers and located in different areas of the country in order to diversify the loan portfolio.[67] Country banks usually did not have the resources to make interregional loans directly. Consequently, the spread of the commercial paper market afforded them opportunities to diversify and thus reduce the risk of their loan portfolio.

An interaction of supply and demand influences contributed to the growth of the commercial paper market. On the supply side, local firms could escape local banking monopolies and high interest rates by offering their own promissory notes for sale on the open market. On the demand side, also, there were strong motives for banks to participate in the commercial paper market. Commercial paper was a very desirable secondary reserve asset for banks, and thus a good investment of surplus funds. In addition, the purchase of open-market paper allowed local banks to diversify their portfolio of earning assets. Which of these effects was the dominant one in the growth of the commercial paper market? Did local firms first sell their paper to note brokers,

[65] Phillips, *Bank Credit*, p. 274.

[66] W. O. Jones, "The Ideal Country Banker," *Proceedings of the Oregon Bankers' Association*, 1908, p. 65.

[67] Greef, *The Commercial Paper House*, p. 336.

leaving local banks with idle funds with which they began to purchase open-market paper, or was the sequence reversed so that the strong demand for commercial paper by banks lured firms into borrowing on the open market?

Such questions are difficult ones to resolve even in specific local markets, and unfortunately, in general, relevant data on local commercial paper markets are not available to answer this question conclusively. However, some figures on the timing of the spread of the commercial paper market into selected cities are presented in Table 33. The timing

Table 33

Spread of the Commercial Paper Market into Selected Cities

City	Approximate date of first sale by local firms to brokers	Approximate date of first sale by brokers to local banks
Akron, Ohio	1902	1906
Columbus, Ohio	1907	1912
Joliet, Ill.	1908	—
Dallas, Texas	1910	1910
Portland, Oregon	1906	1908
Spokane, Wash.	1911	1911

Source: C. A. Phillips, *Bank Credit* (New York: Macmillan Company, 1920), p. 135. Reprinted with the permission of Mr. C. A. Phillips.

sequences there suggest that local firms sold their obligations before local banks began to buy paper, implying that the demand for open-market paper was created by local firms first borrowing in the open market. Of course, the demand for paper by distant banks may have induced local firms to borrow on the open market, so no general overall timing sequence may be necessarily inferred.

Thus far, motives for issuing and purchasing commercial paper have been discussed to establish some of the reasons for the growth of the open market. Now we shall examine

181

the expansion itself in the postbellum period, first in terms of its spread geographically and then in terms of increases in volume.

The open market in commercial paper began to develop in the United States in the early nineteenth century and is chronicled extensively in A. O. Greef's *The Commercial Paper House in the United States*. In the antebellum period the great majority of the dealers in negotiable paper acted as brokers, rather than as buyers and sellers of notes. They would not buy the note directly from its maker, but rather would try to find a customer for it. Because of this practice, they were generally known as "note brokers" or "bill brokers," because they made no commitment to purchase the notes themselves and functioned only as intermediaries or brokers. In contrast, the commercial paper house, which developed somewhat later, purchased the paper it later offered for sale outright. The house first bought all the paper which it later marketed, but it also served the same intermediary function as the note broker.[68]

In the antebellum period, commercial paper operations, unsurprisingly, developed in such Eastern financial centers as Boston, New York, and Philadelphia. But even at those early dates the commercial paper market was not confined to large Eastern cities. It spread to smaller cities in the East; for example, a commercial paper operation was established in Hartford as early as 1855. Furthermore, the open market was by no means limited to the East. By 1850 a number of brokers seem to have been active in Cincinnati and somewhat later in St. Louis. The South was not excluded either. Open-market operations in notes seem to have been going on in New Orleans since the 1840s, spreading to Louisville by 1860.[69] The commercial paper market then appears to have been an established fact not only in Eastern cities, but also in some larger Southern and Western cities in the late antebellum period.

[68] Ibid., p. 31.   [69] Ibid., pp. 25–26.

The westward expansion of commercial paper dealers was somewhat inhibited by the Civil War and the subsequent monetary uncertainty until the resumption of specie payments. Nevertheless, twenty-four Boston notebrokers were listed in the 1867 *Massachusetts Register and Directory of the United States and Canada*.[70] The number of note dealers indicates quite a competitive market. As a result, in 1863 *Bankers' Magazine* complained: "During the last ten years relations between the mercantile class and banks have changed. Before that merchants relied on banks for accommodation. Since then the practice has been growing of relying more and more on bill-brokers for money borrowed by the negotiation of notes. This change of method in the use of deposits and of borrowing money is confined to the large cities. . . . In this way brokers and private banks have acquired an extraordinary power over the money market."[71]

Over the early postbellum period commercial paper dealings spread westward into Midwestern cities. Note brokers began to become respectable in Chicago in the 1870s, and private banking houses began dealing in commercial paper around 1880; by 1902 some ten commercial paper houses had been established in Chicago. Similarly, brokers were combining open-market paper dealings with security brokerage in Indianapolis as early as 1871. By 1875 note brokers had moved to Minneapolis and St. Paul; by 1881 "bankers and brokers" were buying and selling notes in Kansas City.[72] Indeed, by the late 1880s commercial paper dealers had firmly established themselves in Midwestern cities, so that at the 1887 American Bankers' Association convention it was noted that there were "dealers long established in the business" operating in Milwaukee and the commercial paper market was "no longer an experiment in the West."[73]

[70] Ibid., pp. 38–39.
[71] "Bank Loans," *Bankers' Magazine*, XXXVII (May 1883), pp. 52, 54.
[72] Greef, *The Commercial Paper House*, p. 39.
[73] Baker, "Commercial Paper," p. 47.

Expansion of commercial paper dealers to the Pacific Coast and far West took place around the turn of the century. Open-market paper operations began in San Francisco, Los Angeles, and Seattle about 1900.[74] Dealings in Portland began somewhat later, about 1906.[75] At the 1908 Oregon Bankers' Association convention it was mentioned that "one of the leading commercial paper firms in New York has recently established a branch in one of the cities of the Pacific Northwest."[76] It was not, however, until 1910 that commercial paper operations began in Dallas.[77] By the beginning of the Federal Reserve period, commercial paper dealers were operating in most major cities from coast to coast.

The westward movement of the commercial paper dealers from the Eastern cities, to Midwestern cities, and ultimately to the Pacific Coast, however, did not necessarily represent an expansion of the interregional flow of funds. If the commercial paper dealer in Kansas City, for example, dealt only in notes of local borrowers, then the impact of the introduction of the commercial paper market on the interregional transfer of funds would be quite small. Gathering detailed information about the location of both the buyers and sellers of commercial paper in various markets is extremely difficult, but a sample of note offering lists strongly suggests that the commercial paper market was a national, rather than a local, one. For instance, a list of offerings of a Boston firm as early as 1873 included paper from borrowers in Cincinnati, Oshkosh, Memphis, St. Louis, and Louisville as well as from the East Coast; another Boston firm's 1874 list included paper from firms in New Orleans, San Francisco, Kansas City, Terre Haute, Columbus, Mississippi, Cedar Rapids, and Mobile.[78]

[74] Greef, *The Commercial Paper House*, p. 39.
[75] Phillips, *Bank Credit*, p. 135.
[76] Jones, "The Ideal Country Banker," p. 66.
[77] Ibid.
[78] Greef, *The Commercial Paper House*, Exhibits 12, 13.

Phillips argued that interregional flows of funds were slow in developing. As late as the late 1880s Eastern bankers were said to be limiting their purchases to Eastern paper, in spite of the fact that attractive Western paper was available, so that 1890 marked the dividing point after which Eastern funds began to flow westward through the commercial paper market.[79] However, no evidence is presented to support this assertion, which seems overstated, if not clearly incorrect, in view of the substantial number of Southern and Western borrowers we have cited on Boston dealers' offering lists even in the early 1870s.

The timing of this geographic expansion of commercial paper dealers does not tell the entire story, however. Even if a paper dealer moved into town, it did not necessarily follow that local borrowers or lenders would avail themselves of his services immediately and in such quantity so as to affect local credit conditions and interest rates. In addition, local banks could have bought commercial paper through correspondents or out-of-town brokers previously. In similar fashion, it would certainly be misleading to argue that the commercial paper market had no effects on a region before a dealer established himself there. Even with no local broker, a borrower could sell his notes on the open market through an out-of-town broker. Indeed, the spread of commercial paper dealers understates the true expansion of the commercial paper market because firms could have been borrowing through the open market and banks could have been buying paper well before a dealer was established in an area. Consequently, in addition to the spread of dealers, the growth of open-market borrowing by firms and the growth of investing bank funds in commercial paper should be examined.

Little information is available directly on the geographic expansion of open-market borrowing by firms. Only a few specific incidents are known of local stringency leading to open-market borrowing, such as the case of St. Joseph,

[79] Phillips, *Bank Credit*, p. 134.

Missouri. Credit demands were said to be persistently above the lending capabilities of local banks, so to meet their demand for funds local firms began to borrow on the open market. Only years later, around 1900, did local St. Joseph banks have the "surplus funds" to invest in commercial paper.[80] Baltimore is said to provide a similar example.[81] However, the practice of widespread open-market borrowing seems to have developed fairly early. By 1884, a Canadian banker noted that American firms from nearly every state in the country were borrowing on the open market on their "one-name unsecured bills."[82] Note brokers appear to have been quite successful in luring customers away from local banks, in view of the number of complaints that the local banks voiced.

On the other hand, somewhat more can be said about the growth of the practice of investing bank funds in commercial paper. First, the distinction should be made between the introduction of the commercial paper market into an area and the actual purchase of paper in substantial amounts so as to have an effect on the composition of bank portfolios. In St. Louis, for instance, even though commercial paper dealers had been established there for some time, banks were said to have been opposed to the purchase of open-market paper "until after the financial strain in that center in 1897," and thereafter invested large sums in commercial paper.[83] Similarly, Kansas City banks, even with an established open market since the 1880s, bought little commercial paper until after 1897.[84] Panics also encouraged the growth of the commercial paper market. The Panic of 1907 was a real boon to growth after several New York banks had been able to meet financial demands for credit only with funds made available by maturing commercial paper.[85]

---

[80] Foulke, *The Commercial Paper Market*, p. 251.
[81] Ibid.
[82] Greef, *The Commercial Paper House*, p. 43.
[83] Ibid., p. 48.   [84] Ibid.
[85] Foulke, *The Commercial Paper Market*, p. 65.

In assessing the spread of the commercial paper market, the role of country banks as purchasers of commercial paper must also be considered. Did the commercial paper market spread westward quite rapidly from city to city, but then move into the countryside only very slowly? Were country banks resistant to the new institution and consequently to innovations in the interregional transfers of funds? Margaret Myers argued that country banks were very conservative in their acceptance of single-name paper, many preferring to discount only their own customers' notes, risking an undiversified portfolio, rather than to buy open-market paper.[86] A banker from Atlanta in 1898 warned: "Lend your money to your regular customers and do not make a rule of buying commercial paper. . . . Do not permit any loans to be made to anyone on single-name paper, unless otherwise secured, no matter what the commercial rating may be."[87] A few years later a Kansas banker noted, "Most of the smaller banks expressing a preference for commercial paper are tenacious in their insistence for two or more good names on each note."[88] Such insistence on double-name paper is rather puzzling in view of the evidence in Table 5 that single-name paper was relatively more abundant in interior regions than in the East. Possibly personal knowledge of the borrower in local loans provided the same increased security to the country banker that additional signers on commercial paper did.

Nevertheless, in spite of these admonitions, country banks had compelling incentives to purchase commercial paper—in order to diversify their portfolio, to hold a secondary reserve, and to provide employment for "surplus funds."

[86] Margaret G. Myers, *The New York Money Market, Volume I: Origins and Development* (New York: Columbia University Press, 1931), p. 231.

[87] W. S. Witham, untitled address, *Proceedings of the American Bankers' Association Convention*, 1898, pp. 128, 130.

[88] C. C. K. Scoville, "The Best Class of Investments for the Average Kansas Bank," *Proceedings of the Kansas Bankers' Association*, 1903, p. 78.

Moreover, paper dealers went to great efforts to sell their wares in the countryside. Commercial paper was offered to country bankers "almost daily whether through the mails or through the travelling representatives of the bond and commercial paper houses who at present radiate from financial centers and press their wares into almost every hamlet."[89] For example, by the 1890s the six major Chicago houses were already maintaining traveling agents to sell open-market paper to country banks throughout the Midwest.[90] To gather business the commercial paper dealer also sent out "scores of telegrams offering money to the borrowers at the market in the country plus his commission. . . ."[91] Consequently, with the use of the telegraph, correspondence, or traveling salesmen, dealers could establish relationships with both borrowers and buyers far away from the main office.[92] How long, then, did it take for the commercial paper market to spread from the cities into the countryside?

The commercial paper market, which was well established in Midwestern cities by the late 1880s,[93] spread through the countryside in the next decade and was well known to most country bankers there by the turn of the century. A speaker at the 1916 meetings of the American Bankers' Association recalled a tour he had taken of the Dakotas and Minnesota in 1897. At that time, he observed, "Note brokers were almost unknown in that section."[94] However, only a few years later, at the 1903 North Dakota Bankers' Association meeting, a speaker seemed to assume that North Dakota bankers were already quite familiar with commercial paper.[95] Around the same time in neighboring Minnesota, banks in only moderate-sized towns were said to be "supplementing

[89] Jones, "The Ideal Country Banker," p. 64.
[90] Melchior Palyi, *The Chicago Credit Market* (Chicago: University of Chicago Press, 1937), p. 96.
[91] Beal, "Effect of Increased Operations," p. 500.
[92] Greef, *The Commercial Paper House*, p. 42.
[93] Baker, "Commercial Paper," p. 47.
[94] Beal, "Effect of Increased Operations," p. 500.
[95] Stevens, "Commercial Paper," p. 29.

their reserves with purchased paper of the highest grade."[96] The purchase of commercial paper with idle funds at that time was "in general practice throughout the Northwest."[97]

Similarly, in Nebraska in 1903 it was observed that the sale of commercial paper there had sprung up only in the last few years, because there was also a surplus of funds there.[98] Another Nebraska banker in 1903 pointed to the large amount of idle funds in the summer and noted that the practice of buying commercial paper with them was becoming quite prevalent with the interior bankers of the state.[99] In the same year in Kansas, "all the banks in the larger towns" and many of the smaller country banks were said to "find it necessary to employ a considerable portion of their funds in carrying this commercial paper made mostly in the East."[100]

The situation is somewhat more ambiguous on the Pacific Coast. Dealers were established in San Francisco, Los Angeles, and Seattle around 1900. However, according to a local banker, Los Angeles banks had only small amounts of funds available for commercial paper purchases until after 1903.[101] A Portland bank official reported that he started to buy commercial paper about 1900; on the other hand, a Boston dealer, having visited Portland and Seattle in 1907, reported that banks there were loaned up and buying almost no outside paper.[102] About 1910 it was noted that operations of commercial paper houses were "well known" to Arizona bankers.[103]

The South deserves special consideration. Lance Davis has argued that the spread of the commercial paper market

[96] Greef, *The Commercial Paper House*, p. 48.
[97] Stevens, "Commercial Paper," p. 31.
[98] Crandall, "Commercial Paper," p. 188.
[99] Royse, "The Critical Season," p. 366.
[100] Scoville, "The Best Class," p. 79.
[101] Greef, *The Commercial Paper House*, p. 49.
[102] Ibid.
[103] James K. Lynch, "Modern Tendencies and Ancient Principles," *Proceedings of the Arizona Bankers' Association*, 1909, p. 50.

was the institutional change responsible for promoting inter-regional transfers of funds and, consequently, interregional capital market integration. The South was essentially a region apart, participating very little in the process of interregional capital market integration going on in the late nineteenth century, and the reason that it was not woven into the fabric of the national market was that the commercial paper market did not develop there, as opposed to all the other regions.[104] To support this assertion he mentions a 1908 statement of a New York banker that the South was the only region of the country not buying commercial paper to any great extent.[105] In addition, the Superintendent of Banks of Minnesota observed in 1911, "The market for commercial paper extends over the length and breadth of this land, excepting some portions of the Southern States."[106]

Was the South in fact isolated from the commercial paper market? In 1906 Festus J. Wade noted that cities such as Little Rock, Dallas, Memphis, and Nashville had become a "field for the commercial note brokers."[107] It also seems to have been distributed in Dallas well before the first commercial paper house was established there in 1910. So commercial paper was known in a number of Southern cities. Furthermore, knowledge of open-market paper does not appear to have been confined to the cities. Even earlier, in 1904, reference was made to country banks in Arkansas, hardly financial centers, buying commercial paper directly from brokers.[108] In 1908 a dealer observed: "Hundreds of small country banks are more and more resorting to commercial paper. We have purchased in one day over $250,000 of commercial paper for a Texas bank."[109] The practice of

[104] Davis, "The Investment Market," pp. 388–390.
[105] Ibid., p. 390.
[106] K. S. Chase, "Registration of Commercial Paper," *Proceedings of the Minnesota Bankers' Association*, 1911, p. 31.
[107] Festus J. Wade, "What Causes Fluctuations in Money Rates?" *Proceedings of the New York Bankers' Association*, 1906, p. 36.
[108] Hilliard, in *Proceedings*, p. 72.
[109] Jones, "The Ideal Country Banker," p. 63.

investing funds in commercial paper seems to have been known to Southern bankers and was increasingly employed. In 1912 a Chicago banker stated: "In the South and West the idea of investment in commercial paper by country banks has been growing in importance every year. As a matter of fact, about ten years ago there were very few bankers in the cities or agricultural towns of our middle Western states who believed in the policy of loaning any money outside of their own community. We have seen a gradual change in this respect however. . . ."[110] This statement is consistent with our evidence indicating that Midwestern country banks began purchasing commercial paper in quantity around 1900 and also indicates that Southern and Western banks also began to purchase open-market paper, although somewhat later. Moreover, the South also participated in other aspects of the interregional capital market, receiving significant inflows of funds through interbank borrowing and direct interregional lending.

The practice of buying or selling commercial paper in an area, then, could and often actually did precede the establishment of a commercial paper dealer. Greef stated that it should not be surprising that both practices seem to have become nationwide some years before commercial paper houses had covered the entire country.[111] By 1901 even "small country banks" were said to have become "heavy purchasers of market paper."[112] In fact, Greef estimated that the market for commercial paper was essentially nationwide by around the turn of the century.[113] A few years later, in 1904, one banker grumbled, ". . . there go out daily from St. Louis or from Chicago anywhere from one to half a dozen circular letters to banks all over the South and West offering them paper made by Tom, Dick, and Harry, issued in territory extending from Maine to California and from Washing-

---

[110] Hazelwood, "Commercial Paper," p. 85.
[111] Greef, *The Commercial Paper House*, p. 42.
[112] Ibid., p. 49.   [113] Ibid., p. 50.

ton to Florida."[114] In 1912 a large paper house failed whose paper "was scattered from Maine to California, and from Canada to Gulf of Mexico" and was sold to 200 or more banks.[115] The commercial paper market essentially covered the United States by the early years of the twentieth century. After the Panic of 1907, which demonstrated the merits of commercial paper as a secondary reserve, Greef thought it likely that the market for commercial paper had become virtually as wide as it has been at any later time.[116]

After charting the geographical expansion of the commercial paper market, we shall now consider its growth in volume. It is not sufficient to know that the commercial paper market became a nationwide one during the period in order to be able to assess the role of commercial paper in interregional transfers of funds; some sense of the importance of commercial paper as an asset is also necessary. Did it constitute a significant proportion of the asset portfolio of the bank? Did the volume of paper sold in the open market increase substantially during the period? Unfortunately, but unsurprisingly, the data are not available to answer these questions. Bank balance sheets cannot be used to determine the proportion of commercial paper held, because commercial paper was not reported as a separate asset. Rather, it was lumped together under "Discounts," which included not only discounts purchased on the open market, commercial paper, but also local discounts. As a result, there is no way to separate out commercial paper holdings from holdings of ordinary discounts.

Instead, contemporary estimates of the volume of commercial paper must be relied upon. In 1882 Alonzo Follet, a New York dealer, failed and at that time had been selling about $100 million of paper per year; at the same time a bank president estimated that New York banks were buying $1 million of commercial paper a day, although Greef

114 Hilliard, in *Proceedings*, p. 69.
115 Franklin, "Commercial Paper," p. 130.
116 Greef, *The Commercial Paper House*, p. 51.

thought these figures exaggerated.[117] From these estimates one cannot infer the size of commercial paper in bank portfolios because it is not known whether all of the purchased paper went into New York bank portfolios. Indeed, that would seem most unlikely, because New York banks regularly bought open-market paper for their correspondents.

A New York banker in 1906 estimated that more than $500 million of commercial paper per year was sold in the New York market. From this figure, Greef concluded that the total volume of commercial paper in the United States at that time was in excess of $1 billion.[118] Estimates of a yearly volume of $2 billion in 1908 and more than $5 billion in 1912 were deemed to be substantially inflated. More realistic is a 1913 estimate, calculating total 1912 sales of commercial paper to be about $1.7 billion.[119] The commercial paper market did grow more rapidly after the Panic of 1907, and Greef estimated total sales volume at the end of our period, 1914, as about $2 billion per year.[120] This indicates something less than a doubling of total sales between 1906 and 1914. The figure that Lance Davis quotes of almost a tripling of sales between 1907 and 1914[121] may be somewhat of an overestimate.

Let us take $1.7 billion to be the total volume of paper sold in 1912. If we assume that the average maturity of a commercial loan was approximately that of commercial paper, six months, we can compute the total volume of loans made by all banks in 1912. A rough calculation then indicates that commercial paper constituted a little more than 5 percent of total loans on average in bank portfolios at the end of our period. This figure is roughly in the same ballpark as the 1931 estimate of Foulke that commercial paper outstanding at any one time averaged from 5 to 12 percent of all unsecured bank loans.[122] In 1921 the volume

---

[117] Ibid., p. 54.
[118] Ibid., p. 56.
[119] Ibid., p. 58.
[120] Ibid., pp. 59–60.
[121] Davis, "The Investment Market," p. 390.
[122] Foulke, *The Commercial Paper Market*, p. 18.

of paper handled by commercial paper houses equalled nearly 10 percent of loans made by national banks that year.[123]

We cannot, however, compute the changes in the proportion of commercial paper to total loans and discounts over time; nor can we calculate regional variations in commercial paper holdings by banks, both of which facts are important in assessing the spread of the commercial paper market.

What effect did the expansion of the commercial paper market have on local competition for loans? Did the note broker prove to be a strong competitor for borrowers against local banks? To judge from the number of complaints from bankers, the westward expansion of note brokers posed a substantial threat to the normal methods of doing business. As early as 1883, *Bankers' Magazine* observed that "brokers and private bankers have acquired an extraordinary power over the money market," although at that time their influence was confined to larger cities.[124]

The inexorable march westward of the commercial paper market led to a denunciation by J. K. Deming of Dubuque of such "modern methods of soliciting business" at the 1892 Iowa Bankers' Association convention. The impersonal note broker disturbed the warm, personal relationships between local banker and borrower. He complained:

> Until recently western bankers were able to maintain their loaning rates regardless of the depression of the eastern markets, but now there has arisen an element which wages constant war on established rates. It is the festive note-broker, who, with his eastern capital, steps in to disturb the harmonious relations between banker and borrower, and just at a time when there seems to be an opportunity to dispose of idle funds at a profitable rate,

[123] Walter McAvoy, "The Economic Importance of the Commercial Paper House," *Journal of Political Economy*, XXX (February 1922), p. 79.

[124] "Bank Loans," p. 54.

the banker is confronted with the alternative of cutting his rate or seeing his loans going to outside dealers.[125]

As the commercial paper market spread, evidence of dissatisfaction on the part of local bankers at the competition offered by note brokers increased. In the early part of the twentieth century, bankers criticized the "demoralizing" effects of underbidding by brokers.[126] Bank customers did not seem constrained by ties of loyalty to their local banks. F. W. Crane, Cashier of the State Savings Loan and Trust Company of Quincy, Illinois, remarked resignedly that "experience has mollified any antagonism the local banker may have felt toward commercial paper. To be sure he has often seen his customer leave him for the lower rates of a broker. . . ."[127] Another banker grumbled:

Borrowers no longer confine themselves to one place, but go where funds can be procured to the greatest advantage. Merchants in the smaller towns go away from home to borrow money and bankers in smaller cities go away from home to procure investments. Often bankers do not feel that they can break the rate locally, but it frequently happens that they will send to the large money centers and buy the paper of their home merchants at a lower rate than they could take the note for direct. ⅛ percent will take many a businessman from home for his accommodation.[128]

By the turn of the century the influence of the commercial paper market certainly seemed to have extended itself into the countryside. N. E. Franklin of Deadwood, South Dakota, recognized the challenge of the note broker to country

[125] J. K. Deming, "Modern Methods of Soliciting Business," *Proceedings of the Iowa Bankers' Association*, 1892, p. 21.

[126] Joseph T. Talbert, "Commercial Paper," *Proceedings of the Minnesota Bankers' Association*, 1908, p. 46.

[127] Crane, "Commercial Paper," p. 131.

[128] Walter H. Hull, ed., *Practical Problems in Banking and Currency* (New York: Macmillan Company, 1907), p. 45.

bankers: "We bankers of the smaller cities and towns have a danger confronting us which we must look squarely in the face. The time is not far distant when note brokerage houses will be offering for sale the paper of our high grade customers at a much lower rate than these customers are now paying us."[129] This competition forced local bankers to reduce their lending rates, because often the borrower would produce a quoted rate from a broker and the local banker would have to meet it or see his customer go elsewhere.[130]

This competition from brokers led to the formation of a committee on credit information by the American Bankers' Association, which issued its report in 1908. It decried the competition of note brokers. "The scramble on the part of note brokers for paper to sell, the eager competition for attractive names which are 'good sellers,' voluntary offers of increased lines of credit, the bidding of low rates of interest, are demoralizing and lead to a general lowering of rates on all commercial loans beyond the point justified by legitimate competition and the supply of loanable funds."[131] It went on to condemn this "heedless competition," which even extended to such practices as reducing commissions to borrower or "sacrificing them altogether" in order to obtain quality paper for their list of offerings.[132]

One effect of this increased competition from note brokers should have been the reduction of local interest rates. In 1887 discount houses in the Midwest were said to have offered paper at 6 percent, as compared with the prevailing bank rates of 8–9 percent.[133] The commercial paper market facilitated the flow of funds among regions, directing funds from areas where they were abundant to areas in which they were scarce. For example, Hartford and Providence were

---

[129] Franklin, "Commercial Paper," p. 130.

[130] Beal, "Effect of Increased Operations," p. 500.

[131] "Report of the Committee on Credit Information," *Proceedings of the American Bankers' Association*, 1908, p. 197.

[132] Ibid., p. 198.

[133] Palyi, *The Chicago Credit Market*, p. 96.

two cities that had large supplies of funds and also were large purchasers of commercial paper.[134] Contemporaries were quite aware of the function of the open market in channeling funds from capital-scarce areas, thus reducing interregional interest-rate differentials. South Dakota bankers were warned that "the banks of the larger cities will be your competitors to the extent that they will control your loaning rate and eventually we will see a uniform rate of interest extending all over the United States."[135] As early as 1903 Nebraska bankers were told that commercial paper was very effective in equalizing interregional demand and supply for funds.[136] In 1922 in assessing the economic effects of the commercial paper house, Walter McAvoy emphasized the role of commercial paper in equalizing demands and supplies of funds across regions.[137]

The modern version of this theory is propounded by Lance Davis. As the commercial paper market spread westward, more and more cities and towns were integrated into the market, which ultimately became a nationwide one. Capital began to move more easily among regions, and as a result of the inflow of funds, rates in high-interest-rate areas began to decline.[138] In Chapter VI the effects of the spread of the commercial paper market on the narrowing interregional interest-rate differentials will be examined.

The commercial paper market represented another institutional response to the problem of interregional transfers of funds. It was a well-developed, open, impersonal market, in contrast to the rediscount and interbank borrowing market, which operated within the framework of the correspondent banking system. The open market in paper also served

[134] Albert Bolles, *Practical Banking*, 7th ed. (New York: Homans Publishing Co., 1890), p. 63.

[135] Franklin, "Commercial Paper," p. 130.

[136] C. F. Bentley, "Commercial Paper as an Investment for Country Banks," *Proceedings of the Nebraska Bankers' Association*, 1903, pp. 174–185.

[137] McAvoy, "Economic Importance," pp. 78–87.

[138] Davis, "The Investment Market," p. 373.

as a substitute for an interstate branch banking system, which was outlawed, just as the correspondent banking system did. This function of the commercial paper market in facilitating interregional flows of funds and substituting for branch banking was noted by Phillips and Greef.[139] Thus, the commercial paper market, even though its origins lay in antebellum times, was another institution that developed rapidly in the postbellum period to promote the interregional transfer of funds.

[139] Phillips, *Bank Credit*, p. 139; Greef, *The Commercial Paper House*, pp. 388–389.

CHAPTER VI

The Process of Capital Market Integration

FRAMING THE HYPOTHESES

REGIONAL interest rates, which were widely dispersed in the antebellum period, converged markedly in the late nineteenth century, as evidenced in Figures 1 through 4. What forces were at work in promoting the development of a national market in short-term capital? Was this integration of regional capital markets the result of institutional changes promoting interregional flows of funds, as Breckenridge had argued was necessary? In this chapter three principal hypotheses about the forces underlying short-term capital market integration in the postbellum United States will be examined: the institutional change hypothesis, the market power hypothesis, and the perfect market hypothesis.

The two major hypotheses concerning this process of integration in the literature assume the existence of an imperfect capital market because of the persistence of interregional interest rate differences. Barriers to capital mobility must have existed between local capital markets or else capital flows would have been induced to equalize the rates. In examining the movement toward short-term capital market integration, Lance Davis emphasizes the role of institutional change. Davis discounts the importance of such mechanisms as direct solicitation of interregional funds and rediscounting in promoting interregional transfers, arguing that their effectiveness was quite limited. It was "doubtful that the volume of funds moved by these techniques would have been sufficient to arbitrage out the regional differentials."[1] Rather, this unexploited possibility for interregional

[1] Lance Davis, "The Investment Market, 1870–1914: The Evolution of a National Market," *Journal of Economic History*, XXV (September 1965) p. 372.

199

arbitrage led to the growth of a new financial market which facilitated the transfer of short-term funds across regions. The important development in the late nineteenth century that wove the segmented regional and local short-term capital markets together into a national one, according to Davis, was the westward spread of the commercial paper market, which drew more and more borrowers and lenders together into one market. In the antebellum period the commercial paper market had been confined primarily to Eastern cities; by the turn of the century it climaxed its westward movement by reaching the Pacific Coast. Davis notes that the timing of this expansion conformed quite closely to the narrowing of interregional interest rate differentials.[2] Thus, the geographic expansion of a new institution, the commercial paper market, was the primary force breaking down the barriers to capital mobility and facilitating interregional transfers of funds.

In contrast to Lance Davis's picture of widespread barriers to interregional transfers of funds, Richard Sylla views the national banking system as a very efficient mobilizer of funds for industrialization by encouraging the concentration of deposits of rural banks in cities, thus facilitating the flow of funds from agriculture into industry. In spite of the efficiency of the national banking system in allocating funds, interest rate differentials also continued to exist because of the influence of the National Banking Act. Interregional and city-country differentials were due primarily to the influence of local monopoly.[3] The erection of legal barriers to entry by the National Banking Act gave country national banks a quasi-monopoly position in the local market.

The tax on state bank notes restricted competition from state banks, according to Sylla, whereas relatively high minimum capital requirements and the prohibition of lending

[2] Ibid.
[3] Richard Sylla, "Federal Policy, Banking Market Structure, and Capital Mobilization in the United States, 1863–1913," *Journal of Economic History*, XXIX (December 1969), pp. 657–685.

on real estate limited competition in small towns among national banks themselves. Such provisions seriously impeded entry in small towns, enabling country bankers there to exercise monopoly power in the form of exacting higher loan rates. Sylla contends, therefore, that the interregional and city-country interest rate differentials reflected the monopoly power possessed by country bankers.[4] This interpretation is roughly consistent with the views of the Populists, who identified monopolistic elements as being responsible for high interest rates in the countryside. Usually Eastern bankers bore the brunt of the Populist wrath, but one observer did identify the national banking laws as "conceived in infamy and . . . for no other purpose but to rob the many for the few."[5]

Sylla thus argues that the barriers to entry established by the National Banking Act deprived large sections of the country of adequate banking services and that the resultant popular dissatisfaction ultimately led to the passage of the Gold Standard Act of 1900. That act lowered the minimum capital requirements for national banks to $25,000 in towns of population less than 3,000. The result was a rapid expansion in the number of national banks chartered, and almost 60 percent of them were formed in the Southern states and West North Central states where entry barriers were supposed to have had their greatest impact.[6] This increase in competition in rural regions eroded away the monopoly power of local country bankers, leading to the convergence of regional interest rates. The Sylla hypothesis is one version of the more general market power hypothesis, which identifies decreases in local monopoly power as the principal influence in narrowing interest rate differentials.

Both of these explanations postulate an imperfect capital market, with Davis emphasizing barriers to interregional

[4] Ibid., p. 685.
[5] John D. Hicks, *The Populist Revolt* (Lincoln: University of Nebraska Press, 1931), p. 92.
[6] Sylla, "Federal Policy," p. 664.

capital mobility and Sylla emphasizing the role of legal barriers to entry in the local banking market. George Stigler, however, criticizes the basic approach of identifying interest rate differentials with capital market imperfections.[7] One should not be too quick in identifying differentials with imperfections; transactions and information costs must also be considered. Finding potential uses of funds and evaluating their risks in distant regions required the use of resources. Thus, the interest rate differentials between regions may have reflected transactions and information costs.[8] If the differentials reflected real costs, then Stigler would argue that no imperfections were present in the capital market. Declines in the interest rate differentials between regions therefore may have reflected decreases in information costs.[9]

[7] George Stigler, "Imperfections in the Capital Market," *Journal of Political Economy*, LXXV (June 1967), p. 288.

[8] Ibid., p. 291.

[9] A transactions costs explanation for the observed interest-rate differentials has been argued by Richard Keehn. Following Sylla, he investigated the effects of local market structures in Wisconsin banking during the period 1870–1900 on bank performance, using the ratio of loans to total assets as the measure of performance, because a bank with monopoly power would restrict loans relative to one operating in a competitive market. He found that differences in the degree of bank competition explained little of the interbank variation in loan ratios and attributed differentials in interest rates to the existence of high transfer costs between markets, which declined over time due to technological improvements in transportation and communication.

However, there is a more direct method of estimating the transfer costs of funds, by examining exchange rates. In a competitive market the exchange rate between cities should reflect the cost of transporting cash from one city to another. Even in the late 1830s, a period before the dramatic advances in transportation and communication, the highest quoted exchange rate was only 2.5 percent. The domestic exchange rates quoted in *Bradstreet's* in the late nineteenth century were substantially smaller. Consequently, transfer costs could account for only a small part of the total observed differentials.

In his disequilibrium growth model of the postbellum economy, Jeffrey Williamson also postulates a fixed per-unit search or information cost incurred with an interregional transfer of funds that is

Such a formulation however is not testable in that form. Declines in interest rate differentials are taken as evidence of decreases in interregional search and information costs; there is no independent measure of information costs to be used in testing this hypothesis. Another factor that could explain interest rate differentials, besides information costs, without having to resort to the assumption of segmented local capital markets, is the difference in the risk of loans across regions.[10] Even in a perfect capital market, interest rates would not have been uniform if local loans differed in

given by existing institutional arrangements.

Information costs are more difficult to get at. It may well have been the case that the freer flow of information had a significant influence in reducing local monopoly, but in its present form it is not a testable hypothesis. We have no independent measure of information costs. Some possibilties might be the number of miles of telegraph line per square mile in an area or else telegram charges, but most likely these would work essentially like a time trend, conveying little information themselves.

Richard Keehn, "Federal Bank Policy, Bank Market Structure and Bank Performance: Wisconsin, 1863–1914," *Business History Review*, XLVIII (Spring 1974), pp. 1–27; Ralph C. H. Catterall, *The Second Bank of the United States* (Chicago: University of Chicago Press, 1903), p. 507; Jeffrey Williamson, *Late Nineteenth-Century American Development* (Cambridge: Cambridge University Press, 1974), p. 129.

[10] Risk to an economist is the spread, the variance or standard deviation, of a probability distribution. Here there is a probability distribution for the expected return on a bank's loan portfolio because of the possibility of default and, possibly in the case of longer maturity loans, changes in capital value due to interest rate movements. The greater the variance of the distribution, the more uncertain, in the literal sense, the outcome is, and hence the more risk there is. If the future loss rate, for example, were known with certainty, there would be no risk. Because individuals are traditionally taken to prefer certain outcomes to uncertain ones, they are usually assumed to be risk-averse. Hence, they must be compensated for holding a risky asset; in other words, they must be paid a risk premium. For more about risk see, for example, William F. Sharpe, *Portfolio Theory and Capital Markets* (New York: McGraw-Hill Book Company, 1970), Part I.

the degree of risk attached to them. Loans that were riskier would have carried higher interest rates, because a premium would have had to have been paid to lenders to compensate them for bearing the additional risk. As long as loans in different regions differed in the degree of risk attached to them, differences in interest rates would be observed even in a perfect national short-term capital market.[11] If Western and Southern loans on average were riskier than Eastern loans, interest rates would be higher in those regions. As early as 1874, the view that Western interest rates were higher because loans were riskier there was argued before a Congressional committee.[12]

Interregional interest rate differentials therefore could also be quite consistent with perfect capital markets if differences in risk are allowed for.[13] Declining interest rate differentials in that case would be evidence of relative decreases in risk in Western and Southern loans. The shift from agriculture to industry in the Midwest may have been responsible for a decrease in the riskiness of Midwestern loans. In addition, an increase in capital intensity of production or the introduction of new farming techniques may have reduced the uncertainty of crop outcomes and concomitantly the risk of loans in agricultural communities. Decreases in the average riskiness of Western and Southern loans, then, might

[11] The risk referred to here must be systematic, or correlated, risk, because all unsystematic, or uncorrelated, risk may be diversified away in the perfect market and hence commands no risk premium.

[12] U.S. Congress, House Committee on Banking and Currency, *Views Expressed before the Committee*, 43rd Congress, 2nd Session, 1874, pp. 136–137.

[13] Lance Davis has argued that the observed interest rate differentials were too large to be accounted for by risk differentials, because substantial differentials remained in the series of net rates of return on earning assets after losses had been subtracted off. He concluded that western loans were not "all that much" riskier. However, Davis implicitly assumes that banks were risk-neutral. It seems more reasonable to characterize them as risk-averse, and therefore much more sensitive to risk. Davis, "The Investment Market," p. 358.

have been responsible for decreases in interregional interest rate differentials, even within the confines of a perfect capital market.

The role of risk needs to be considered explicitly. If risk were properly accounted for, it might well have been the case that the national short-term capital market was already a perfect market in the late nineteenth century, that barriers to capital mobility were not important during this period, as opposed to the presumptions of the previous two theories that we have examined. We shall refer to this theory, that interest rate differentials were reflections only of risk differentials and that decreases in the riskiness of Western loans in turn led to narrowing interest rate differentials, as the perfect market hypothesis.[14]

Smiley attributes some part of the continuing interregional interest rate differentials to regional differences in risk pre-

[14] The rationale for the perfect market hypothesis discussed in the previous paragraph is based on essentially exogenous decreases in risk in interior regions. As observed in note 11, all risk was systematic risk. However, the fact that the correspondent banking system facilitated interregional transfers of funds, as described in Chapters IV and V, suggests an alternative form of the perfect market hypothesis. The growth of the correspondent banking system and links among banks in the postbellum period enabled more and more banks to diversify their loan holdings across regions, eliminating unsystematic risk, and thereby reducing interregional risk and interest rate differentials. No exogenous forces acting upon riskiness are called for; risk premiums decrease endogenously, due to forces within the capital market. Once again, the capital market would have been a perfect one. The problem is that as high-risk, high-return Western loans are added to more portfolios, with the diversification process reducing their unsystematic risk to zero, there most likely would have been a flow of short-term funds from East to West, from areas where local loans were relatively uncorrelated with agricultural ones. In Chapter IV, however, we saw that flow of short-term capital, on the contrary, was most probably from West to East. In any case, whatever the cause of the risk reduction, the test for a perfect national market remains the same: the insignificance of the effect of changes in local banking market structure on local interest rates.

miums and suggests that high loss rates during the depressed years of the 1890s[15] made interior bankers more risk-averse, so that the slower rate of convergence of regional interest rates after 1900 was due to differing regional risk premiums.[16] The risk premium has two components: the amount of risk itself, measured as the variance or standard deviation of the probability distribution of expected returns, and the reaction to that risk, the degree of risk aversion. Smiley does not carefully distinguish between these, and it is not clear which factor is supposed to be the principal influence on the differing regional risk premiums. More important, however, is the fact that Smiley makes no attempt to measure risk premiums; indeed, he has no well-defined model of interest rate determination at all in which to assess the effects of risk.

Rockoff focuses on a slightly different type of risk, the risk of bank failure. He finds that between 1870 and 1914 the correlation between regional failure rates of national banks and regional profit rates was positive and statistically significant. Moreover, there is evidence of convergence of regional failure rates. To be sure, the absolute magnitudes of the failure rates were small, but, depending on the degree of risk aversion of the public, investment in national bank shares may well have been discouraged, especially because shareholders were liable up to twice the amount of their investment. Rockoff emphasizes, however, the effects of the possibility of bank failure on depositors rather than on investors. Because deposits in almost all states were not insured, a premium was placed on a reputation for soundness

[15] In Figures 3 and 4 we saw that progress toward interest rate convergence was in fact reversed during the depression years of the mid-1890s, which may well have been due to heavy default losses of interior banks, which were hit harder by the more distressed conditions in agriculture.

[16] Two other explanations for the retardation in the rate of convergence are offered in note 39. Gene Smiley, "Interest Rate Movement in the United States, 1888–1913," *Journal of Economic History*, XXXV (September 1975), pp. 602, 604.

by depositors; this enabled such banks to earn above-average rates of return, especially in areas such as the West where the failure rate was relatively high.[17] To the extent that national banks, because of their larger capitalization requirements, were more identified with soundness by the public, they may have been able to attract more customers and exact higher returns from them than state or private banks.

Another hypothesis concerning interest rate convergence, but one that is not tested explicitly here, is that of Jeffrey Williamson, which emphasizes changes in real factors on the demand side of the capital market. All of the previous hypotheses have explained capital market integration by changes within the capital market, changes in the supply of funds. Williamson, on the other hand, focuses on a relative decline in the demand for funds in the Midwest. He finds in his model that the rate of labor force shift to the Midwest stops by the early 1880s, with a resulting decline in investment demand there. Stability in the relative price of grain may have reduced the demand for agricultural capital. Moreover, the railroad declined in relative importance in the Midwest in the 1870s.[18] Thus, a decline in the demand for funds caused Midwestern interest rates to fall relative to Eastern rates. The explanation for capital market integration is found in real forces exogenous to the capital market rather than in changes within the capital market itself. For one thing, this hypothesis offers no explanation for the similar declines in Western and Southern interest rates. The pattern of net flows predicted by the Williamson hypothesis, from Midwest to East, is not confirmed by the estimates of interregional flows in Chapter IV. Finally, the inclusion of demand influences, measured by the deviations from the trend of gross farm income by state in our regressions, which are discussed later in this chapter, for twenty-five

[17] Hugh Rockoff, "Regional Interest Rates and Bank Failures, 1870–1914," *Explorations in Economic History*, XIV (January 1977), pp. 90-95.

[18] Williamson, *Late Nineteenth-Century*, p. 131.

agricultural states indicated that shifts in income, and hence the demand for loans, did not seem to be significant influences on the pattern of local interest rates, although this is certainly not a conclusive test because Williamson referred to shifts in demand due to changes primarily on the industrial rather than the agricultural side.

Thus we are presented with a range of explanations of the trend toward short-term capital market integration in the late nineteenth century. Lance Davis emphasizes structural changes in the capital market, in particular, the spread westward of the commercial paper market, bringing more and more banks and firms into the national open market for funds. On the other hand, Richard Sylla is more concerned with legal barriers established by the National Banking Act, such as high minimum capital requirements and the prohibition of mortgage lending, restricting the flow of funds than with structural barriers. In both cases, however, country bankers were assumed to have enjoyed quasi-monopoly positions in the local market, as a result of impediments to the free flow of capital. In contrast, the perfect market hypothesis does not assume segmented regional capital markets, but rather explains the narrowing interest rate differentials in terms of relative decreases in risk on Western loans.

In order to assess the influence of the effects emphasized in these three major hypotheses on the pattern of local interest rates, the important factors affecting the level of interest rates must be taken explicitly into account. In other words, a model of local interest rate determination is needed to distinguish between the effects of changing risk and changing levels of local monopoly power on local interest rates. Because we wish to examine the influence of local monopoly power on local interest rates, it is assumed that the local bank has monopoly power in the loan market. A mean-variance model of bank portfolio selection, in which the bank is assumed to be risk-averse and thus takes into consideration the risk characteristics as well as the yields of the assets in its portfolio, was developed in which the loan market is imperfectly competitive. Under very general conditions[19] the equilibrium expected loan rate may be expressed as the sum of a risk premium and a monopoly premium.[20] Thus, the influences of risk and local monopoly on local loan rates may be separated out.

The theoretical relationship between expected loan rates on the one hand and a risk premium and monopoly premium on the other was first transformed into one in terms of observables and then the regression was estimated for country national banks and for reserve city national banks during the period 1893–1911. The construction of the basic local interest rate data, pictured in an aggregate form in Figure 2, is discussed in Appendix A. A bank density index, the total number of banks—national, state, and private—per capita is taken as a proxy for the monopoly premium. An alternative measure of the degree of concentration of local markets, the average number of banks per town in the state, produced very similar results. The sample variance of the loss rate on loans over the previous five years is taken as a measure of loan riskiness.[21] The material that follows,

[19] The demand curve for loans must be downward-sloping.

[20] The monopoly premium includes the inverse of the elasticity of demand for loans, so that if the loan market is competitive, the elasticity of loan demand is infinite, and the monopoly premium reduces to zero. For the complete derivation, see John A. James, "Portfolio Selection with an Imperfectly Competitive Asset Market," *Journal of Financial and Quantitative Analysis*, XI (December 1976), pp. 831–846.

[21] Such a measure allows the bank's recent experience with defaults to affect the perceived degree of risk. Rockoff's emphasis on the risk of bank failure is well taken, but nevertheless, not incorporated into the framework of the mean-variance analysis here. If the public turned to national banks because of their reputation for soundness, which allowed them in turn to earn above-average rates of return, the failure rate that should have most directly influenced their behavior was the state bank failure rate, or else the difference between the state and national bank failure rates. Unfortunately such a series is not available in many areas. In any case, the national bank failure rate is likely to be quite highly correlated with the loss rate on loans, which is included in the estimated equation.

describing tests of the three major explanations for the convergence of regional short-term interest rates based on those estimated equations, summarizes econometric work that is reported in more detail elsewhere.[22]

PERFECT MARKET HYPOTHESIS

The perfect market hypothesis holds that differences in risk alone could account for the observed interregional interest rate differentials and that decreases in the risk of Western loans could account for the narrowing of those differentials. Indeed, in a set of regressions of the sample variance of the loss rate, our measure of risk, on a time trend over the period 1893–1911 for country banks by state in virtually every state the estimated coefficient of the time trend was significantly negative. Risk on commercial loans diminished in almost every state over the period.[23] Was this decline in risk reflected in significant decreases in local interest rates? The effects of changes in risk as opposed to changes in local monopoly power on the pattern of interest rates may be distinguished in regressions based on our model of local interest rate determination. Cross-section time-series regressions, ones that contain observations in time series for several different areas grouped together, so that both variance over time and over different geographical areas is

[22] For the transformation of the theoretical relationship into terms of measurable variables and the estimation process, see John A. James, "Banking Market Structure, Risk, and the Pattern of Local Interest Rates in the United States, 1893–1911," *Review of Economics and Statistics*, LVIII (November 1976), pp. 453–462. For the hypotheses tests, see John A. James, "The Development of the National Money Market, 1893–1911," *Journal of Economic History*, XXXVI (December 1976), pp. 878-897.

[23] John A. James, "The Evolution of the National Money Market, 1888–1911" (unpublished Ph.D. dissertation, MIT, 1974), pp. 483–484.

included, indicated that risk was a significant factor in accounting for interregional interest rate differences across reserve cities, but not across country banks. In about one-third of the states the risk variable was found to have had a significant influence on country bank interest rate movements, although there was marked regional variation in its impact. Virtually every state in the South, for example, showed risk to be a significant variable. However, the magnitude of this influence on average was quite small, so that decreases in risk could account for only a small part of the observed narrowing of differentials.

If capital markets had not been segmented, local banks would have possessed no monopoly power, and as a result local banking market structure would have had no effect on local interest rates. However, the monopoly power index proved to be a significant influence on local interest rates for both country and reserve city banks in the cross-section time series. Consequently, the perfect market hypothesis must be rejected. Even though the narrowing of risk differentials could account for some part of the observed narrowing of interest rate differentials, local monopoly power remained a very important factor. In order for banks to possess some degree of local monopoly power, capital markets must have been segmented to some extent. Existing institutions, such as the correspondent banking system, although they did facilitate the interregional transfer of short-term funds and did serve as a substitute for the prohibited branch banking system, apparently were not successful in achieving a perfect national market in short-term capital. A study of market structure revealed that institutions developed or adapted to promote interregional capital flows, but market performance had to be studied also to determine if such institutions in fact eliminated market imperfections. As a result, the two hypotheses based on market imperfections, the institutional change and market power hypotheses, must now be considered.

INSTITUTIONAL CHANGE HYPOTHESIS

The postbellum national short-term capital market must have been imperfect to some extent, because changes in interest rates in different regions could not be accounted for by changes in risk alone. If the short-term capital market was segmented into local or regional markets to some degree, what forces were at work reducing the barriers to capital mobility? The institutional change hypothesis emphasized the westward expansion of the commercial paper market in bringing borrowers and lenders from different sections of the country together. How can such a hypothesis be tested? No information is available on the volume of the flow of funds through the commercial paper market among regions. Here instead we shall assess whether the introduction of the commercial paper market into an area had a substantial impact on local interest rates by comparing the timing of the spread of the commercial paper market with the pattern of local interest rate changes, following a *post hoc ergo propter hoc* type of analysis, which is not without its difficulties.

First, the westward expansion of the commercial paper market was not as clear-cut and easily identifiable a process as Davis had pictured in chronicling the westward march of commercial paper house openings.[24] Interior banks were never really isolated from the commercial paper market because they could always have purchased paper through their New York correspondents, which virtually every country bank possessed. So a country bank could well have participated in the open market without having a local dealer. In addition, we have also seen that commercial paper houses could be operating in a region, either buying or selling paper, well before a dealer was established there. By 1869 dealers were already using the telegraph to make contacts and distribute their offerings.[25] Another method of dealing with

[24] Davis, "The Investment Market," p. 371.

[25] Albert O. Greef, *The Commercial Paper House in the United States* (Cambridge, Mass.: Harvard University Press, 1938), p. 98.

customers far away from the dealer's office was the traveling representative, or salesman. In 1908 a banker made reference to the "travelling representatives of the bonds and commercial paper houses who at present radiate from financial centers and press their wares into almost every hamlet."[26] C. A. Phillips also commented, "A large proportion of the paper handled is now sold by travelling representatives, who work in regularly assigned territory."[27] In view of these considerations, the distinction between areas in which the commercial paper market did and did not exist is much less clear. The spread of the open market was a much more gradual process than a hopping from one city to another.

Furthermore, just because a commercial paper house was established in a city in a given year does not necessarily mean that it began to exert an influence on interest rates there immediately. Rather, it might have done a very small volume of business at first, and only after several years have risen to such a position of importance as to influence local rates. By a similar token, it is very difficult to assess the influence of a commercial paper house in a city on country banks in an area. Did the fact that a commercial paper house was established in Kansas City mean that Kansas country banks bought paper from it and that firms in small Kansas towns sold paper to it? It is difficult to say. In Minneapolis or St. Paul a note broker was in operation as early as 1879,[28] but it was not until around 1900 that it was noted that banks in moderate-sized Minnesota towns had become purchasers of commercial paper.[29] So the introduction of a commercial paper house into a region did not mean that country banks necessarily availed themselves of it immediately, and hence its effects might not show up right away.

---

[26] W. O. Jones, "The Ideal Country Banker," *Proceedings of the Oregon Bankers' Association*, 1908, p. 64.

[27] Chester A. Phillips, *Bank Credit* (New York: Macmillan Company, 1920), p. 139.

[28] Greef, *The Commercial Paper House*, p. 39.

[29] Ibid., p. 48.

Nevertheless, in tests of the commercial paper hypothesis, tests of timing must be relied upon, because these are the only available pieces of information. The introduction of the commercial paper market into an area might have affected local loan rates through both shifts in the demand for and in the supply of commercial paper. On the supply side, local firms, after the appearance of a commercial paper dealer, had another form of financing available to them and, as a result, were offered an opportunity to escape the local banking monopoly. Consequently, the spread of commercial paper into an area should have reduced the monopoly power of local banks.

On the demand side, the commercial paper market allowed banks to diversify their portfolios across regions. Small country banks previously restricted to making loans in the local areas, where default risks on loans are likely to be highly correlated, could then in effect make loans in other regions and industries, where the risks were independent or only weakly correlated with those on local loans, through purchasing commercial paper. Giving the bank a wider geographical area over which to loan enabled it to diversify away some of the local risk (such as weather conditions) and thus to reduce the risk on its total portfolio. So there should have been, as a result, a decrease in the variance of the loss rate on the loan portfolio. The interest rate on local loans should fall because commercial loans had become less risky due to the reduction of unsystematic risk.

First, on the demand side, did the purchase of commercial paper allow local banks to diversify, thereby reducing portfolio risk and interest rates? Even though commercial paper houses were established there in the 1880s, banks in St. Louis and Kansas City did not start investing substantial sums in open-market paper until after 1897.[30] A test for a downward shift in the coefficient of the risk variable, the sample variance of the loss rate, in other words, a Chow test, indicated that after 1897 there was a definite reduction in the risk

[30] Ibid.

premium in Kansas City, but not in St. Louis. Similarly, country banks in several Midwestern states became regular purchasers of commercial paper around the turn of the century.[31] Once again, however, the test results are mixed. In two cases, North Dakota and Minnesota, there is evidence of a downward shift in loan riskiness, whereas in Kansas and Nebraska there is not. Another possible effect of portfolio diversification through the purchase of commercial paper is a fall in the loss rate on loans, because banks would have been better able to reduce the number of defaults in their loan portfolio. Strictly speaking, it is not a necessary consequence, because changes in risk refer only to changes in the variance of the probability distribution of expected returns rather than to changes in the mean, but it does appear to be a likely result. In seven reserve cities, however, there was no evidence of a significant downward shift in the loss rate after banks there began to purchase open-market paper.[32]

Effects on the supply side have usually been thought to have been more immediate and more important. The introduction of a commercial paper dealer into an area enabled local firms to borrow from thousands of banks across the United States by selling their paper to the note broker, who

[31] A report at the Minnesota Bankers' Association convention noted that around 1900 country banks in Minnesota were "supplementing their reserves with purchased paper of the highest grade." About the same time many banks in North Dakota "were familiar with commercial paper," and seasonal buying of open-market paper "was in general practice throughout the Northwest." Nebraska banks had also begun to buy commercial paper by 1900, as had banks in Kansas. Ibid.

[32] It has been noted that St. Louis and Kansas City banks began to buy substantial amounts of commercial paper only after 1897. Minneapolis banks did not begin to purchase large amounts of paper until after the Panic of 1893, even though note brokers had been established there since the early 1880s. Similarly, Los Angeles banks invested little in commercial paper until after 1903, even though brokers had been established there a few years earlier. Portland banks began buying paper around 1908, whereas Dallas banks started about 1910.

215

then in turn offered it to banks in other areas. As a result, local banks were more limited in the monopoly premiums that they could exact on loans, so there should have been a drop in local interest rates. A given market structure, then, should have been associated with a smaller degree of monopoly power after the introduction of the commercial paper market. The results of a test for a shift in the monopoly power coefficient after the date when local firms began to sell commercial paper (another Chow test) for four reserve cities[33] are mixed. San Francisco shows a definite decrease in the monopoly power of local banks after the introduction of the commercial paper market, and Portland shows some influence, whereas in Columbus and Dallas there seems to be no effect at all.

These tests have thus far relied on the exact timing of the introduction of the commercial paper market, which in view of the difficulties in identifying the spread of the market may be too stringent a test. A weaker test therefore was performed for nineteen Eastern and Midwestern reserve cities,[34] where the commercial paper market had been established prior to the late 1880s, during the period 1888–1911 to determine whether the degree of local monopoly power associated with a given market structure was diminishing over time, as opposed to a decrease in monopoly power caused

[33] 1900 is marked as the date of the earliest operations in commercial paper in San Francisco. In several other cities we can establish the approximate date of the first sale of paper by local firms to brokers. In Columbus the first sale took place about 1907, whereas local banks did not start buying paper until 1912. Local firms in Portland began selling to brokers in 1906; by 1908 a New York banker told the Oregon Bankers' Association that its region "is beginning to attract the attention of dealers in commercial paper." Commercial paper operations in Dallas began about 1910. Greef, *The Commercial Paper House*, p. 39; Phillips, *Bank Credit*, p. 135; Jones, "The Ideal Country Banker," p. 66.

[34] Boston, New York, Albany, Philadelphia, Pittsburgh, Baltimore, Washington, Brooklyn, Cincinnati, Cleveland, Chicago, Detroit, Milwaukee, St. Louis, Kansas City, Omaha, St. Joseph, Minneapolis, and St. Paul.

by more banks and increased competition. In no city did there seem to be a decrease in the level of monopoly power associated with a specified market structure over time, as would have happened if the local bank monopolies had been eroded by the growth of the commercial paper market.

The introduction of the commercial paper market into an area does not, on the whole, seem to have made a significant impact on local interest rates, either through offering opportunities for portfolio diversification and thereby risk reduction in local loan portfolios or through the reduction of monopoly power of local banks. To be sure, the evidence is somewhat mixed, and in certain local markets, such as Kansas City or San Francisco, the commercial paper market may have had a significant impact, but there does not seem to be an overall pattern of decreases in local interest rates after the appearance of a commercial paper dealer through either demand-side or supply-side effects.

Just as the patterns of interest rates in local markets do not lend strong support to the commercial paper hypothesis, the general patterns of regional interest-rate movements do not seem to be consistent with the pace of expansion of the commercial paper market either. Consider again the plots of the regional interest rate differentials in Figures 3 and 4. The pattern of interest rate movements does not seem to be highly correlated with the spread of the commercial paper market. In Region IV, the North Central Region, where the commercial paper market was well established in the 1880s, there was nevertheless a continual narrowing of the interest rate differential with the East. If the commercial paper market was the principal institutional change leading to narrowing differentials, there should not have been a decline in the regional differential until after the open market had been established in the region. Country banks in the Great Plains did not begin buying commercial paper until 1900; but there were substantial declines in the Region V differentials before 1900. The commercial paper market did not reach the Pacific Coast until 1900. Once again, however, there were substantial interest rate declines in Region VI, the Pacific states, before 1900. On closer inspection, the pattern of regional interest rate movements does not seem, contrary to Davis's assertion, to be consistent with the timing of the expansion of the commercial paper market.

MARKET POWER HYPOTHESIS

According to Richard Sylla, on the other hand, the crucial event that reduced the monopoly power of country banks and thus led to a narrowing of interregional interest rate differentials was the passage of the Gold Standard Act of 1900, which amended the National Banking Acts to allow the formation of national banks with a minimum capital of $25,000 in towns with a population under 3,000. He observed that this legal barrier to entry was eliminated by the stroke of a pen, and that the liberalization of requirements resulted in a rapid increase in the rate of formation of country national banks and consequently a diminution of local monopoly power and of local loan rates primarily in Western and Southern regions.[35] A change in market structure brought about by lowered legal barriers to entry therefore decreased local monopoly premiums, resulting in the convergence of regional interest rates.

What were the effects of the Gold Standard Act of 1900? Lowering the barriers to entry should have resulted in a rapid increase in the number of country banks.[36] Consider Figure 5,

[35] Sylla, "Federal Policy," pp. 663, 665–670.

[36] One other provision of the 1900 Act that may have encouraged national bank formation was the change in national bank note issue requirements. Prior to 1900 national banks could issue notes on only 90 percent of the par or market value, whichever was lower, of their government bond holdings. The Gold Standard Act allowed notes to be issued on 100 percent of the par or market value of bond holdings. Consequently, note issue became more profitable after 1900. See Phillip Cagan, *Determinants and Effects of Changes in the Stock of Money, 1875–1960* (New York: Columbia University Press, 1965), pp. 93–95.

showing the growth of national, state, and private banks between 1877 and 1909, drawn from National Monetary Commission statistics. After 1900 the number of national banks rose quite rapidly, but state banks expanded very rapidly as well. If the legal barriers to entry in the National Banking Act had been the principal influences on the rate of growth of banks, no influence on the formation of state banks should be observed; if anything, the rate of formation of state banks should have decreased with the lowering of capital requirements for national banks. In fact, after 1900 the rate of formation of both national and state banks increased dramatically, suggesting that they were affected by some common influence, such as the business cycle. In the first decade of the twentieth century, when business revived, the rate of bank formation should also have increased. Indeed, a crude business cycle index does just as well in accounting for the increase in the number of banks per capita by state after 1900 as a dummy variable representing the passage of the Gold Standard Act.

Moreover, a simple examination of the resultant increase in numbers of national banks in small towns overstates the effects of the new law. Many of the new national banks may have been merely conversions or reorganizations of existing state banks, so that the net change in the number of banks in the state may have been quite small. Thornton Cooke in a 1901 article discussed the immediate effects of the Gold Standard Act of 1900 in lowering capital requirements, a law that had been anticipated. In the six months after the passage of the law not one new, as opposed to converted, national bank was established in North Dakota. In South Dakota and Missouri only one was added, and in Nebraska and Kansas only two were added.[37] In North Dakota, South Dakota, Nebraska, Kansas, and Missouri the new national banking law resulted in a net addition of exactly six banks

[37] Thornton Cooke, "The Effect of the New Currency Law on Banking in the West," *Quarterly Journal of Economics*, XV (February 1901), pp. 278–279.

during the six-month period. In contrast, eighty-five new state banks and ten new private banks were organized there during the same period.

The new national banking law did have more substantial effects in some other states. In Texas, where state banks were still forbidden, thirty-four new national banks were organized during the period. In Iowa, where the minimum capital requirement was $25,000, so that a new bank was subject to the same minimum requirement whether it was state or national, thirty-two new national banks were organized.[38] In states where minimum state bank capital requirements were relatively high, such as Iowa or Texas (where it was infinite), the lower national bank capital requirements did significantly increase the number of new national banks. On the other hand, in areas such as the Great Plains states where state capital requirements were relatively low, the new national law had little effect on net.

Furthermore, consider Figures 3 and 4 again. Most of the decline in interregional interest rate differentials occurred prior to 1900 rather than after as the Sylla hypothesis asserts. As noted previously, the process of capital market integration slowed and even retrogressed somewhat in some areas, such as the Midwest, after 1900.[39] In addition, the Sylla hypothesis fails to explain the significant narrowing of the differentials before 1900. So the pattern of interest rate differentials predicted by this hypothesis is the exact opposite of that which is observed.

[38] Ibid., p. 280.

[39] In spite of retardation in the rate, overall progress toward convergence of regional interest rates continued after 1900. This slowing of the narrowing of differentials after 1900 may have been influenced by shifts in demand, as Williamson argues. It may also, however, have been evidence of diminishing returns in the growth of banks. The twentieth bank established in an area would probably have less of an effect on the state of competition and the level of local monopoly power than the second or third bank. For a measure of the average reduction in interregional differentials, the square root of the average of squared differentials of other regions with the East, see James, "Development of the National Money Market," p. 880.

The cross-section time-series regression for country banks indicates that differences in the number of banks per capita across states is an important factor in accounting for interstate differences in interest rates during the period 1893–1911. In the time-series regressions for country banks by state the bank density index, the monopoly power variable, proved to be a significant explanatory variable for the pattern of local interest rates in most non-Eastern states.[40] Moreover, the simulated effects of the changes in bank density during the period, calculated by multiplying the change in the bank density index by its estimated coefficient for each state, accounted for almost all of the observed declines in local interest rates of country banks in most states, especially in the South and Midwest.[41] The reduction of local monopoly

[40] The influence of local monopoly power on local interest rates was most evident in the South and Midwest, where virtually every state showed a significant coefficient. In the West, on the other hand, only about one-quarter of the states showed local monopoly power to be a significant effect on interest rates, and in general the estimated coefficients there were smaller than in other regions. The poor performance of the bank density index variable may be due to the fact that such a measure implicitly assumes a uniform distribution of banks and population across the state. In the West, where population was concentrated in widely spaced small towns, banking markets may have been much more strictly defined, with less interaction between local markets than elsewhere. In other words, the assumption about population distribution may not be that appropriate for the Western states. In the East, where population was relatively stable and banks grew relatively little also (see Table 36), local monopoly power also seemed to explain little of the variation in interest rates.

[41] The special case of the South should be noted here briefly. The rate of decline of Southern interest rate differentials, as seen in Figures 3 and 4, was much slower than those for other interior regions, a phenomenon that Davis attributes to the slowness of the spread of the commercial paper market in the South. In fact, decreases in monopoly power account for almost all of the observed decline in Southern interest rates; the real question is why that rate of decrease was so much slower in the South relative to other regions.

The answer most probably lies in the South's unique population structure, which allowed the local monopoly power of banks there to persist much longer than elsewhere. The South was primarily a rural region, with relatively few towns and virtually no cities. In

power was important, but it was eroded by the growth of state, rather than national, banks. One of the main short-comings of the Sylla hypothesis is that it focuses only on changes in the number of national banks, essentially neglect-ing state banks. State banks remain on the periphery to Sylla despite the fact the spread of deposit banking had made them good substitutes for national banks, as argued in Chapter II, a conclusion also supported by Keehn in his study of post-bellum Wisconsin banking.[42] Furthermore, state banks out-

---

1900 only 22 percent of the Southern population lived in incorpo-rated areas, as compared with the next most rural region, the West, which had a proportion almost double that of the South. This rural character enabled country banks to exert a significant degree of monopoly power. With a widely dispersed population the number of banks that could be supported in a given area was quite limited. In addition, the greater distances between banks also limited the extent to which the monopoly power of nearby banks would be eroded by new entry. Even in as sparsely populated an area as the West, popu-lation was relatively concentrated in urban areas, thus reducing the monopoly power of a given bank.

In a 1909 cross-section regression of local country bank interest rates by state on minimum state capital requirements (representing barriers to entry) and distance of a major city in the state from New York (representing distance from national financial markets), a dummy variable for the South was significantly positive, indicating that interest rates were higher there than in the rest of the country, other things being equal. Moreover, in the regression population density, formerly a highly significant explanatory variable, dropped into insignificance when the Southern dummy was added. It was this element of spatial monopoly that also gave Southern general stores their local monopoly power and allowed them to function as quasi-financial institutions in lieu of banks in many rural areas. Davis, "The Investment Market," p. 389; U.S. Census Office, *1900 Census of Population* (Washington, D.C.: U.S. Government Printing Office, 1903), p. lxviii; Roger Ransom and Richard Sutch, "Debt Peonage in the Cotton South after the Civil War," *Journal of Economic His-tory*, XXXII (September 1972), p. 647; Roger Ransom and Richard Sutch, "Documenting Monopoly Power in the Rural South: the Case of the General Store," Southern Economic History Project, No. 15 (Riverside, Calif., April 1976).

[42] Keehn, "Federal Bank Policy," p. 27.

numbered and grew more rapidly than national banks after the early 1890s, as shown in Figure 5.

In Table 34 the ratio of national banks to total commercial banks declines steadily until 1900, the date of the passage

Table 34

Growth of State and National Banks, 1896–1910
(number of banks on June 30)

Year	Total Commercial Banks	National Banks	State Banks	Percent National Banks
1896	11,474	3,689	7,785	32.1
1897	11,438	3,610	7,828	31.5
1898	11,530	3,581	7,949	31.0
1899	11,835	3,582	8,253	30.2
1900	12,427	3,731	8,696	30.0
1901	13,424	4,163	9,261	31.0
1902	14,488	4,532	9,956	31.2
1903	15,814	4,935	10,879	31.2
1904	17,037	5,330	11,707	31.2
1905	18,152	5,664	12,488	31.2
1906	19,786	6,047	13,739	30.5
1907	21,361	6,422	14,939	30.0
1908	22,531	6,817	15,714	30.2
1909	23,098	6,886	16,212	29.8
1910	24,514	7,138	17,376	29.1

Source: *All-Bank Statistics* (Washington, D.C., 1959), pp. 30–49.

of the Gold Standard Act. After 1900 the proportion of national banks to all commercial banks increases, but toward the end of the decade the percentage of national banks declines once again. A similar story is told by the number of new banks formed in Table 35. Only in the year immediately following the passage of the Gold Standard Act, 1901, did national banks make a significant dent in the total number of new banks established per year, and then national banks as a percentage of the total decreased steadily after that year.

223

Table 35

New Banks Created, by Year, 1897–1910
(as of June 30)

Year	Total Banks	National Banks	State Banks	Percent National Banks
1897	−36	−79	43	—
1898	92	−29	121	—
1899	305	1	304	0.3
1900	592	149	443	25.1
1901	997	432	565	43.3
1902	1064	369	695	34.6
1903	1326	403	923	30.3
1904	1223	395	828	32.2
1905	1115	334	781	29.9
1906	1634	383	1251	23.4
1907	1575	375	1200	23.8
1908	1170	395	775	33.7
1909	567	69	498	12.1
1910	1436	252	1184	17.5

Source: *All-Bank Statistics* (Washington, D.C., 1959), pp. 30–49.

National banks, therefore, did not constitute a sizable amount of new banks formed. In addition, the greatest growth in state banks was exactly in those regions where monopoly was supposed to have been the strongest—the South, Midwest, and West—and with the exception of the South, where the declines in interest rates were the greatest. In New England the number of state banks in 1909 was exactly the same as in 1879, and in the Eastern states the increase in state banks was quite small. Table 36, compiled from National Monetary Commission statistics,[43] presents the numbers and percentage changes of state banks by regions.

The growth of state banks certainly appears to be an im-

[43] Consequently, the state bank totals are slightly underestimated relative to the *All-Bank Statistics* series.

Table 36

Numbers and Percentage Increase of State Banks
by Areas by Decade, 1879–1909

	1879	*1889*		*1899*		*1909*	
Region	*No.*	*No.*	*Percent Increase*	*No.*	*Percent Increase*	*No.*	*Percent Increase*
New England	19	22	16	23	5	19	−17
Eastern	189	253	34	334	32	387	16
Southern	204	464	127	1,071	131	3,312	209
Midwestern	295	675	129	1,594	136	3,717	133
Western	42	528	1,157	956	81	3,026	216
Pacific	64	155	142	275	77	831	202
Total	813	2,097	158	4,253	102	11,292	165

Source: George E. Barnett, *State Banks and Trust Companies since the Passage of the National Bank Act* (Washington, D.C.: U.S. Government Printing Office, 1911), p. 202.

portant phenomenon of the period with which Sylla does not deal directly, but it did evoke some degree of attention from contemporaries. "Almost every municipal community throughout the length and breadth of our country has its banking institution and in many of the small aggregations of not more than 1,000 population we find more than one banking institution prospering."[44] Needless to say, this proliferation of banks was not looked upon favorably by some of the bankers themselves: "So numerous have country banks become that a state of competition exists, so excessive as seriously to threaten the welfare of the banks, and, to a material degree, demoralize the people through too cheap credit."[45] Another banker complained that "more than a fair average profit cannot be realized. . . . It is whether . . .

[44] A. E. Padgett, "The Multiplication of Banks," *Proceedings of the South Carolina Bankers' Association*, 1908, p. 126.
[45] "Country Credit Methods," *Proceedings of the Maryland Bankers' Association*, 1914, p. 47.

225

suitable amendments to state laws should not be interposed to prevent more than a limited number of banks to the local assessed valuation."[46] In Chapter II we noted that towns as small as Battle Creek, Iowa, with a population of 688 in 1915, had three banks; North Liberty, Iowa, with a population of under 200, had two banks in 1918.[47] Indeed, Cootner and Carson argue that many small population centers were "overbanked" by 1900.[48]

The impressive growth of state banks in the postbellum period was in large part a response to the legal restrictions imposed on national banks. The handicap of the loss of the power of note issue diminished rapidly in importance as the use of deposits grew immediately after the Civil War. On the other hand, the state bank form of organization had some competitive advantages over national banks. National banks were prohibited from loaning on real estate, whereas in almost all cases state banks could loan on mortgages. National bank capital requirements were relatively high; state bank capital requirements were usually lower.

The role of state bank minimum capital requirements will be discussed in more detail here, but consider private banks for a moment. These unincorporated banks were in general not subject to state regulations such as minimum capital requirements. Interior private banks were on the whole quite small and provided banking facilities for very small towns that could not support a state bank with larger capital requirements. For example, in Wisconsin in 1890 one-third of private banks had capitals less than $5,000 and two-thirds of them had capitals less than $15,000.[49] Chartered banks,

[46] T. H. Hinchman, *Banks and Banking in Michigan* (Detroit: M. Graham, 1887), p. 170.

[47] Howard H. Preston, *History of Banking in Iowa* (Iowa City: State Historical Society of Iowa, 1922), p. 354.

[48] Paul Cootner and Deane Carson, "The Structure of Competition in Commercial Banking in the United States," in Commission on Money and Credit, ed., *Private Financial Institutions* (Englewood Cliffs, N.J.: Prentice-Hall, 1963), p. 66.

[49] Theodore A. Andersen, *A Century of Banking in Wisconsin* (Madison: State Historical Society of Wisconsin, 1954), pp. 62–63.

then, could not maintain complete monopolies in small towns if private banks could be established. In fact, how could any bank possess local monopoly power as long as private banks could be established with no minimum capital requirements restricting entry?[50] The public, however, seemed to put a premium on soundness, and to feel more comfortable with chartered banks as a result. So private banks were not very close substitutes for chartered banks. Such an argument is very similar to Rockoff's suggestion that the premium placed on bank soundness gave national banks an advantage in regions with high failure rates. It may be argued here, however, that with their certainly non-negligible capital requirements state banks were viewed by the public as being close substitutes for national banks; the real division in terms of expected soundness came instead between chartered and unchartered banks. Private banks did act as an offset to the restrictions of high minimum capital requirements and undoubtedly contributed significantly to the narrowing of interregional interest rate differentials in the 1870s and early 1880s shown in Figure 1; but because they were not wholly favorably regarded by the public, they were not close enough substitutes to eliminate local monopoly power entirely.

Capital requirements were intended to provide a buffer between the bank's creditors and losses that the bank might incur. If the bank had no capital, losses would fall directly on the creditors rather than on the stockholders, and hence the greater the likelihood of losses to depositors. In many states it was felt that the population of the town was a rough index of the amount of business that would be done by a bank there, so capital requirements for state banks, like those for national banks, were graduated, increasing with town population. As we are concerned with the entry of state banks in small towns and rural areas in interior regions, we

[50] In South Dakota in 1897 apparently two private banks did operate with no capital at all. Thornton Cooke, "Distribution of Small Banks in the West," *Quarterly Journal of Economics*, XII (October 1897), p. 71.

shall consider only state bank minimum capital requirements here.

Table 37 shows the minimum capital requirements for state banks in 1909. The Gold Standard Act of 1900 low-

Table 37

Minimum Capital Requirements for State Banks, 1909

East		Midwest	
Maine	$ a	Ohio	$25,000
New Hampshire	a	Indiana	25,000
Vermont	a	Illinois	25,000
Massachusetts	a	Michigan	20,000
Rhode Island	a	Wisconsin	10,000
Connecticut	a	Minnesota	10,000
New York	25,000	Iowa	25,000
New Jersey	50,000	Missouri	10,000
Pennsylvania	25,000	Kansas	10,000
Delaware	a	Nebraska	10,000
Maryland	10,000	North Dakota	10,000
		South Dakota	10,000
South		West	
Virginia	$10,000	Colorado	$10,000
West Virginia	25,000	New Mexico	30,000
North Carolina	5,000	Arizona	0
South Carolina	0	Utah	10,000
Georgia	15,000	Wyoming	10,000
Florida	15,000	Montana	20,000
Alabama	15,000	Idaho	10,000
Mississippi	10,000	Nevada	10,000
Louisiana	10,000	Washington	10,000
Texas	10,000	Oregon	10,000
Arkansas	0	California	25,000
Tennessee	0	Oklahoma	10,000
Kentucky	15,000		

a Capital determined individually.

Source: George E. Barnett, *State Banks and Trust Companies since the Passage of the National Bank Act* (Washington, D.C.: U.S. Government Printing Office, 1911), p. 43.

ered national bank capital requirements in towns of under 3,000 population to $25,000. From Table 37 we can see that such a reduction should have had relatively little influence on net bank formation if state and national banks were close substitutes, because in the great majority of states the minimum capital requirement was already below $25,000. There does seem to be a geographical pattern to the range of capital requirements. In New England states in which state banks were incorporated by special act, the capital was fixed for each bank by the legislature.[51] In the Eastern states and the most easterly states in the Midwest, such as Ohio, Indiana, and Illinois, the minimum capital requirements were relatively high, usually around $25,000. On the other hand, in the less dense, more rural states of the South and West, the minimum requirements were usually much lower, ranging mostly between $10,000 and $15,000. In 1909 there were only four states that had no minimum capital requirements for state banks—Arizona, Arkansas, South Carolina, and Tennessee. In these states, state banks were organized under the business incorporation law and like other corporations the size of capital was at the discretion of the incorporators.[52]

The Comptroller of the Currency's *Annual Report* for 1895 reported state bank capital requirements for that year. Those figures, together with the change in minimum capital requirements between 1895 and 1909, are reported in Table 38. In 1895 in a number of states that did not have specific banking incorporation laws, the amount of capital was individually determined by the legislature, so no direct comparison between 1895 and 1909 can be made for those states. In the states that can be compared directly, there is no general pattern of upward or downward trend. On the whole, in states in which the capital requirement was rela-

[51] George E. Barnett, *State Banks and Trust Companies since the Passage of the National Bank Act* (Washington, D.C.: U.S. Government Printing Office, 1911), p. 36.
[52] Ibid.

Table 38

Minimum Capital Requirements for State Banks, 1895,
and Change in Minimum Requirements, 1895–1909

	1895 Minimum	Change 1895–1909		1895 Minimum	Change 1895–1909
East			*Midwest*		
Maine	a		Ohio	25,000	0
New Hampshire	a		Indiana	25,000	0
Vermont	50,000		Illinois	25,000	0
Massachusetts	a		Michigan	15,000	+5,000
Rhode Island	a		Wisconsin	25,000	−15,000
Connecticut	a		Minnesota	10,000	0
New York	25,000	0	Iowa	25,000	0
New Jersey	50,000	0	Missouri	10,000	0
Pennsylvania	50,000	−25,000	Kansas	5,000	+5,000
Delaware	a		Nebraska	5,000	+5,000
Maryland	50,000	−40,000	North Dakota	5,000	+5,000
			South Dakota	5,000	+5,000
South			*West*		
Virginia	10,000	0	Colorado	30,000	−20,000
West Virginia	25,000	0	New Mexico	30,000	0
North Carolina	a		Arizona	a	
South Carolina	0	0	Utah	25,000	−15,000
Georgia	25,000	−10,000	Wyoming	a	
Florida	15,000	0	Montana	20,000	0
Alabama	50,000	−35,000	Idaho	a	
Mississippi	0	+10,000	Nevada	a	
Louisiana	100,000	−90,000	Washington	25,000	−15,000
Texas	b		Oregon	a	
Arkansas	a		California	5,000	+25,000
Tennessee	0	0	Oklahoma	a	
Kentucky	a				

a Capital determined individually.
b No state banks.

Source: U.S. Comptroller of the Currency, *Annual Report*, 1895 (Washington, D.C.: U.S. Government Printing Office, 1895), pp. 38–60, 111–169.

tively high in 1895 there is generally a decrease in requirements. On the other hand, several states in the Great Plains —Kansas, Nebraska, North Dakota, and South Dakota— where capital requirements were the lowest in the country, $5,000, raised minimum requirements to $10,000, after finding banks with a very small capital unsatisfactory.[53] Other states found even somewhat larger capital requirements still unsatisfactory. The Michigan bank commissioner in 1898 urged that the section authorizing formation of banks with a capital of $15,000 in towns of less than 1,000 population be repealed, and in 1899 the minimum capital requirement in Michigan was raised to $20,000.[54] In general, during this period there is a convergence toward minimum capital requirements of about $10,000 to $15,000 from both above and below.

Did these low minimum capital requirements, especially the $5,000 minimum in the Great Plains states, actually encourage the formation of banks in small towns and thereby erode local monopoly? In North and South Dakota in 1896 virtually all state banks were located in towns with a population of 1,000 or less. In North Dakota forty-seven out of seventy-one state banks had a capital of $10,000 or less; in South Dakota it was forty-eight out of seventy-six. In the same year three-quarters of both Kansas and Nebraska state banks had capitals of under $25,000, the level to which the national bank requirement was lowered in 1900. More than one-half of the state banks in Missouri were located in towns with a population not larger than 1,000. In addition, most private banks were also located in small towns. Thirteen towns in Nebraska with a population of less than 100 had state banks, and there were eight such villages in Kansas and seven in Missouri.[55] Clearly, low minimum capital requirements did encourage the development of banking in small towns, although relatively few state banks were lo-

[53] Ibid., p. 40.   [54] Ibid.
[55] Thornton Cooke, "Distribution of Small Banks in the West," p. 71.

cated in larger towns.[56] The high capital requirements prevented the establishment of national banks in small towns, but banking services were provided there by state banks instead.

What effect did state bank minimum capital requirements have on the structure of interest rates? A cross-section regression for country banks by state of local interest rates in 1909 on 1909 state minimum capital requirements, representing barriers to entry, and the distance of a major city in the state from New York, representing the ease of capital flow from the national to the local market, showed that the size of the minimum capital requirement was an extremely important influence on the level of local interest rates. The lower the state minimum capital requirements, the lower the local loan rates, other things being equal.

In addition, a regression of the changes in country bank interest rates by state for the period 1888–1911 on 1909 state minimum capital requirements indicated that they were also important explanatory factors of the pattern of local interest rates over time. The 1909 capital requirement was significantly associated with the total decline in local interest rates. So states in which there were lower state bank capital requirements experienced larger falls in interest rates, other things being equal.

Lower state bank minimum capital requirements therefore were associated both with lower interest rates across states at a point in time, in the cross section, and with larger decreases in local interest rates over time, in time series. They allowed more banks to be established in small towns, because entry barriers were lower, and as a consequence the monopoly power of local banks was decreased.[57]

---

[56] Cooke explains this by asserting a preference for national banks on the part of the public, which might have been based on the belief that national banks were relatively sounder. Ibid., p. 72.

[57] As a further test, if lowered state capital requirements eroded local monopoly positions, there should be a relationship between state bank capital requirements and the estimated coefficients of the monopoly power variable from the time series regressions. The esti-

Another major factor that encouraged the growth of state banks after the mid-1880s was the liberalization of incorporation laws in many states. Because "the practice of granting exclusive privileges to particular individuals invited competition for these legislative favors," in the words of Millard Fillmore, Comptroller of New York, in his 1849 report,[58] the system of granting special charters began to come into increasing disfavor in the period before the Civil War. Following the model of the 1838 New York state banking law, the National Banking Acts established a system of free banking. Thus, special legislative approval was not needed for the chartering of individual banks. Any group of individuals that fulfilled the specified requirements could receive a national bank charter.

In contrast, incorporation in many states after the Civil War was a quite difficult process. The extreme case was the Texas Constitution of 1876, which prohibited the chartering of state banks, a ban that remained in effect until 1905. In the Midwest, where several states had passed general banking laws before the Civil War, the state banking laws were in effect nullified by the National Banking Act, because they had been originally written to cover the chartering of banks of issue. In Illinois between 1870 and 1888 the state legislature granted no bank charters at all because of the constitutional prohibition of special charters and the absence of a general banking law; thus the establishment of national banks was clearly encouraged. A free banking law was not passed in Illinois until 1887.[59] As late as 1870, with the ex-

---

mated coefficients by state were regressed on 1909 minimum capital requirements for state banks and state population density at the approximate midpoint of the period, 1900. There was a highly significant relationship between the size of the capital requirement and the degree of local monopoly power. In other words, the lower the state capital requirement, the lower the degree of local monopoly power.

[58] Barnett, *State Banks and Trust Companies*, p. 26.

[59] Don M. Dailey, "The Development of Banking in Chicago before 1890" (unpublished Ph.D. dissertation, Northwestern University, 1934), pp. 309, 355.

ception of two or three states, the special charter was the only method of incorporating a bank in the Southern and Eastern regions.[60]

In several of the Midwestern "free banking" states after the effective prohibition on state bank note issue made the then-existing incorporation laws obsolete, they were repealed and banks were allowed to incorporate under the "business incorporation law," which applied to all manufacturing and mercantile companies. Barnett noted that prior to 1887 there were general incorporation laws explicitly for banks in only a very few states, but such laws were adopted by almost all states fairly rapidly thereafter.[61] Many Western states adopted free banking provisions in their constitutions about this time—North Dakota, South Dakota, Montana, Wyoming, Idaho, and Washington in 1889; Utah, in 1895.[62] Most Southern states adopted general banking rules in the decade of the 1890s, from Mississippi in 1890 to Alabama in 1901 and Virginia in 1902.[63] The New England states remained resistant to the trend toward free state banking until after the turn of the century. However, by 1910 all states in the East except Delaware and Maryland had adopted general banking laws.[64] Barnett distinguishes three periods in state bank incorporation after the Civil War. Between 1865 and 1875 most banks were incorporated under special acts; from 1875 to 1887 incorporation under the "business incorporation law" was the most common; and after that the general banking law became almost universal.[65]

Sylla, then, was certainly correct in identifying differences in local monopoly as a principal cause of the interregional differences in interest rates and also in attributing the nar-

[60] Barnett, *State Banks and Trust Companies*, p. 32.
[61] Ibid., p. 33.
[62] Leonard C. Helderman, *National and State Banks* (Boston: Houghton Mifflin Company, 1931), p. 161.
[63] Barnett, *State Banks and Trust Companies*, p. 31.
[64] Helderman, *National and State Banks*, p. 162.
[65] Barnett, *State Banks and Trust Companies*, p. 34.

rowing of those differentials to declines in local monopoly power. Indeed, the time-series regressions for country banks by state indicate that increases in the bank density index, and hence declines in local monopoly power, account for the great part of the observed declines in interest rates. However, Sylla was not correct in analyzing the mechanism that eroded this monopoly power. The lowering of national bank capital requirements by the Gold Standard Act of 1900 did not produce the observed pattern of narrowing differentials and, moreover, did not seem to lead to a very large increase in the total number of banks. Sylla concentrated on the national banks and neglected the role of the state banks, which were much more numerous and grew rapidly over the period.

High minimum capital requirements for national banks did restrict entry in small towns, but state banks developed as substitutes. Differences in state bank minimum capital requirements were important in accounting for cross-sectional differences and also for declines in local interest rates over time. States with lower capital requirements experienced more rapid growth in state banks and more rapid declines in interest rates.

Local monopoly power was eroded initially by the rapid growth of private banks immediately after the Civil War. The rapid growth of state banks began in the late 1880s, when the spread of deposit banking had made the loss of the power of note issue much less important and the passage of general banking laws in most states had made the incorporation of state banks much easier. Lower minimum capital requirements also encouraged the growth of state banks, which was primarily responsible for the diminution of local monopoly power, not the expansion of national banks. The erosion of these monopoly premiums of country banks in turn led to the narrowing of interregional interest rate differentials.

CHAPTER VII

Summary

THE postbellum economy in the United States experienced substantial shifts in both the nature and location of economic activity, heightening the need for interregional and intersectoral transfers of funds. The national banking system was widely criticized as being inadequate for the tasks. It was usually viewed as a cause of economic instability, rather than as a promoter of stabilization, and as unsuited for the interregional transfer of funds to promote economic growth.

The tendencies to crises in the national banking system perhaps may have been exacerbated by the concentration of balances in New York, but the central problem was the inelasticity of reserves and the absence of a lender of last resort, not the structure of the national banking system itself. Ultimately, the Federal Reserve system was appended to the national banking system to resolve this difficulty. The existence of differentials among regional interest rates was taken as evidence of market imperfections, and, as a result, the system was deemed inadequate to promote interregional capital flows. To determine its success, the structure of the interregional short-term capital market and also its performance, the forces promoting the narrowing of the interregional interest rate differentials must be analyzed.

First of all, a distinction must be drawn between the legal structure and constraints of the postbellum banking system, and the manner in which banks actually operated. Nineteenth-century banks were traditionally viewed as being severely constrained in their portfolio choice by a number of legal and theoretical restrictions, such as usury laws or the real-bills doctrine, but that does not seem to have been an accurate picture of actual bank operations. In fact the nineteenth-century banking system was quite adaptable in responding to institutional constraints. The postbellum banking system also encompassed more than just the national banking system. State and private banks developed rapidly as a result of the restrictions placed on national banks, serving as substitutes, especially in rural areas and small towns. For example, the National Banking Act prohibited loans on real estate security to national banks until 1913. This restriction was one of the principal factors contributing to the growth of state banks and trust companies during the late nineteenth century, which for the most part functioned under less severe restraints. Similarly, in response to high minimum capital requirements for national banks, state banks with relatively small capital requirements also developed rapidly during the period.

Moreover, even though the legal structure of the banking system was fragmented into a large number of unit banks spread across the country, these unit banks did not operate as isolated entities. Rather, banks in different areas were linked together in the sophisticated and extensive structure of the correspondent banking system. The system of city correspondents enabled even small country banks to have access to national financial markets. The correspondent banking system represented a response to the prohibition of branch banking and offered a mechanism to promote the interregional flows of funds and information.

Interbank lending and rediscounting usually took place within the framework of the correspondent banking system. Direct interregional lending and investment in bank stock were also methods used in transferring capital. Although the correspondent banking system represented a nonmarket response to the problem of interregional transfers, an open market also developed to facilitate the flow of funds, the commercial paper market. Davis identifies the westward expansion of the commercial paper market as the central event in the gradual process of integration, but the commercial paper market in fact was only one of several channels of the interregional short-term capital market. The national money market therefore was quite an extensive and fairly well-developed institution. The examination of structure alone certainly creates a presumption in favor of capital market integration or at least of the view that local markets were partially integrated together. It seems clear that local capital markets were not completely segmented or isolated.

During the postbellum period there was a marked convergence of regional interest rates, which has been taken as evidence of the development over the period of a national capital market. In view of the strains placed on the financial system by the shifts in the nature and location of economic activity in the postbellum period and of the fact that the national capital market in the antebellum period appeared to have been in a continuous state of disequilibrium, the observed convergence of regional short-term interest rates is quite remarkable. Were the institutions of the banking system large enough and extensive enough to be adequate in promoting the interregional transfer of funds and hence a perfect national short-term capital market? What forces were responsible for the pronounced narrowing of interregional interest rate differentials in the period after the Civil War?

Cost differentials may be ruled out as an explanation for the observed differentials and their narrowing. Even though the smaller banks in interior regions incurred higher operating costs, the cost differential with average-sized Eastern banks was quite small. High interest rates in the interior on average were associated with high profit rates for national banks, but the higher rates of return may have been compensation for bearing greater risk in interior regions or due to local monopoly power.[1] To assess the performance of the

[1] National banks by regions that earned higher profit rates also experienced greater variability in their rates of return. Consider the relationship between the mean and variance of the series of the ratio of net profits to capital and surplus of national banks by region for

market in the convergence of regional interest rates, the patterns of local interest rates were examined within the context of a mean-variance model of bank asset selection that allowed for the existence of a monopolistic local loan market; the local loan rate then could be separated into a risk premium, because previous studies had not explicitly taken risk into account, and a monopoly premium component.

If existing financial institutions had been successful in creating a perfect national market in short-term capital, then interregional interest rate differentials should have been reflections only of regional differences in risk and the narrowing of differentials should have been the result of the relative decline in riskiness of interior loans. For country banks, risk premiums did indeed decline over time. In some areas the declines in risk were significant, but overall the magnitudes of the decreases in risk differentials could account for only a small part of the narrowing of interest rate differentials. Moreover, contrary to the existence of a perfect market, local banking market structure had a significant influence on the level of local interest rates across areas, for both country and reserve city banks. The interregional capital market therefore was not a perfect market, such that there was free mobility of funds and risk alone could account for geographical differences in interest rates. Although the structure of the interregional capital market did facilitate financial flows, it achieved only partial integration of the short-

the period 1870–1900. See Keith Powlison, *Profits of the National Banks* (Boston: Gorham Press, 1931), pp. 105–106.

Region	Mean	Variance
New England	6.39%	4.09
Eastern	7.83	2.84
Southern	9.06	5.40
Midwestern	8.93	5.46
Western	11.24	25.33
Pacific	12.56	38.30

term capital market. Other institutions, such as state banks and trust companies, did develop to bypass National Banking Act regulations; the correspondent banking system spread and the commercial paper market developed in lieu of the prohibited branch banking system. However, they were not completely successful in eliminating market imperfections. The performance of the market has to be studied in addition to the pattern of institutional change. Although contemporary criticisms of the banking system for the most part ignored the extent to which interregional flows of funds were facilitated in spite of National Banking Act restrictions, they were at least partially justified in that barriers to free capital mobility did exist.

The short-term capital market, then, was segmented into local markets to some degree. The two major explanations of the convergence of regional interest rates over the period, the institutional change and the market power hypotheses, are both based on the possession of local monopoly power by banks in the interior. In the institutional change hypothesis it is diminished by the introduction of the commercial paper market into a Western area, resulting in a capital inflow from the East. The spread of the market westward was said to have allowed a larger flow of capital into high-interest-rate areas, thereby promoting the equalization of local interest rates across regions. However, hypotheses tests indicated that the timing of the expansion of the commercial paper market seemed to have had little influence on the pattern of local interest rate decline. In the case of reserve cities, test of the effects of the introduction of the commercial paper market in a city on local interest rates produced no overall pattern of significance, although to be sure in some areas there were significant results. More generally, the pace of westward expansion of the market did not fit well with regional interest rate movements. For example, the commercial paper market reached the cities in the Pacific states only about the turn of the century, whereas in fact country bank interest rates in that region had been declining at a substantial rate long before that.

The market power hypothesis was also based on at least a partially segmented capital market. The Sylla hypothesis, emphasizing the role of the Gold Standard Act of 1900 in reducing capital requirements for country national banks, thereby lowering barriers to entry and eroding the local monopoly power of existing national banks, first of all does not fit the observed pattern of interest rate differentials; it predicts a dramatic narrowing of interregional differentials after 1900, whereas in actuality we observe exactly the opposite pattern, with the progress toward integration slowing rather than accelerating after 1900.

The Sylla hypothesis with its concentration on national banks also neglects the growth of state banks, which were more numerous than and grew more rapidly than national banks over the later part of the postbellum period. The erosion of local monopoly power accounts for almost all of the observed decline in local interest rates in most states in our regressions for the period 1893–1911, but it was due to the growth of state rather than national banks. Contrary to Redlich's assertion that "state banks couldn't defeat the national banking system,"[2] state banks were close substitutes for national ones soon after the end of the Civil War. National Banking Act restrictions, such as the prohibition of lending on real estate and high minimum capital requirements, spurred the formation of state banks, which in almost all cases were subject to more liberal regulations. As a result, the number of state banks in small towns and rural areas increased dramatically, thus reducing the local monopoly power of existing banks. For example, in Chapter VI the effects of lower state bank minimum capital requirements, an easily quantifiable bank regulation, were examined; both

[2] Fritz Redlich, *The Molding of American Banking: Men and Ideas* (New York: Johnson Reprint Co., 1968), p. 178.

over time and across areas, lower minimum state bank capital requirements are associated with greater declines in interest rates through encouraging the growth of state banks. Sylla was correct in emphasizing the role of local monopoly in interest rate differentials, but not in identifying the causes of its erosion.

In addition, our estimates suggest that unless the Eastern interregional balance-of-trade surplus was enormous, close to $1 billion per year during the period 1900–1910, the direction of short-term capital flow must have been from West to East, a result consistent with the observations of contemporaries concerning the concentration of funds in New York through the system and consistent also with the role of New York as a financial intermediary, importing short-term capital and exporting long-term capital. This pattern of short-term capital flow, from West to East, supports the market power hypothesis, in which the crucial element is the number of banks in the local market, not necessarily an increase in the supply of funds. If state banks were established with local funds, then there could have been a decline in local interest rates without a capital inflow. On the other hand, if the destruction of barriers to interregional capital mobility, such as by the spread of the commercial paper market, had been the principal factor in reducing interregional interest rate differentials, the net flow of short-term capital would have been from East to West.

The influences on the convergence of regional interest rates were complex, and the relative reduction in the riskiness of Western loans played some part. Lack of interest rate data prevents a systematic examination of the performance of the national capital market in the period immediately following the Civil War; response to the disequilibrium of the Civil War, relative reductions in the riskiness of interior loans, and the growth of private banks, all may not be ruled out as forces influencing interest rate convergence in the earlier part of the postbellum period. However, in the later part changes in the legal framework by states, such as lower

minimum capital requirements and more liberal incorporation laws, thus encouraging the growth of state banks after
the mid-1880s, appear to have been the most important factors in accounting for the observed decreases in differentials,
whereas reductions in the barriers to interregional capital
mobility seemed much less significant. The role of institutional change was central in the erosion of local monopoly
power, but it was in state banking regulations rather than in
the expansion of the commercial paper market or in liberalization of national banking requirements.

Data Appendix

INTEREST RATES

IN his study of capital market integration, Lance Davis constructed what have become the basic measures of performance in short-term capital market integration for the pre-Federal Reserve period, gross and net returns on earning assets of national banks.[1] To the extent that the composition of earning asset portfolios differed across regions, differences in the rates of return on earning assets would not be fully reflective of differences in the rate of return on loans. For example, if loans were especially risky in a particular area, the bank may have chosen to hold a larger proportion of relatively safe assets, such as bankers' balances, than they would have otherwise; as a result, the rate of return on earning assets may substantially understate the actual loan rate. To the extent that Western banks held more bankers' balances than Eastern banks, as Sylla argues, Davis's proxy, the rate of return on earning assets, would understate Western interest rates and thus also understate the interregional differential. In addition, because we want to test the market power hypothesis, we need to consider explicitly the effects of banking concentration. If we are examining the effects of local market structures on local loan rates, we should consider a smaller unit than the region, which Davis uses.

In this section the construction of the basic data employed in this study, average rates of return on the loan and discount portfolios of country national banks by state and of reserve city national banks, is described. Just as for Davis,

[1] Lance Davis, "The Investment Market, 1870–1914: The Evolution of a National Market," *Journal of Economic History*, XXV (September 1965), pp. 360–365.

the primary sources of information are the annual reports of the U.S. Comptroller of the Currency. All national banks were required to report their balance sheets on five call dates per year, unannounced in advance. Income statements, on the other hand, were reported semiannually.[2] From 1869 to 1914 net earnings of national banks, gross earnings less losses and operating expenses, were reported, but only after 1888 were gross earnings explicitly reported. Unfortunately, the unavailability of gross earnings figures for earlier dates limits the construction of local interest rate data and hence explicit examination of the forces promoting regional interest rate convergence to the period after 1888, even though the process had begun earlier in the postbellum period, as shown in Figure 1.

The time period covered here therefore extends from 1888, the first date for which gross earnings are reported, until 1911 for country banks by state;[3] for reserve cities the interest rate series runs from 1888 or whenever the reserve city was established until 1911. Because the gross earnings series are semiannual, the interest rate series are also of semiannual periodicity.[4] 1911 is chosen as the end date because in following years gross earnings were reported annually rather than semiannually.

In the derivation of the interest rate series, returns on other earnings assets are subtracted from the gross earnings

[2] Between 1888 and 1906 the six-month periods ended on March 1 and September 1, the former period including the harvest season. In 1907 the report dates were changed to January 1 and July 1, so that from 1907 to 1911 the time periods were July to January and January to July. Because the former period still includes the harvest season, this shift should have little effect on our estimates.

[3] Except for North and South Dakota, 1890–1911; Oklahoma, 1891–1911.

[4] Linear interpolation between call dates was employed to convert the balance sheet figures into data of semiannual periodicity. For a detailed description of the process, see John A. James, "The Evolution of the National Money Market, 1888–1911" (unpublished Ph.D. dissertation, MIT, 1974), pp. 399–403.

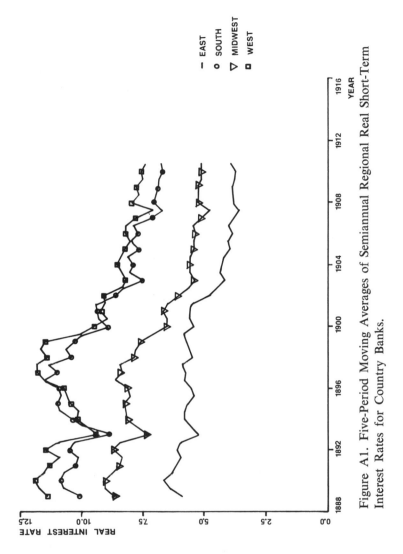

Figure A1. Five-Period Moving Averages of Semiannual Regional Real Short-Term Interest Rates for Country Banks.

of the bank, leaving the return on loans and discounts as a residual, and from total returns to loans the average rate of return on loans can be computed.[5] For a detailed discussion of asset and liability entries in a national bank balance sheet, see Alcorn[6] or several other contemporary banking textbooks.[7] Here only five major categories of earning assets will be considered: Loans and Discounts, Bonds for Circulation, Bonds for Deposits, Other Stocks and Bonds, and Due from Banks.

"Bonds for Circulation" represents government bonds held as security against the issue of national bank notes. "Bonds for Deposits" represents bonds deposited with the Treasury as security against deposits of public funds[8] to which we add "U.S. Bonds on Hand." "Due from Banks" represent bankers' balances on deposit in other banks, so that they are assets of the bank in question; here they include

[5] Smiley has recently derived series of average rates of return on private earning assets for national banks by a similar technique, also using data from the Comptroller of the Currency reports. However, as opposed to the average return on the loan and discount portfolio derived here, the rate of return on private earning assets also includes the returns on stocks, securities, and non-U.S. bonds. Additional reasons why the series derived here are probably more accurate than the Smiley ones are discussed in note 26 to Chapter I. Gene Smiley, "Interest Rate Movement in the United States, 1888–1913," *Journal of Economic History*, XXXV (September 1975), p. 595.

[6] Edgar G. Alcorn, *The Duties and Liabilities of Bank Directors* (Columbus, Ohio: Financial Publishing Co., 1908), pp. 138–151.

[7] For example, Horace White, *Money and Banking,* 5th ed. (Boston: Ginn and Co., 1911), pp. 205–215; Davis Dewey and Martin Shugrue, *Banking and Credit* (New York: Ronald Press Co., 1922), pp. 126–141; William H. Kniffin, Jr., *The Practical Work of a Bank* (New York: The Bankers' Publishing Co., 1915), pp. 261–274.

[8] At first only U.S. bonds were accepted as security, but later other bonds became acceptable. For simplicity we assume "Bonds for Deposit" to be composed homogeneously of U.S. bonds; because it is only a small item on the balance sheet, this assumption should have no serious effects.

"Due from National Banks" plus "Due from State Banks" plus "Due from Reserve Agents."

Thus, the total return on the loan and discount portfolio may be written:

$$TR = GE - r_{US} (BC + BD) - r_{BB} DB - r_{RRB} OSB$$

where TR is the total return on the loan and discount portfolio; GE is gross earnings; BC is Bonds for Circulation; BD is Bonds for Deposit; DB is Due from Banks; OSB is Other Stocks and Bonds; r_{US} is the average interest rate on government bonds; r_{BB} is the interest rate on bankers' balances; and r_{RRB} is the interest rate on prime railroad bonds.

The Comptroller of the Currency classified total holdings of U.S. bonds used as security for circulation by yields. From such a table the average interest rate on all government bonds held for circulation may be calculated. This rate is applied to the Bonds for Circulation holdings of all country and reserve city banks, implicitly assuming that the bond portfolio of each bank had its holdings distributed among bonds of different coupon values in the same proportions as the national aggregate. In addition, this rate is applied to Bonds for Deposits holdings, under the assumption that the relative proportions of different coupons there were the same as for Bonds for Circulation, a simplification for which there is some justification. First of all, Bonds for Deposits were small relative to Bonds for Circulation, so we are defiling only a small part of total bank holdings of government bonds by this assumption. In 1900 U.S. bonds held for purposes other than circulation equalled 38 percent of Bonds for Circulation; in 1905, 16 percent; in 1910, 9 percent. Also, in any given year the vast majority of government bonds were of one particular coupon, so the composition of Bonds for Circulation and Bonds for Deposits should have been quite similar. For example, in 1899, 4 percent bonds constituted 63 percent of the U.S. bonds held to secure circulation; in 1905, 2 percent bonds amounted to 98 percent.

Macaulay's index of yields on railroad bonds[9] is used as the rate of return on Other Stocks and Bonds, because railroad bonds constituted a majority of nongovernment securities in bank portfolios. In 1908 railroad bonds made up 66 percent of bond holdings other than governments of national banks.[10] The interest rate on bankers' balances in New York remained virtually constant at 2 percent throughout the period.[11] We also assume that the bank has no sources of income other than the returns on earning assets, a reasonable assumption because the profit on services such as exchange, issuing cashier's checks, and so on must have been relatively quite small.

A simple procedure to get the rate of return on the loan and discount portfolio would be to divide the total return by the average value of loans and discounts outstanding over the period. However, we are interested in calculating the stated rate on loans rather than the realized, or net, rate; these figures differ because some loans were defaulted on. Therefore, because the denominator, average loans and discounts over the period, contains some loans on which the bank will not realize any income, the expression would measure the realized rate on the loan portfolio rather than the original rate; in order to approximate the stated rate instead, the denominator has to be purged of defaulted loans. Losses during the period are thus subtracted from Loans and Discounts in the denominator to yield an expression for the average interest rate on loans.

This formulation also implicitly assumes that returns from loans were realized within the same period in which they were made or else that loans and discounts were relatively

---

[9] Frederick Macaulay, *Some Theoretical Problems Suggested by the Movements of Interest Rates, Bond Yields, and Stock Prices in the United States since 1856* (New York: National Bureau of Economic Research, 1938), pp. A141–A161.

[10] U.S. Comptroller of the Currency, *Annual Report*, 1909 (Washington, D.C.: U.S. Government Printing Office, 1909), p. 9.

[11] See Appendix B.

constant over time. The influence of the real-bills doctrine, however, ensured that commercial loans would be short-term, whether in fact they were self-liquidating or not. Most loans were about six months in length; very few were for longer than a year. If the average length of loans was around six months, then most loans made in one semiannual period would not have been realized until the next one. If the bank was growing rapidly, loans made in period $t - 1$ being repaid in period t would be substantially smaller than the amount of loans outstanding in period t appearing in the denominator, and hence the calculated interest rates would be biased downward. To compensate for this effect, "Loans and Discounts" in the denominator is lagged one period. Thus the expression for the average rate of return on the loan and discount portfolio may be written as

$$R_t = \frac{GE_t - r_{US} \ (BC_t + BD_t) - r_{BB} \ DB_t - r_{RRB} \ OSB_t}{(LD_{t-1} - LOSSES_t)}$$

In 1910 the Comptroller of the Currency collected figures for the average rate of interest charged on time loans by national banks.[12] The figures, by state, unfortunately do not include reports from all banks and also combine country and reserve city banks together. Nevertheless, the Pearson correlation coefficient between these reports of average interest rates charged on loans by state on June 30, 1910,[13] and the computed average rate of return on loans for country banks was 0.92.[14] So our computed interest rates seem to be quite faithful reflections of actual ones.

[12] U.S. Comptroller of the Currency, *Annual Report*, 1910, pp. 768–769.

[13] Another difference is that the Comptroller figures represent the average rate on loans at a point in time, whereas the computed series are semiannual averages.

[14] In our calculated series it is impossible to separate out the rate of return on demand loans from that on time loans, which might account for some of the deviation between average "actual" and computed values. However, the magnitude of the differential should not be too substantial, because outside of the Pacific states demand loans

COMPARISON OF BRADSTREET'S INTEREST RATE SERIES WITH
THOSE DERIVED FROM THE COMPTROLLER'S REPORTS

A source of information about local financial conditions in cities outside of New York was *Bradstreet's*, a weekly trade journal, in which average weekly rates of discount were reported for principal commercial cities during our period.[15] Interest rates reported in *Bradstreet's* comprised the basic data in R. M. Breckenridge's study of interregional interest rate differentials, shown in Table 1. In the previous section the computed interest rate series derived from the Comptroller's reports were compared with average loan rates of national banks presented in the 1910 *Annual Report*; in this section the interest rate series derived from *Bradstreet's* reports will be compared with our computed series for selected reserve cities.

The local interest rate figures employed by Goodhart, discussed in Chapter IV, were collected for 1902–1913 from *Dun's Review*, also a weekly business journal that reported economic conditions in major cities. The discussion here of the methods of collection of local discount rates is applicable to both the rates reported in *Bradstreet's* and the ones appearing in *Dun's Review*. Local discount rates in both series

---

constituted only about 20 percent of total country bank loans. In addition, as is pointed out later, the Comptroller's study found the average interest rate on demand loans to be only slightly below that on time loans, although such a finding is rather suspicious. See U.S. Comptroller of the Currency, *Annual Report*, 1910, pp. 768–769.

[15] Cities reported during at least some part of our time period include: Boston, New York, Baltimore, Hartford, Philadelphia, Providence, Cincinnati, Chicago, Pittsburgh, New Orleans, St. Louis, Portland, Me., Richmond, Buffalo, Memphis, San Francisco, Milwaukee, Indianapolis, Cleveland, Detroit, St. Paul, Nashville, Louisville, Minneapolis, Kansas City, St. Joseph, Charleston, S.C., Los Angeles, Duluth, Galveston, Mobile, Omaha, Savannah, Atlanta, Birmingham, Houston, Portland, Ore., Salt Lake City, Little Rock, Dallas, Tacoma, Seattle, Denver, Montreal, and Toronto. It may be noted that not all of the cities reported in *Bradstreet's* were reserve cites.

Table A1

Regional Interest Rates, Unadjusted, 1888 I–1911 II
(percent)

Year	East	South	Midwest	West
1888 I	4.560	8.093	7.137	9.498
II	4.664	8.202	7.268	9.248
1889 I	5.229	8.381	7.475	9.638
II	5.038	8.732	7.254	8.953
1890 I	5.286	8.832	7.266	10.441
II	5.297	8.733	6.972	8.694
1891 I	5.306	8.774	7.297	10.029
II	4.639	8.287	6.510	8.596
1892 I	4.543	7.377	6.571	8.543
II	4.277	7.902	6.357	8.135
1893 I	4.620	8.072	6.775	8.834
II	4.442	7.457	5.807	7.310
1894 I	3.660	6.098	4.788	5.805
II	4.017	8.018	5.853	7.343
1895 I	4.008	7.866	6.012	7.424
II	3.754	8.034	5.686	7.096
1896 I	4.022	7.853	6.025	8.402
II	3.886	7.754	5.647	8.279
1897 I	3.702	6.660	5.009	6.359
II	3.729	7.640	6.062	7.815
1898 I	4.113	7.437	5.693	9.246
II	4.013	7.907	5.502	7.280
1899 I	3.520	6.745	5.265	9.076
II	4.177	7.397	4.741	7.283
1900 I	4.350	7.231	5.685	7.857
II	5.308	8.500	6.034	6.528
1901 I	4.358	7.328	5.432	8.491
II	3.839	7.626	4.375	6.545
1902 I	3.955	7.141	5.164	8.006
II	3.603	7.041	4.597	6.859
1903 I	4.192	6.769	5.142	8.086
II	3.670	7.157	4.588	6.766
1904 I	3.658	6.325	5.051	7.765
II	3.670	7.406	4.607	6.594

Table A1 (*continued*)

Year	East	South	Midwest	West
1905 I	3.420	6.719	4.877	8.082
II	3.456	7.035	4.542	6.413
1906 I	3.512	6.715	5.080	7.887
II	3.581	7.014	4.568	5.961
1907 I	3.257	6.840	4.729	8.214
II	3.691	6.822	4.784	7.246
1908 I	3.629	5.903	4.796	7.061
II	3.412	6.125	4.429	5.914
1909 I	3.448	6.537	5.263	7.893
II	3.697	6.890	4.802	7.245
1910 I	4.081	7.050	5.470	8.529
II	4.129	7.470	5.376	7.649
1911 I	4.294	7.007	5.733	6.166
II	4.500	6.914	5.302	6.974

were reported by local "stringers." In smaller cities reporting was sometimes quite erratic, with no reports at all appearing for long periods.[16] Goodhart, however, argues that the erratic nature of the reporting may lead one to underestimate the reliability of the data, because in many cases no report meant no change in local money market conditions; a change in rates would have been an event of which local reporters would have taken notice.[17]

Goodhart also considers the possibility of errors in reporting to have been relatively unlikely. Mistakes or purposive errors in reporting by banks were most probably unlikely. Similarly, purposive errors in reporting by local stringers of fallacious data sent in to satisfy requests for information were thought to be unlikely also. In the latter case, the dilatory reporter could just vaguely report conditions in the money market to be the same, so there would be little in-

[16] C. A. E. Goodhart, *The New York Money Market and the Finance of Trade, 1900–1913.* (Cambridge, Mass.: Harvard University Press, 1969), p. 200.

[17] Ibid., pp. 200–201.

centive to falsify the record completely.[18] He thus concludes the picture of extreme rigidity of interest rates in interior cities to be fairly accurate.

However, in Chapter IV it was argued that there is a *prima facie* case for the implausibility of such stable interior rates. Thin markets should have been much more volatile than the well-developed Eastern money markets. Moreover, in the time-series regressions the estimates of the seasonality component in country bank interest rates in agricultural areas turned out to be quite substantial.[19] Local interest rate stability in the face of substantial seasonality fluctuations was very unlikely. For example, Goodhart's data show no changes in rates at all in New Orleans over the entire year of 1910, and also complete interest rate stability in Kansas City in 1907, 1909, and 1910.[20]

A similar argument applies to the longer run. Just as it is implausible that interior interest rates were constant over the year, being immune to seasonal influences, it is also very implausible that such rates would have been constant for several years at a time and that the volatility of interest rates decreased with the thinness of the market. *Dun's Review* reported Kansas City rates as being virtually constant, with only two brief aberrations, for four years, between 1907 and 1910.[21]

The *Bradstreet's* series between 1886 and 1901 also show a number of smaller cities with very stable rates, although this stability is probably not as widespread as in the *Dun's* series. St. Joseph interest rates were absolutely rigid between 1894 and 1901, for example. Because there was a severe decline in the price level during the 1890s, if in fact nominal interest rates had been quite stable, then real rates in these

[18] Ibid., p. 201.

[19] The Comptroller series for individual cities seem to have a much greater seasonal component than the respective *Bradstreet's* series. The residuals of the Comptroller's series regressed on a time trend exhibit very distinct seasonal patterns, in contrast to many *Bradstreet's* series.

[20] Goodhart, *The New York Money Market*, p. 91.

[21] Ibid.

interior cities would have risen sharply during the 1890s, a result that appears suspect.

The *Bradstreet's* reports often cited a range of interest rates in particular cities. Rather than reflecting the size of the discount attached to paper of greater risk or longer maturities, Breckenridge argued that the margin indicated the high and low rates on local paper for the week because *Bradstreet's* quoted only first-class, double-name paper.[22] In the calculations here, a simple average of the high and low rates was taken to represent the weekly rate of discount, which in turn was incorporated into semiannual averages of the same timing (September–March, March–September) as the computed series. Figures A2 and A6 present five-pe-

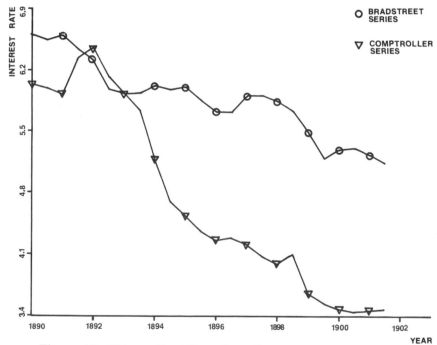

Figure A2. Chicago Short-Term Loan Rates.

[22] R. M. Breckenridge, "Discount Rates in the United States," *Political Science Quarterly*, XIII (March 1898), pp. 121–122.

256

riod moving averages of the *Bradstreet's* series and the series computed from the Comptroller's reports for the period 1889–1901 for Chicago, New Orleans, Pittsburgh, Omaha, and San Francisco, a sample of representative cities.

Nominal interest rates generally fell sharply during the 1890s. The New York commercial paper rate declined about 2 percentage points before turning up toward the end of the decade.[23] In Figure A2 for Chicago both series declined over the 1890s, but the fall in the Comptroller's series was much sharper; the Comptroller's series also leveled out at the end of the decade, just as the New York commercial paper rates did. A similar relationship between the *Brad-*

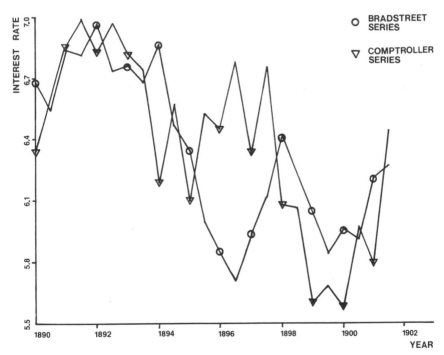

Figure A3. New Orleans Short-Term Loan Rates.

[23] Macaulay, *Some Theoretical Problems,* pp. A150–A152.

257

street's and Comptroller's series was evidenced in the St. Louis rates. The relatively small nominal declines in the *Bradstreet's* series meant that real rates would have been rising sharply in the early 1890s and then rapidly dropping in the latter part of the decade for St. Louis, Pittsburgh, and Omaha, as well as for Chicago. On the other hand, the real rates computed from the Comptroller's interest rate series for those cities show much steadier rates of decrease over the period.[24]

The stability of nominal rates noted by Goodhart is evidenced in Figures A4 and A5. In Pittsburgh the *Bradstreet's* rates seemed quite stable over the long term, with two sharp drops in the first part of the 1890s; however, the rate remained absolutely constant for a two-year period between 1896 and 1898. In Omaha, *Bradstreet's* rates also remained absolutely stable between 1895 and 1897 and also in 1889 and 1890. In contrast, in both cities the rates computed from the Comptroller's data show very definite long-run declines.

Figures A3 and A6 present the New Orleans and San Francisco interest rates. In both of these cities the difference between the two different measures of local interest rates is relatively small; they fit together quite well. One possible explanation for this variation in the strength of correlation between the *Bradstreet's* and Comptroller's series across cities is differences in the accuracy of reporting of local money rates to *Bradstreet's*. It is not known how those quotations were collected locally; thus it may well have been the case that some local reporters were more assiduous and conscientious than others. So the New Orleans and San

[24] Real rates of interest here were computed by imposing an *a priori* lag structure for the determination of price expectations as discussed in note 28 to Chapter I. Because we are interested only in the effects of real factors on the pattern of local interest rates and hence on interregional interest rate differentials, we need to separate out the influences of changes in the price level. Hence, all the interest rates used in the regressions underlying the hypotheses tests discussed in Chapter VI are real rates rather than nominal ones.

Francisco *Bradstreet's* series could possibly be much more accurate than those reported from other cities.

Generally the Comptroller's series lay below the *Bradstreet's* series in most cities, such as in Chicago or Omaha, with San Francisco being an exception. Similarly, our estimates of country bank loan rates usually were lower than those local rates quoted in the 1910 *Annual Report*. How, then, can we account for the lower values that are derived from the Comptroller's data?

One possibility for which we have seen some evidence through the extraordinary stability of some *Bradstreet's* rates is inaccurate reporting of local *Bradstreet's* stringers.[25]

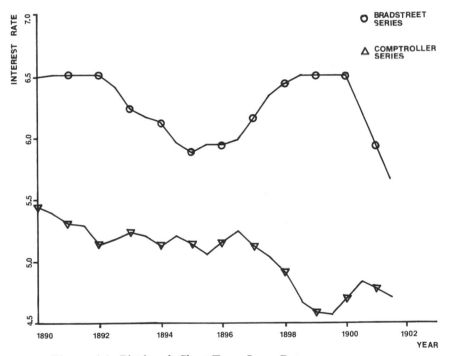

Figure A4. Pittsburgh Short-Term Loan Rates.

[25] Another possibility is that to some extent the two series are measuring different things. The Comptroller's series represents the

259

Moreover, the Comptroller's series represents an average rate of return on the entire loan portfolio, whereas demand loans constituted a substantial proportion of the portfolio in some areas. For example, in 1910 demand loans made up 24 percent of the total loan portfolio of national banks outside New York City, "that ratio being only slightly lower than for New York banks."[26] If demand loans usually carried

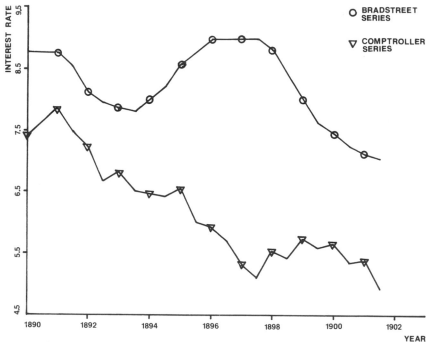

Figure A5. Omaha Short-Term Loan Rates.

average interest rate on loans, whereas the *Bradstreet's* reports supposedly represent the quoted rate on first-class, double-name paper. In many localities the money market was probably not as well organized and borrowers so uniform that substantial numbers of them received the quoted rate, so this in part might account for the relative stability of the *Bradstreet's* rates.

[26] U.S. Comptroller of the Currency, *Annual Report*, 1910, p. 4.

lower interest rates than time loans, their inclusion would pull down the interest rate estimates from the Comptroller of the Currency data. The 1910 *Annual Report,* however, reported this differential to be quite small; as of June 30, 1910, interest rates on time loans of national banks averaged 7.33 percent, while interest rates on demand loans averaged 7.00 percent.[27] However, in view of the low open-market call loan rates, one might be skeptical of the small magnitude of this differential.

In view of the facts that the stability of *Bradstreet's* and *Dun's Review* interest rates contradict our theoretical inferences about the volatility of thin versus thick markets.

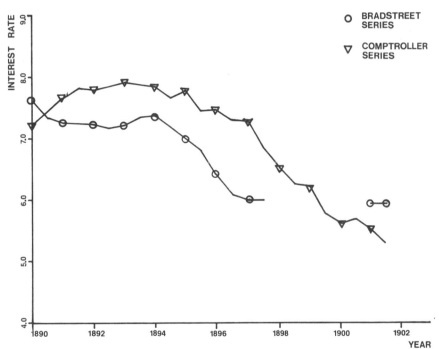

Figure A6. San Francisco Short-Term Loan Rates.

[27] Ibid., p. 777.

and that the movements of the nominal and real local interest rate series derived from the Comptroller's data paralleled movements of known open-market rates over the period while the *Bradstreet's* series did not, we might conclude that the rates derived here from the Comptroller's *Reports* are more accurate representatives of local interest rates than those reported in *Bradstreet's*.

The years after the turn of the century were generally ones of high interest rates, so there was no downward pressure. Two 1906 articles mention 2 percent as the rate on bankers' balances,[24] and several textbooks refer simply to 2 percent as the going rate on bankers' balances.[25] Finally, at the end of the period, during the Federal Reserve hearings, the 2 percent rate was often cited.[26]

Over the last part of the nineteenth century and the first part of the twentieth, therefore, the rate paid by New York banks on bankers' balances remained virtually stable at 2 percent. Indeed, reference was made to the "inflexibility" of interest rates paid by New York banks.[27] Even under substantial downward pressure in the 1890s, the rate fell below 2 percent for only brief periods. In 1890 there were 108 banks in New York City with 47 national ones; in 1910 there were 113 with 39 national ones.[28] Only a small part of this total participated actively in the competition for country deposits, but the constancy of the rate on bankers' balances is clearly indicative of an extremely competitive banking market in New York in the postbellum period.

---

in Chicago and Boston. Two years earlier a number of banks in Boston reduced their rates on interbank deposits to 2 or 2½ percent. *Bankers' Magazine*, LXIV (April 1894), p. 788; *Bankers' Magazine*, XLII (July 1892), pp. 61–62.

[24] George M. Coffin, "The New York Rate of Interest," *Bankers' Magazine*, LXXII (January 1906), p. 46; Festus J. Wade, "What Causes Fluctuations in Money Rates?" *Proceedings of the New York State Bankers' Association*, 1906, p. 36.

[25] For example, see Horace White, *Money and Banking*, 5th ed. (Boston: Ginn and Co., 1911), p. 212.

[26] U.S. Senate, Banking and Currency Committee, *Hearings on HR7837 (S2639)*, 63rd Congress, 1st Session, pp. 1293, 1354.

[27] C. F. Bentley, "Commercial Paper as an Investment for Country Banks," *Proceedings of the Nebraska Bankers' Association*, 1903, p. 184.

[28] Myers, *The New York Money Market*, p. 244.

Bibliography

Alcorn, Edgar G. *The Duties and Liabilities of Bank Directors.* Columbus: Financial Publishing Co., 1908.

Alhadeff, David A. *Monopoly and Competition in Banking.* Berkeley: University of California Press, 1954.

American Bankers' Association. *Proceedings,* 1881–1911.

Andersen, Theodore A. *A Century of Banking in Wisconsin.* Madison: State Historical Society of Wisconsin, 1954.

Andrew, A. Piatt. "The Crux of the Currency Question," *Yale Review,* n.s. II (July 1913), pp. 595–620.

————. "The Influence of the Crops upon Business in America," *Quarterly Journal of Economics,* XX (May 1906), pp. 323–353.

————, ed. *Statistics for the United States, 1867–1909.* Washington, D.C.: U.S. Government Printing Office, 1910.

Andrews, T. W. "Banking Methods—Ancient and Modern," *Proceedings of the South Carolina Bankers' Association,* 1905, pp. 69–86.

Armstrong, Leroy, and Denny, J. O. *Financial California.* San Francisco: Coast Banker Publishing Co., 1916.

Arrington, Leonard J. "Banking Enterprises in Utah, 1847–1880," *Business History Review,* XXIX (December 1955), pp. 312–334.

Bagehot, Walter. *Lombard Street.* New York: Scribner, Armstrong, and Co., 1873.

Baker, W. H. "Commercial Paper," *Proceedings of the American Bankers' Association,* 1887, pp. 45–47.

Balabanis, H. P. *The American Discount Market.* Chicago: University of Chicago Press, 1935.

"Bank Loans," *Bankers' Magazine,* XXXVII (May 1883), pp. 809–811.

"Bank Losses—How Caused and Their Consequences," *Bankers' Magazine,* XXXIX (August 1884), pp. 134–137.

Bankers' Magazine (and Statistical Register), Vols. XXIV–LXXXIII, 1870–1911.

Barnett, George E. *State Banks and Trust Companies since the*

Passage of the National-Bank Act. Washington, D.C.: U.S. Government Printing Office, 1911.

Barsalow, F. W. "The Concentration of Banking Power in Nevada: An Historical Analysis," *Business History Review*, XXIX (December 1955), pp. 350–363.

Beach, W. E. *British International Gold Movements and Banking Policy: 1881–1913.* Cambridge, Mass.: Harvard University Press, 1935.

Beal, Thomas P., Jr. "Effect of Increased Operations of Note Brokers upon the Earnings of Commercial Banks," *Proceedings of the American Bankers' Association*, 1916, pp. 499–506.

Beckhart, Benjamin H., ed. *Business Loans of American Commercial Banks.* New York: Ronald Press Co., 1959.

———. *The New York Money Market, Volume III: Uses of Funds.* New York: Columbia University Press, 1932.

———, and Smith, James G. *The New York Money Market, Volume II: Sources and Movements of Funds.* New York: Columbia University Press, 1932.

Bell, Frederick W., and Murphy, Neil B. "Impact of Market Structure on the Price of a Commercial Banking Service," *Review of Economics and Statistics*, LI (May 1969), pp. 210–213.

Bell, Spurgeon. "Profit on National Bank Notes," *American Economic Review*, II (March 1912), pp. 38–60.

Bentley, C. F. "Commercial Paper as an Investment for Country Banks," *Proceedings of the Nebraska Bankers' Association*, 1903, pp. 174–185.

Blair, William. *Historical Sketch of Banking in North Carolina.* New York: B. Rhodes and Co., 1899.

Blye, A. W. "Collection of Country Checks," *Proceedings of the American Bankers' Association*, 1885, pp. 135–137.

Board of Governors of the Federal Reserve System. *All-Bank Statistics, 1896–1955.* Washington, D.C.: U.S. Government Printing Office, 1959.

Bogue, Allan G. *From Prairie to Corn Belt.* Chicago: University of Chicago Press, 1963.

———. *Money at Interest.* New York: Russell and Russell, 1955.

Bolles, Albert S. *The National Bank Act and its Judicial Meaning,* 2nd ed. New York: Homans Publishing Co., 1888.

Bolles, Albert S. "Notes on Banking in New York City," *Bankers' Magazine*, XLIII (April 1889), pp. 721-727.

————. *Practical Banking*, 7th ed. New York: Homans Publishing Co., 1884.

Bradstreet's, Vols. XIV–XXXVIII, 1886–1910.

Breckenridge, R. M. "Branch Banking and Discount Rates," *Bankers' Magazine*, LVIII (January 1899), pp. 38–52.

————. "Discount Rates in the United States," *Political Science Quarterly*, XIII (March 1898), pp. 119–142.

Brokaw, C. L. "A Study in Bank Investments," *Proceedings of the Kansas Bankers' Association*, 1908, pp. 37–48.

Bryan, Alfred C. "History of State Banking in Maryland," *Johns Hopkins Studies in Historical and Political Science*, Ser. XVII. Baltimore, 1899.

Buck, Solon J. *The Agrarian Crusade*. New Haven, Conn.: Yale University Press, 1921.

Cagan, Phillip. *Determinants and Effects of Changes in the Stock of Money, 1875–1960*. New York: Columbia University Press, 1965.

Caldwell, Stephen A. *A Banking History of Louisiana*. Baton Rouge: Louisiana State University Press, 1935.

Cameron, Rondo, ed. *Banking and Economic Development*. New York: Oxford University Press, 1972.

———— et al. *Banking in the Early Stages of Industrialization: A Study in Comparative Economic History*. New York: Oxford University Press, 1967.

Cannon, J. G. *Clearing Houses*. Washington, D.C.: U.S. Government Printing Office, 1910.

Carson, Deane, ed. *Banking and Monetary Studies*. Homewood, Ill.: Richard D. Irwin, 1963.

Cartinhour, Gaines T. *Branch, Group, and Chain Banking*. New York: Macmillan Company, 1931.

Case, J. H. "The Desirability of Commercial Paper as a Bank Investment," *Proceedings of the New Jersey Bankers' Association*, 1912, pp. 30–40.

Catterall, Ralph C. H. *The Second Bank of the United States*. Chicago: University of Chicago Press, 1903.

Chapman, John M., and Westerfield, Ray B. *Branch Banking*. New York: Harper & Brothers, 1942.

Chase, K. S. "Registration of Commercial Paper," *Proceedings of the Minnesota Bankers' Association*, 1911, pp. 30–44.

Clayton, B. F. "The Banker and His Customer," *Proceedings of the Iowa Bankers' Association,* 1892, pp. 34–40.

Coffin, George M. "The New York Rate of Interest," *Bankers' Magazine,* LXXII (January 1906), pp. 44–48.

Commercial and Financial Chronicle, Vols. XLIV–XCII, 1888–1911.

Commission on Money and Credit, ed. *Private Financial Institutions.* Englewood Cliffs, N.J.: Prentice-Hall, 1963.

Conference on Research in Income and Wealth, ed. *Output, Employment, and Productivity in the United States after 1800.* New York: Columbia University Press, 1966.

———. *Trends in the American Economy in the Nineteenth Century.* Princeton, N.J.: Princeton University Press, 1960.

"The Convention of the Arkansas Bankers' Association," *Bankers' Magazine,* XLVI (June 1892), pp. 941–950.

Conway, Thomas, Jr., and Patterson, Ernest M. *The Operation of the New Bank Act.* Philadelphia: J. B. Lippincott Co., 1914.

Cooke, Thornton. "Branch Banking for the West and South," *Quarterly Journal of Economics,* XVIII (November 1903), pp. 97–113.

———. "Distribution of Small Banks in the West," *Quarterly Journal of Economics,* XII (October 1897), pp. 70–72, 105–109.

———. "The Effect of the New Currency Law on Banking in the West," *Quarterly Journal of Economics,* XV (February 1901), pp. 277–286.

Cooley, Thomas, and DeCanio, Stephen. "Varying-Parameter Supply Functions and the Sources of Economic Distress in American Agriculture, 1866–1914," NBER Working Paper No. 57 (September 1974).

Coulter, E. Merton. *The South during Reconstruction, 1865–1877.* Baton Rouge: Louisiana State University Press, 1947.

Cox, Albert H., Jr. "Regulation of Interest Rates on Bank Deposits," *Michigan Business Studies,* XVII, No. 4, 1966.

Crandall, Noble. "Commercial Paper," *Proceedings of the Nebraska Bankers' Association.* 1903, pp. 185–188.

Crane, F. W. "Commercial Paper Purchased from Brokers," *Proceedings of the Illinois State Bankers' Association,* 1916, pp. 130–139.

Dailey, Don M. "The Development of Banking in Chicago before 1890." Unpublished Ph.D. dissertation, Northwestern University, 1934.

Davis, A. M. *The Origins of the National Banking System.* Washington, D.C.: U.S. Government Printing Office, 1910.

Davis, Lance E. et al. *American Economic Growth.* New York: Harper & Row, 1972.

————. "Capital Immobilities and Finance Capitalism: A Study of Economic Evolution in the United States, 1820–1920," *Explorations in Entrepreneurial History*, 2nd series, I (Fall 1963), pp. 88–105.

————. "The Investment Market, 1870–1914: The Evolution of a National Market," *Journal of Economic History*, XXV (September 1965), pp. 355–399.

————. "The New England Textile Mills and the Capital Markets: A Study of Industrial Borrowing, 1840–1860," *Journal of Economic History*, XX (March 1960), pp. 1–30.

————, and North, Douglass C. *Institutional Change and American Economic Growth.* Cambridge: Cambridge University Press, 1971.

Dawes, Charles G. *The Banking System of the United States.* Chicago: Rand, McNally and Co., 1894.

Deming, J. K. "Modern Methods of Soliciting Business," *Proceedings of the Iowa Bankers' Association*, 1892, pp. 19–22.

Dewald, William. "The National Monetary Commission: A Look Back," *Journal of Money, Credit, and Banking*, IV (November 1972), pp. 930–956.

Dewey, Davis. *State Banking before the Civil War.* Washington, D.C.: U.S. Government Printing Office, 1910.

————, and Shugrue, Martin. *Banking and Credit.* New York: Ronald Press Co., 1922.

Dowrie, George W. *American Monetary and Banking Policies.* New York: Longmans, Green and Co., 1930.

Dunbar, Charles F., "The Bank Note Question," *Quarterly Journal of Economics*, VII (October 1892), pp. 55–77.

————. *Chapters on the Theory and History of Banking.* New York: G. P. Putnam's Sons, 1891.

————. *Economic Essays.* New York: Macmillan Company, 1904.

————. *Laws of the United States relating to Currency, Finance, and Banking.* Boston: Ginn and Co., 1897.

Economic Essays in Honour of Gustave Cassel. London: George Allen and Unwin Ltd., 1933.

Engerman, Stanley. "A Note on the Economic Consequences of the Second Bank of the United States," *Journal of Political Economy*, LXXVIII (July/August 1970), pp. 725–728.

Erickson, Erling A. *Banking in Frontier Iowa, 1836–1865*. Ames: Iowa State University Press, 1971.

Fels, Rendigs. *American Business Cycles, 1865–1897*. Chapel Hill: University of North Carolina Press, 1959.

Finney, Katherine. *Interbank Deposits*. New York: Columbia University Press, 1958.

Fiske, Amos K. *The Modern Bank*. New York: D. Appleton and Co., 1904.

Flechsig, Theodore G. "The Effect of Concentration on Bank Loan Rates," *Journal of Finance*, XX (May 1965), pp. 298–311.

Fogel, Robert, and Engerman, Stanley, ed. *The Reinterpretation of American Economic History*. New York: Harper & Row, 1971.

Forgan, James B. *Recollections of a Busy Life*. New York: Bankers' Publishing Co., 1924.

Foulke, Roy A. *The Commercial Paper Market*. New York: Bankers' Publishing Co., 1931.

———. *The Sinews of American Commerce*. New York: Dun and Bradstreet, 1941.

Franklin, N. E. "Commercial Paper," *Proceedings of the South Dakota Bankers' Association*, 1912, pp. 126–131.

Friedman, Milton. *The Interpolation of Time Series by Related Series*, NBER Technical Paper 16. New York: National Bureau of Economic Research, 1962.

———, and Schwartz, Anna. *A Monetary History of the United States*. Princeton, N.J.: Princeton University Press, 1963.

———. *Monetary Statistics of the United States*. New York: Columbia University Press, 1970.

Gallman, Robert E., and Davis, Lance E. "The Share of Savings and Investment in Gross National Product during the 19th Century in the U.S.A.," in *Fourth International Conference of Economic History, Bloomington, Indiana, 1968*. Paris: Mouton, 1973, pp. 437–466.

Gerschenkron, Alexander. *Ecnomic Backwardness in Historical Perspective*. New York: Frederick A. Praeger, 1965.

273

BIBLIOGRAPHY

Gibbons, J. S. *The Banks of New York, Their Dealers, The Clearing House, and the Panic of 1857.* New York: D. Appleton and Co., 1858.

Gilbert, Claude. "Country Credit Methods," *Proceedings of the Maryland Bankers' Association*, 1914, pp. 43–53.

Goldfeld, Stephen. "The Demand for Money Revisited," *Brookings Papers on Economic Activity*, 3, 1973, pp. 577–638.

Goodhart, C. A. E. *The New York Money Market and the Finance of Trade, 1900–1913.* Cambridge, Mass.: Harvard University Press, 1969.

——. "Profit on National Bank Notes, 1900–1913," *Journal of Political Economy*, LXXIII (October 1965), pp. 516–522.

Gordon, W. C. "The Necessity of Credit Statements and the Desirability for Uniformity Thereof," *Proceedings of the American Bankers' Association*, 1916, pp. 521–528.

Greef, Albert O. *The Commercial Paper House in the United States.* Cambridge, Mass.: Harvard University Press, 1938.

Green, George D. *Finance and Economic Development in the Old South.* Stanford, Calif.: Stanford University Press, 1972.

Gurley, John G., and Shaw, Edward S. "Financial Aspects of Economic Development," *American Economic Review*, XLV (September 1955), pp. 515–538.

——. "Financial Structure and Economic Development," *Economic Development and Cultural Change*, XV (April 1967), pp. 257–268.

Gurney, E. R., "A Study in Liquidation," *Proceedings of the Missouri Bankers' Association*, 1911.

Hague, George. "One-Name Paper," *Proceedings of the American Bankers' Association*, 1884, pp. 64–70.

Hammond, Bray. *Banks and Politics in America.* Princeton, N.J.: Princeton University Press, 1957.

Hammond, C. W. "Clearings of Country Collections," *Proceedings of the American Bankers' Association*, 1890, pp. 106–111.

Harris, Seymour, ed. *American Economic History.* New York: McGraw-Hill Book Company, 1961.

Hazelwood, C. B. "Commercial Paper as a Secondary Reserve for West Virginia Banks," *Proceedings of the West Virginia Bankers' Association*, 1913, pp. 83–92.

274

Helderman, Leonard C. *National and State Banks*. Boston: Houghton Mifflin Company, 1931.

Henson, G. N. "Selection of Loans," *Bankers' Magazine*, XLVII (February 1894), pp. 613–616.

Hepburn, Alonzo B. *A History of Currency in the United States*. New York: Macmillan Company, 1903.

Hicks, John D. *The Populist Revolt*. Lincoln: University of Nebraska Press, 1931.

Hilliard, H. P. Untitled address, *Proceedings of the Michigan Bankers' Association*, 1904, pp. 65–75.

Hinchman, T. H. *Banks and Banking in Michigan*. Detroit: M. Graham, 1887.

Hodgman, Donald. *Commercial Banks Loans and Investment Policy*. Champaign: University of Illinois Press, 1963.

Hoffman, Charles. *The Depression of the Nineties*. Westport, Conn.: Greenwood Publishing Corp., 1970.

Hogan, John V. "Bond Investments by National Banks," *Journal of Political Economy*, XXI (November 1913), pp. 843–849.

Hollander, Jacob H. "Security Holdings of National Banks," *American Economic Review*, III (December 1913), pp. 793–814.

Homer, Sidney. *A History of Interest Rates*. New Brunswick, N.J.: Rutgers University Press, 1963.

Hughes, Jonathan R. T. *The Vital Few*. Boston: Houghton Mifflin Company, 1965.

Hull, Walter, ed. *Practical Problems in Banking and Currency*. New York: Macmillan Company, 1907.

Huntington, A. T., and Mawhinney, Robert J. *Laws of the United States Concerning Money, Banking, and Loans, 1778–1909*. Washington, D.C.: U.S. Government Printing Office, 1910.

Hurst, J. M. "Interest on Balances and Its Regulation by Open Market Rates," *Proceedings of the Idaho Bankers' Association*, 1916, pp. 59–67.

"Interest on Bank Balances," *Bankers' Magazine*, XV (August 1865), pp. 124–125.

"Interest on Country Deposits," *Bankers' Magazine*, XXXIX (December 1884), pp. 414–415.

"Interest on Deposits," *Bankers' Magazine*, XXXIV (November 1879), pp. 339–340.

BIBLIOGRAPHY

"Interest on Deposits," *Bankers' Magazine*, XLI (December 1886), pp. 454–455.

Jacoby, Neil, and Saulnier, Raymond. *Business Finance and Banking.* New York: National Bureau of Economic Research, 1947.

James, F. C. *The Growth of Chicago Banks*, 2 vols. New York: Harper & Bros., 1938.

James, John A. "Banking Market Structure, Risk, and the Pattern of Local Interest Rates in the United States, 1893–1911," *Review of Economics and Statistics*, LVIII (November 1976), pp. 453–462.

———. "The Conundrum of the Low Issue of National Bank Notes," *Journal of Political Economy*, LXXXIV (April 1976), pp. 359–367.

———. "The Development of the National Money Market, 1893–1911," *Journal of Economic History*, XXXVI (December 1976), pp. 878–897.

———. "The Evolution of the National Money Market." Unpublished Ph.D. dissertation, MIT, 1974.

———. "A Note on Interest Paid on New York Bankers' Balances in the Postbellum Period," *Business History Review*, L (Summer 1976), pp. 198–202.

———. "Portfolio Selection with an Imperfectly Competitive Asset Market," *Journal of Financial and Quantitative Analysis*, XI (December 1976), pp. 831–846.

Jenkins, Charles. "Collection of Country Checks," *Proceedings of the American Bankers' Association*, 1884, pp. 56–58.

Jones, W. O. "The Ideal Country Banker," *Proceedings of the Oregon Bankers' Association*, 1908, pp. 47–70.

Jonung, Lars. "The Behavior of Velocity in Sweden, 1871–1913," Nationalekomiska Institution, University of Lund, 1976.

Kane, Thomas P. *The Romance and Tragedy of Banking.* New York: Bankers' Publishing Co., 1923.

Keehn, Richard. "Federal Bank Policy, Bank Market Structure, and Bank Performance: Wisconsin, 1863–1914," *Business History Review*, XLVIII (Spring 1974), pp. 1–27.

Kemmerer, E. J. *Seasonal Variations in the Relative Demand for Money and Capital in the United States.* Washington, D.C.: U.S. Government Printing Office, 1910.

Kniffin, William H., Jr. *American Banking Practice*. New York: McGraw-Hill Book Company, 1921.

————. *Commercial Banking*, 2 vols. New York: McGraw-Hill Book Company, 1923.

————. *Commercial Paper*, 3rd ed. New York: Bankers' Publishing Co., 1924.

————. *The Practical Work of a Bank*, 5th ed. New York: Bankers' Publishing Co., 1919.

Knox, John Jay. *A History of Banking in the United States*. New York: B. Rhodes and Co., 1903.

Krueger, Leonard B. *History of Commercial Banking in Wisconsin*. Madison: University of Wisconsin Press, 1933.

Langston, L. H. *Practical Bank Operation*. New York: Ronald Press Co., 1921.

Laughlin, J. Laurence, ed. *Banking Reform*. Chicago: National Citizens' League, 1912.

Lee, Everett S. et al. *Population Redistribution and Economic Growth*, 3 vols. Philadelphia: American Philosophical Society, 1957.

Lockhart, Oliver C. "The Development of Interbank Borrowing in the National Banking System, 1869–1914," *Journal of Political Economy*, Part I, XXIX (February 1921), pp. 138–160; Part II, XXIX (March 1921), pp. 222–240.

Lynch, James K. "Banking in Theory and Practice," *Proceedings of the Arizona Bankers' Association*, 1910, pp. 30–41.

————. "Modern Tendencies and Ancient Principles," *Proceedings of the Arizona Bankers' Association*, 1909, pp. 42–53.

Macaulay, Frederick. *Some Theoretical Problems Suggested by the Movements of Interest Rates, Bond Yields, and Stock Prices in the United States since 1856*. New York: National Bureau of Economic Research, 1938.

McAvoy, Walter. "The Economic Importance of the Commercial Paper House," *Journal of Political Economy*, XXX (February 1922), pp. 78–87.

McGrath, A. J. "The Northern Banker Passing on Paper Offered by the Southern Banker," *Proceedings of the Georgia Bankers' Association*, 1905, pp. 98–102.

Mints, Lloyd W. *A History of Banking Theory*. Chicago: University of Chicago Press, 1945.

Mitchell, Waldo. *The Uses of Bank Funds*. Chicago: University of Chicago Press, 1925.

Moore, Geoffrey, ed. *Business Cycle Indicators, Vol. II*. Princeton, N.J.: Princeton University Press, 1961.

"The Morality of Usury," *Bankers' Magazine*, XXXIV (June 1880), pp. 956–958.

Morrill, E. N. "Reminiscences of Banking in Kansas," *Proceedings of the Kansas Bankers' Association*, 1905.

Moulton, H. G. "Commercial Banking and Capital Formation," *Journal of Political Economy*, Part I, XXVI (May 1918), pp. 484–508; Part II, XXVI (June 1918), pp. 638–663; Part III, XXVI (July 1918), pp. 705–731; Part IV, XXVI (November 1918), pp. 849–881.

Myers, Margaret G. *The New York Money Market, Volume I: Origins and Development*. New York: Columbia University Press, 1931.

Noyes, A. D. *Forty Years of American Finance: 1865–1907*. New York: G. P. Putnam's Sons, 1909.

Padgett, A. E. "The Multiplication of Banks," *Proceedings of the South Carolina Bankers' Association*, 1908, pp. 125–134.

Palyi, Melchior, *The Chicago Credit Market*. Chicago: University of Chicago Press, 1937.

Patchin, Sydney A. "The Development of Banking in Minnesota," *Minnesota History Bulletin*, II (August 1917), pp. 111–168.

Patten, Claudius B. *Practical Banking*, 5th ed. New York: B. Rhodes and Co., 1891.

"Payment of Interest on Deposits," *Bankers' Magazine*, LXI (August 1900), pp. 157–158.

"Payment of Interest on Deposits," *Bankers' Magazine*, LXIX (August 1904), p. 136.

"Payment of Interest on Deposits," *Bankers' Magazine*, LXXX (May 1910), p. 873.

Perloff, Harvey et al. *Regions, Resources, and Economic Growth*. Lincoln: University of Nebraska Press, 1960.

Phillips, Chester A. *Bank Credit*. New York: Macmillan Company, 1920.

———, ed. *Readings in Money and Banking*. New York: Macmillan Company, 1920.

Pollard, Sidney. "Fixed Capital in the Industrial Revolution in Britain," *Journal of Economic History*, XXIV (September 1964), pp. 299–314.

Powlison, Keith. *Profits of the National Banks.* Boston: Gorham Press, 1931.

Pred, Allan A. *Urban Growth and the Circulation of Information: the United States System of Cities, 1790–1840.* Cambridge, Mass.: Harvard University Press, 1973.

Preston, Howard H. *History of Banking in Iowa.* Iowa City: State Historical Society of Iowa, 1922.

Ransom, Roger, and Sutch, Richard. "Debt Peonage in the Cotton South after the Civil War," *Journal of Economic History*, XXXII (September 1972), pp. 641–669.

———. "Documenting Monopoly Power in the Rural South: The Case of the General Store," Southern Economic History Project, Working Paper No. 15, Riverside, Calif., April 1976.

———. "The Ex-Slave in the Postbellum South: A Study of the Economic Impact of Racism in a Market Environment," *Journal of Economic History*, XXXIII (March 1973), pp. 131–148.

Redlich, Fritz. *The Molding of American Banking: Men and Ideas,* 2 vols. New York: Johnson Reprint Co., 1968.

"Report of the Committee on Credit Information," *Proceedings of the American Bankers' Association*, 1908, pp. 195–207.

Report of the Monetary Commission of the Indianapolis Convention. Chicago: University of Chicago Press, 1898.

Riefler, Winfield W. *Money Rates and Money Markets in the United States.* New York: Harper & Brothers, 1930.

Rockoff, Hugh. "Regional Interest Rates and Bank Failures, 1870–1914," *Explorations in Economic History*, XIV (January 1977), pp. 90–95.

———. "Varieties of Banking and Regional Economic Development in the United States," *Journal of Economic History*, XXXV (March 1975), pp. 160–177.

Rogers, G. A. "Loaning Money," *Proceedings of the Kansas Bankers' Association*, 1905, pp. 133–140.

Royse, E. "The Critical Season in Banking in Nebraska," *Proceedings of the Nebraska Bankers' Association*, 1903, pp. 364–367.

BIBLIOGRAPHY

Schroeder, W. G. Untitled address, *Proceedings of the Okla-homa-Indian Territory Bankers' Association,* 1907, pp. 63–64.
Scott, William A. *Money and Banking.* New York: Henry Holt and Co., 1910.
————. "Rates on the New York Money Market, 1896–1906," *Journal of Political Economy,* XVI (May 1908), pp. 273–298.
Scoville, C. C. K. "The Best Class of Investments for the Average Kansas Bank," *Proceedings of the Kansas Bankers' Association,* 1903, pp. 72–80.
Selden, Richard T. *Trends and Cycles in the Commercial Paper Market,* NBER Occasional Paper No. 85. New York: National Bureau of Economic Research, 1963.
Sharpe, William F. *Portfolio Theory and Capital Markets.* New York: McGraw-Hill Book Company, 1970.
"Should Bank Deposits Bear Interest?" *Bankers' Magazine,* XXX (February 1876), pp. 596–598.
Shreve, B. J. "Country Checks and Country Bank Accounts," *Bankers' Magazine,* LVI (February 1898), pp. 221–231.
Smiley, Gene. "Interest Rate Movements in the United States, 1888–1913," *Journal of Economic History,* XXXV (September 1975), pp. 591–620.
Smith, C. T. Untitled address, *Proceedings of the Georgia Bankers' Association,* 1917, pp. 117–120.
Smith, Walter Buckingham. *Economic Aspects of the Second Bank of the United States.* Cambridge, Mass.: Harvard University Press, 1953.
Southworth, Shirley D. *Branch Banking in the United States.* New York: McGraw-Hill Book Company, 1928.
Sparks, Earl S., and Carver, Thomas N. *History and Theory of Agricultural Credit in the United States.* New York: Thomas Y. Crowell Co., 1932.
Sprague, O. M. W. "Branch Banking in the United States," *Quarterly Journal of Economics,* XVII (February 1903), pp. 244–260.
————. "The Distribution of Money between the Banks and the People since 1893," *Quarterly Journal of Economics,* XVIII (August 1904), pp. 513–528.
————. *History of Crises under the National Banking System.* Washington, D.C.: U.S. Government Printing Office, 1910.

Stevens, E. M. "Commercial Paper," *Proceedings of the North Dakota Bankers' Association*, 1903, pp. 29–31.

Stevenson, Russell, ed. *A Type Study of American Banking: Non-Metropolitan Banks in Minnesota.* Minneapolis: University of Minnesota Press, 1934.

Stigler, George. "Imperfections in the Capital Market," *Journal of Political Economy*, LXXV (June 1967), pp. 287–292.

Sumner, William G. "History of Banking in the United States," in *A History of Banking in All Leading Nations, Vol. I.* New York: Journal of Commerce and Commercial Bulletin, 1896.

Swartz, D. G. "Interest on Deposits," *Bankers' Magazine*, XXIV (March 1870), pp. 665–670.

Sylla, Richard. "American Banking and Growth in the Nineteenth Century: A Partial View of the Terrain," *Explorations in Entrepreneurial History*, IX (Winter 1971–1972), pp. 197–227.

———. "The American Capital Market, 1846–1914, A Study of the Effects of Public Policy on Economic Development." Unpublished Ph.D. dissertation, Harvard University, 1968.

———. "Federal Policy, Banking Market Structure, and Capital Mobilization in the United States, 1863–1913," *Journal of Economic History*, XXIV (December 1969), pp. 657–686.

———. "Forgotten Men of Money: Private Bankers in Early U.S. History," *Journal of Economic History*, XXXVI (March 1976), pp. 173–188.

Talbert, Joseph T. "Commercial Credits," *Proceedings of the New York Bankers' Association*, 1908, pp. 76–91.

———. "Commercial Paper," *Proceedings of the Minnesota Bankers' Association*, 1908, pp. 36–53.

Taylor, F. M. "The Final Report of the Indianapolis Monetary Commission," *Journal of Political Economy*, VI (June 1898), pp. 293–322.

Thomas, Rollin G. "The Development of State Banks in Chicago." Unpublished Ph.D. dissertation, University of Chicago, 1930.

Tostlebe, Alvin S. *Capital in Agriculture: Its Formation and Financing since 1870.* Princeton, N.J.: Princeton University Press, 1957.

Trescott, Paul. *Financing American Enterprise.* New York: Harper & Row, 1963.

BIBLIOGRAPHY

U.S. Bureau of the Census. *Historical Statistics.* Washington, D.C.: U.S. Government Printing Office, 1960.

————. *Thirteenth Census of the United States: 1910. Vols. II–III: Population, 1910. Reports by States, with Statistics for Counties, Cities and Other Civil Divisions.* Washington, D.C.: U.S. Government Printing Office, 1913.

U.S. Census Office. *Tenth Census, 1880. Vol. I: Statistics of the Population of the United States.* Washington, D.C.: U.S. Government Printing Office, 1883.

————. *Eleventh Census, 1890. Vol. I: Report on Population of the United States.* Washington, D.C.: U.S. Government Printing Office, 1895–1897.

————. *Twelfth Census, 1900. Vols. I–II: Population.* Washington, D.C.: U.S. Government Printing Office, 1901–1902.

————. *Abstract of the Twelfth Census of the United States, 1900.* Washington, D.C.: U.S. Government Printing Office, 1903.

U.S. Comptroller of the Currency. *Annual Report, 1870–1918.* Washington, D.C.: U.S. Government Printing Office, 1870–1918.

U.S. Congress, House of Representatives. *Investigation by a Select Committee of the House of Representatives Relative to the Causes of the General Depression in Labor and Business, etc.* House Miscellaneous Document No. 29. 45th Congress, 3rd Session, 1879.

————. *Investigation by a Select Committee of the House of Representatives Relative to the Causes of the General Depression in Labor and Business, etc.* House Miscellaneous Document No. 5, 46th Congress, 2nd Session, 1880.

————. *Investigation of the Financial and Monetary Conditions in the United States under House Resolutions Nos. 429 and 504 before the Subcommittee on Banking and Currency,* 2 vols. 62nd Congress, 3rd Session, 1912.

————, Committee on Banking and Currency. *Hearings before the Committee on Banking and Currency on H.R. 8149.* 53rd Congress, 3rd Session, 1894.

————, Committee on Banking and Currency. *Views Expressed before the Committee on Banking and Currency.* 43rd Congress, 2nd Session, 1874.

U.S. Congress, Senate Committee on Banking and Currency. *Hearings before the Committee on Banking and Currency on H.R. 7837 (S. 2639)*, 3 vols. 63rd Congress, 1st Session, 1913.

U.S. National Monetary Commission. *Report*. Washington, D.C.: U.S. Government Printing Office, 1911.

Van Fenstermaker, J. "The Development of American Commercial Banking: 1782–1837," Bureau of Economic and Business Research Series No. 5, Kent State University, 1965.

Wade, Festus J. "What Causes Fluctuations in Money Rates?" *Proceedings of the New York Bankers' Association*, 1906, pp. 35–41.

Warren, George F., and Pearson, Frank A. *Prices*. New York: John Wiley & Sons, 1933.

Watkins, Leonard L. *Bankers' Balances*. Chicago: A. W. Shaw Co., 1929.

————. "Commercial Banking Reform in the United States," *Michigan Business Studies*, VIII, No. 5, 1938.

Westerfield, Ray B. *Banking Principles and Practice*. New York: Ronald Press Co., 1924.

White, Horace. *Money and Banking*, 4th ed. Boston: Ginn and Co., 1912.

Williamson, Jeffrey G. *Late Nineteenth-Century American Development*. Cambridge: Cambridge University Press, 1974.

Willis, H. Parker. *American Banking*. Chicago: La Salle Extension University, 1916.

Witham, W. S. Untitled address, *Proceedings of the American Bankers' Association*, 1898.

Woodward, C. Vann. *Origins of the New South, 1877–1913*. Baton Rouge: Louisiana State University Press, 1951.

Wright, Benjamin C. *Banking in California, 1849–1910*. San Francisco: H. S. Crocker Co., 1910.

Wright, Ivan. *Bank Credit and Agriculture*. New York: McGraw-Hill Book Company, 1922.

Wylie, James R. Untitled address, *Proceedings of the Michigan Bankers' Association*, 1901, pp. 36–39.

Yohe, William P., and Karnosky, Davis S. "Interest Rates and Price Level Changes," *Federal Reserve Bank of St. Louis Review*, LI (December 1969), pp. 19–36.

Zartman, Lester. *Investments of Life Insurance Companies*. New York: Henry Holt and Co., 1906.

Index

acceptances, 53–56; bank, 53–55; trade, 53–56, *see also* discounts: double-name paper. *See also* bills of exchange

agriculture, shift from to industry, 4

Alcorn, Edgar G., 248

American Bankers' Association, 57, 72, 82, 92, 196

bank note issue, *see* National Banking Acts: note issue provisions, profitability of note issue under

bankers' balances, 102–113, 132, 157; as use of surplus funds, 126; competitive market in New York for, 110–111, 264, 267; concentration in New York of, 95–99, 103, 104, 106–108, 112, 113n, 119–121, 148, 170, 236, *see also* pyramiding of reserves; defined, 105; growth of, 97, 105–107; opposition to interest payment on, 112–113, 264; rates on New York, 96–97, 250, 263–267; relationship to call loan market, 103–104, 118–119; *withdrawals*: during Panics, 119–120; seasonal, 136–137: traditional theory, 126–127, Goodhart theory, 127–128, estimates of, 134

Bankers' Magazine, 79, 112, 143, 183, 194, 264–265

banks and banking system, 236–238; American vs. British, 57, 62;

balance sheet entries: 46–47, 248–251; bonds for circulation, 248, 249; bonds for deposits, 248, 249; due from banks, 47, 154, 248–249, *see also* bankers' balances; due to banks, 47, *see also* bankers' balances; loans and discounts, 248, 250, 251; other stocks and bonds, 248, 250; clearings, 139n; credit departments, 72–73, 101; functions of, 6–7; growth of, 25, 89; portfolio diversification, 47–51, 88, 179–180; role in economic development of, 3; stock, interregional holdings of, 170–174, 237; structure and performance of, 7, 13, 236, 238. *See also* correspondent banking system; national banks; private banks; state banks

Barnett, George, 36, 43, 234

bill brokers, 41. *See also* commercial paper market: dealers

bills of exchange, 51–56; defined, 51; importance, 52–53; *kinds*: bank acceptances, 54; demand bills, 52; time bills, 52; trade acceptances, 53–54; 55–56; relation to real-bills doctrine, 60. *See also* checks

bills of lading, 63–64

Bolles, Albert S., 68

bonds, railroad, 50–51, 249–250

285

Library of Congress Cataloging in Publication Data

James, John A.   1946–
    The capital market.

    1. Finance—United States—History.   2. Financial
institutions—United States—History.   3. Saving and
investment—United States—History.   4. Capital—
United States—History.   I. Title.
HG181.J345   332.4   77–85540

ISBN 0–691–04218–7

DATE DUE

DEC 1 0 '86			